Paul and Virtue Ethics

Paul and Virtue Ethics

Building Bridges between New Testament Studies and Moral Theology

Daniel J. Harrington, SJ
and
James F. Keenan, SJ

A SHEED & WARD BOOK

ROWMAN & LITTLEFIELD PUBLISHERS, INC.
Lanham • Boulder • New York • Toronto • Plymouth, UK

Published by Rowman & Littlefield Publishers, Inc.
A wholly owned subsidiary of The Rowman & Littlefield Publishing Group, Inc.
4501 Forbes Boulevard, Suite 200, Lanham, Maryland 20706
http://www.rowmanlittlefield.com

Estover Road, Plymouth PL6 7PY, United Kingdom

British Library Cataloguing in Publication Information Available

Library of Congress Cataloging-in-Publication Data

Harrington, Daniel J.
  Paul and virtue ethics : building bridges between New Testament studies and moral
theology / Daniel J. Harrington and James F. Keenan.
      p. cm.
  Includes bibliographical references and index.
  ISBN 978-0-7425-9959-8 (cloth : alk. paper) — ISBN 978-0-7425-9961-1 (electronic)
  1. Christian ethics—Catholic authors. 2. Christian ethics—History. 3. Bible. N.T.
Epistles of Paul—Criticism, interpretation, etc. 4. Ethics in the Bible. I. Keenan, James
F. II. Title.
  BJ1249.H375 2010
  241—dc22
                            2010022581

∞™ The paper used in this publication meets the minimum requirements of American
National Standard for Information Sciences—Permanence of Paper for Printed Library
Materials, ANSI/NISO Z39.48-1992.

Printed in the United States of America

Dedicated to

Lisa Sowle Cahill, beloved friend and colleague

Contents

PART III—OTHER VIRTUES AND CHRISTIAN LIFE

PART IV—THE VIRTUES AND SOCIAL AND SEXUAL ISSUES

Prologue

This book is the companion to our *Jesus and Virtue Ethics: Building Bridges between New Testament Studies and Moral Theology* (Lanham, MD: Sheed & Ward, 2002). As we finished that book, we recognized the need for another volume that would treat the relevant topics in the context of the early church and its spread from the Holy Land into the urban centers of the Greco-Roman world.

The apostle Paul is the focus of this volume. Of the twenty-seven writings that comprise the New Testament canon, thirteen of them are ascribed to Paul and another (Acts) tells at great length the story of Paul's "conversion" and missionary journeys. Most of our attention here goes to the seven uncontested Pauline letters; that is, those letters that almost all New Testament scholars regard as having been composed directly by Paul: Romans, 1 and 2 Corinthians, Galatians, Philippians, 1 Thessalonians, and Philemon. Some parts of Acts are used to flesh out details in Paul's biography. Materials from the Pastorals (1 and 2 Timothy, Titus) and from Colossians and Ephesians—all generally regarded as Deuteropauline, or having been written later in Paul's name—are treated, especially near the end of the chapters on the Pauline virtues and vices and on social ethics according to Paul, respectively. For the most part, however, we rely on the undisputed Pauline letters to give us our best access to the voice of Paul. For a basic introduction to Paul and his letters, see Harrington's *Meeting St. Paul Today* (Chicago: Loyola Press, 2008).

Once more, our moral theological approach is through virtue ethics. Again, we define virtue ethics broadly. The basic questions are "Who am I?" "What do I want to become?" and "How do I get there?" In answering these questions, our primary guide is Paul.

Our book has four major parts. Part I treats the shape of virtue ethics in general and of Paul's virtue ethics in particular, Paul's views on the human condition before and after Christ, conversion and the human condition, the various contexts of Paul's ethical teachings, and the understanding of experience and conscience in moral theology today. Part II focuses on the three theological virtues—faith, love or charity, and hope—as they are treated by Paul and by Thomas Aquinas. We regard Thomas as a biblical theologian, since he not only lectured extensively on Scripture and wrote biblical commentaries but also often dealt with important questions that the biblical writers left open and calling for answers. Part III considers other virtues and Christian life by looking at various "natural" virtues (and vices) according to Paul, how these virtues are treated in theology today, the communal context of Pauline ethics, Christian ethics and the need for humility, and the role of the Eucharist in Pauline theology and Christian life. Part IV discusses various issues in the areas of social ethics and sexual morality, respectively, as they are dealt with by Paul and in Christian virtue ethics today, with particular attention to the importance of relational self-understanding in these matters.

Our thesis is that the concerns of Christian virtue ethics provide a good lens for reading Paul's letters, and that Paul and his letters provide a good lens for understanding Christian virtue ethics. Paul's moral teaching is based squarely on Jewish and Christian theology and on the Christ-event (especially Jesus' death and resurrection) in particular. His "ethical" teachings are generally not timeless moral maxims. Rather, they are shaped by and flow from Paul's fundamental convictions about the saving significance of Jesus' life, death, and resurrection. They are intelligible only when their theological roots are recognized and respected. Again, our work is intended as a "heuristic probe"—an effort at stimulating discovery and dialogue. While there may be some necessary overlaps between our two volumes, we have generally avoided repeating material already treated at some length in *Jesus and Virtue Ethics*. We believe that our two books taken together give a good introduction to how ethics/morality was treated in the earliest phases of the Christian movement, provide material for further and deeper conversations about the relationship between Scripture and moral theology, and contribute to realizing the Second Vatican Council's goal of "the perfecting of moral theology" by drawing "more fully on the teaching of Holy Scripture" (*Optatam totius* 16). As in the earlier book, we are seeking to build bridges between two theological disciplines, biblical studies and moral theology, that have seldom engaged in extensive dialogue and collaboration.

We are Jesuit priests who teach at Boston College. Harrington is professor of New Testament in the School of Theology and Ministry, while Keenan is professor of moral theology/christian ethics in the Department of Theology. We have taught many courses together on the New Testament and virtue ethics, first at the Weston Jesuit School of Theology in Cambridge, Massachusetts, and then at Boston College. Harrington was the principal writer for the prologue and chapters 2, 3, 5, 7, 9, 11, 13, 15, 17, 19, and 21. Kenan was the principal writer for chapters 1, 4, 6, 8, 10, 12, 14, 16, 18, 20, and 22, as well as the epilogue. Harrington seeks to present the Pauline material in a concise and objective style, while Keenan responds by ranging widely in the Catholic theological tradition (especially Augustine and Thomas Aquinas), modern developments in moral theology, classical artwork, popular culture, Scripture, and personal experience. A glance at our extended table of contents will show what we are trying to do. We have generally quoted the Bible according to the New Revised Standard Version.

We are especially grateful to our students, who have enriched our theological understanding and our global vision.

We dedicate this book to our beloved friend and colleague at Boston College, Professor Lisa Sowle Cahill. She has written wisely and well on many topics covered in our work and we have learned much from her publications and her personal example.

Part One

THE SHAPE OF
CHRISTIAN VIRTUE ETHICS

Chapter One

Virtue Ethics and Fundamental Moral Theology

Renewed interest in virtue ethics arises from a dissatisfaction with the way we do ethics today. Most discussions about contemporary ethics consider major controversial actions: abortion, gay marriage, nuclear war, gene therapy, and so on. These discussions basically dominate contemporary ethics.

Virtue ethicists have different interests. We are not primarily concerned with particular actions, but rather with persons. We believe that the real discussion of ethics is not primarily the question about what actions are morally permissible, but about who we should become. In fact, virtue ethicists, following Alasdair MacIntyre's proposal, expand that question into three key, related ones: "Who are we?" "Who ought we to become?" and "How are we to get there?" I now turn to each of these questions.

THE NATURE OF VIRTUE ETHICS

No question is more central for virtue ethics than the identity question "Who are we?" To virtue ethicists, the question is the same as "Are we virtuous?" To answer this first question, we must focus on two major considerations. First, what standards are we to measure ourselves against? Second, how will we know whether we are measuring fairly?

Regarding the first point, two of the most important works in ethics attempt to assist us by naming the basic virtues. In the *Nichomachean Ethics*, Aristotle gives us eleven different virtues that are necessary for citizens to engage. Friendship, magnanimity, and practical wisdom are some of these. In the "Second Part" of the *Summa Theologiae*, Thomas Aquinas takes from Plato, Cicero, Ambrose, Gregory, and Augustine the four cardinal virtues: prudence, justice, temperance, and fortitude. To these he adds the three

3

theological virtues: faith, hope, and charity. He states that the first four we can acquire through deliberately willed and enjoyed habitual right action; the latter three are gifts from God. These virtues help us answer the question of self-understanding.

But how can we know whether we are answering the question objectively? Here Aristotle suggests that we can know ourselves by considering how we act in spontaneous situations: We "discover" ourselves when we act in the unplanned world of ordinary life. We may believe that we are particularly brave or cowardly, but that assessment is only correct if it conforms to how we actually behave in the unanticipated concrete situation. Self-knowledge is key, therefore, but a self-knowledge that is critical and honest, not one based on wishful thinking.

MacIntyre's second question embodies a vision of the type of person we ought to become. Though we use Thomas's four cardinal virtues to find out how virtuous we actually are, we could use those same four virtues to determine who we ought to become. For certainly, if we are honest in the first question, then some virtues are not as fully acquired by us as are others. In fact, for the honest person, the virtues are not what we acquire in life; they are what we pursue.

We use the virtues, therefore, to set the personal and social goals that we encourage ourselves to seek. Thomas and others call this goal the "end." That is, the middle question sets an end that we should seek. That end is a type of person or community shaped by the virtues. Setting this end means that the fundamental task of the moral life is to develop a vision and to strive to attain it. Inasmuch as that vision is who we ought to become, then, the key insight is that we should always aim to grow. As a person- and community-oriented ethics, virtue ethics insists that without growth, we cannot become more moral.

Setting such an end describes then another way that virtue ethicists are different from other ethicists. Rather than examining actions and asking whether we should perform them or not, virtue ethicists say that we ought to set ends for the type of people we believe we should become and should pursue. Thus, to the extent that we are examining our lives and seeking ways of improving ourselves for the moral flourishing of our world, to that extent we are engaging virtue ethics.

As we will see in the next chapter, for Paul these questions are compelling: He answers the first question as a converted disciple of Christ, but he looks to the second question with the eyes of eschatological faith.

Turning to the third question, in order to get to the end, we need prudence. For many years prudence has had a terrible reputation, being thought of as caution or self-interest. "Be prudent" means "Don't get caught," "Be extra careful," "Watch out!" But for Aristotle and Thomas, prudence is not simply caution. Prudence is rather the virtue of a person whose feet are on the ground and who thinks both practically and realistically. Prudence belongs to the person who not only sets realistic ends, but sets out to attain them. The prudent person is precisely the person who knows how to grow.

Being prudent is no easy task. From the medieval period until today, we believe that it is easier to get something wrong than to get it right. For today we still assert that if only one component of an action is wrong, the whole action is wrong.

Prudence is even more complicated when we try to figure out the appropriate ways of becoming more virtuous. Prudence must be attentive to detail, anticipate difficulties, and measure rightly. Moreover, as anyone who has watched children knows, we are not born with prudence. Actually, we acquire it through a very long process.

Finding prudence is finding the middle point: All of prudence is precisely getting to the middle point or the "mean" between extremes. As Thomas says, "Virtue is the mean." The mean is located where there is adequate tension for growth—neither too little nor too much. That mean is not fixed. The mean of virtue is not something set in stone; rather, it is the mean by which only specific persons or communities can grow. This is another reason why prudence is so difficult: No two means are the same.

Finding the mean of the right tension depends on who the persons or communities are. In a manner of speaking, a virtue ought to fit a person the way a glove fits one's hand. There is a certain tailor-made feel to a virtue, which prompts Thomas to call virtue "one's second nature."

Virtue ethics is, therefore, a proactive system of ethics. It invites all people to see themselves as they really are, to assess themselves and see who they can actually become. In order both to estimate oneself and to set desired goals, it proffers the virtues for both. Moreover, it invites all people to see that they set the agenda not only of the end, but also of the means to accomplish that end. Virtuous actions, like temperate drinking or courageously facing our fears, are the prudential means for achieving the end of becoming more virtuous persons.

Virtue ethics encompasses our entire lives. It sees every moment as the possibility for acquiring or developing a virtue. To underline this point, Thomas held that every human action is a moral action. That is, any action that we knowingly perform is a moral action because it affects us as moral persons. Whatever we do makes us become what we do.

Thomas saw every human action as an "exercise." Though some of us go through life never examining the habits we engage in, Thomas suggests to us that we ought to examine our ways of acting and ask ourselves if they are making us more just, prudent, temperate, and brave. If they are, they are virtuous exercises.

When we think of exercise, we think of athletics. The person who exercises by running eventually becomes a runner, just as one who dances becomes a dancer. From that insight Thomas, like Aristotle before him, sees that intended, habitual activity in the sports arena is no different from that in any other arena of life. If we can develop ourselves physically, we can develop ourselves morally by intended, habitual activity.

Virtue ethics sees, therefore, the ordinary as the terrain on which the moral life moves. Thus, while most ethics make their considerations about rather controversial material (genetics, abortion, war, etc.), virtue ethics often engages the commonplace. It is concerned with what we teach our children and how; with the way we relate with friends, family, and neighbors; with the way we live our lives. Moreover, it is concerned not only with whether a physician (for example) maintains professional ethics (for instance, whether he or she keeps professional secrets or observes informed consent with patients) but is equally concerned with his or her private life, with whether he or she knows how to respect the confidences of friends or respects the privacy of family members. In a word, before the physician is a physician, he or she is a person. It is one's life as a person with which virtue ethics is first concerned.

As opposed to dilemma-based ethics, virtue ethics is proactive, concerned with the ordinary, and all-encompassing. Dilemma-based ethics—which captures so much of our time, imagination, and energy—presents ethics as an emergency room in which suddenly a previously unknown person arrives in a catastrophic state: needing an organ transplant, assisted suicide, or an abortion. In that context, the moral agent is little more than a reactor to other people's dilemmas.

Virtue ethics looks at the world from an entirely different vantage point, moving ahead with less glamour and drama, but always seeing the agent not as reactor, but as actor: knowing oneself, setting the agenda of personal ends and means in both the ordinary and the professional life.

The virtues are then heuristic guides that collectively aim for the right realization of human personal and social identity. The word *heuristic* means something that can serve as an aid to learning, discovery, or problem solving by experimental means. The virtues are called heuristic because they point us in the general direction of finding out what type of persons we ought to become. In this sense they are also teleological—that is, end-oriented. As teleological virtues, they need to be continually realized and redefined; their final definition remains outstanding. Their nature is, then, historically dynamic; being in themselves goal oriented, they resist classicist constructions but rather require being continually understood, acquired, developed, and reformulated.

The historical dynamism of the virtues applies correspondingly to the anthropological vision of human identity that guides us in our pursuit of the virtues. That vision is also, in its nature, historically dynamic. As we grasp better who each and every human person can become, to that extent we need to reformulate our understanding of the virtues. As we determine our anthropological vision, we subsequently designate corresponding virtues to fill in or "thicken" the image of the human that we aim at.

Thus Aristotle's elitism led him to discuss virtues primarily for those who could be magnificent. While he designated other virtues for educated men, he did not develop any for women or slaves. But as philosophers and theologians further developed a more inclusive anthropology, they needed virtues that substantiated this more democratic framework. Of course, Paul, who so promotes community, is also inclusive. He recognizes the Jewish disciples of Jesus, as well as Gentiles who had become disciples after Jesus' resurrection. But he is more than communal and more than inclusive. Indeed, he is the great democratizer, leveling the distinctions between slave and free, man and woman, and Greek and Jew (see Galatians 3:28). And in this, he is far different from Aristotle.

The dialectical interplay between these historically dynamic concepts of an anthropological vision of human identity and the corresponding human virtues can be seen from a variety of viewpoints. Years ago, Dietmar Mieth, for instance, outlined the changes of values among historical and economic societies and described the prototype of each society in terms of its prototypical virtuous person. Likewise, Clodovis Boff proposed a set of virtues that pointed heuristically toward a liberating anthropology for the poor.

Underlying the teleological nature of the virtues is then an implicit belief in the progress of ethical thought. For instance, Anne Patrick described how the historical narrative of a particular person as prototypically virtuous can be seen in hindsight as oppressive. In her essay "Narrative and the Social Dynamics of Virtue," she examined the canonization of Maria Goretti and suggested that it implicitly proposed a woman's chastity as a social virtue of greater importance than a woman's own life. Patrick presumed an ethically objective progression in our insights in the shift from a classical patriarchal anthropology (wherein chastity was the signature virtue for women) to a more egalitarian, liberation anthropology where justice was the hallmark virtue for both genders.

Patrick's progress is not simply descriptive but rather normative. Progress in articulating and proposing both an anthropological vision and the corresponding virtues doesn't just happen. Ethicists and moralists have then the quadruple task of critically reflecting on the contemporary situation to see whether existing anthropologies and the corresponding constellations of virtues inhibit or liberate members of our global community, of perceiving new horizons of human possibility, of expressing the possible ways that virtue can attain those horizons, and of making politically possible the actual new self-understanding and self-realization. This final task is often overlooked: Too often ethicists and moralists think that our work ends with written proposals, but inasmuch as ethical insight *to be ethical* must end in action, similarly the task of the ethicist must end in political action, an insight that Aristotle routinely affirmed.

In their political actions, moralists must ask themselves what type of persons we are promoting. The appropriateness of a particular virtue is ascertained by the articulation of our anthropological vision. Sometimes, whether or not a particular virtue aims to advance our vision depends not on the virtue itself, but rather on its relationship to the constellation of other virtues. For instance, in the essay by Patrick, by itself chastity is an important virtue, but the priority of place it received in the patriarchal description of the virtuous woman does not make it, in that case, an effective tool for the right realization of women. In a similar way, Karen Lebaqcz and Shirley Macemon raised the case of pastors who notoriously underpay their staff claiming that their employees must be "patient." The authors argued that patience is an auxiliary virtue of justice and if there is no justice, then patience is a vice. Particular virtues can be as underestimated as they are overestimated.

A dialectic emerges. As we further determine our anthropological vision, to that extent we further amend or reformulate our virtues. But it is a full dialectic in that we cannot further determine our anthropological vision without actually appropriating the virtues that help us have a fresh perspective on humanity. This brief sketch of virtue ethics provides us with an impetus to further investigate its appropriateness for today.

RESPONDING TO CRITICISMS REGARDING VIRTUE ETHICS

Let me turn then to the reasons why I think some moralists hesitate to turn to virtue ethics. First, our anthropological self-understanding is profoundly relational, and virtues are usually described as perfecting particular powers of individual agents. Second, the notion of perfecting stands as a real Pelagian affront to contemporary Christian sensibilities. Third, it is not evident that virtue ethicists can supply normative guidance for action. Fourth, because certain virtue theories can embody a very powerful summons to uniformity, leaders of right-wing organizations (fascists and socialists as well as certain contemporary fundamentalist Christian movements) often make appeals to these virtues. I shall address each of these, spending considerable time on the first challenge regarding relationality.

I have argued elsewhere that we need a virtue ethics that perfects not internal powers but rather ways that we are related. If we take the cardinal virtues as they are proposed in Thomas Aquinas, we find that they perfect four corresponding, hierarchically organized powers: the practical reason, the will, the concupiscible, and the irascible. Just as these powers inhere in a particular hierarchy, so do the virtues. Temperance and fortitude are predominantly at the service of justice. Prudence determines the right choice of means for each of the virtues, but it especially looks to recommend the just action, since justice governs all exterior principles. In a manner of speaking, the anthropological identity of the virtuous person is simply the just one.

In this light, the classical, cardinal virtues endorse an anthropology that inhibits greatly the present theological agenda. As far as I see it, three reasons merit replacing them. First, contemporary writers repeatedly express dissatisfaction with the insufficiency of justice. For the most part, they offer hyphenated constructs, the most famous being "love-justice," which attempts to acknowledge that while working for the equality of all persons, we still maintain partial relationships that need to be nurtured and sustained. But the hyphen is distracting. It suggests that it is one virtue. For this reason, Paul Ricoeur saw them rightly as two and placed them in a tension between two distinct and sometimes opposed claims. Ricoeur's insight that the virtues are distinct and at times opposing stands in contrast with Thomas's strategy of the cardinal virtues, where their unity is harmonious. Only when another virtue stands as a fully equal heuristic guide can there be a dialectical tension wherein the virtues challenge and define one another, and as Ricoeur suggested, "may even be the occasion for the invention of responsible forms of behavior."

Second, the modern era insists that moral dilemmas are not based on the simple opposition of good and evil but, more frequently, on the clash of goods—thus a constellation of heuristic guides that already resolves the priority of one virtue over another by which a preconceived hierarchical structure preempts realism. We cannot propose heuristic guides that prefabricate solutions when the concrete data is still forthcoming.

Third, the primary identity of being human is not as an individual with powers needing perfection, but as a relational rational being whose modes of relationality need to be made virtuous or to be rightly realized.

I propose that our identity is relational in three ways: generally, specifically, and uniquely. Each of these relational ways of being demands a cardinal virtue: As a relational being in general, we are called to justice; as a relational being specifically, we are called to fidelity; as a relational being uniquely, we are called to self-care. These three virtues are cardinal. Unlike Thomas's structure, none is ethically prior to another; they have equally urgent claims and they should be pursued as ends in themselves. We are not called to be faithful and self-caring in order to be just, nor are we called to be self-caring and just in order to be faithful. None is auxiliary to the others. They are distinctive virtues with none being a subset or subcategory of the other. They are cardinal. The fourth cardinal virtue is prudence, which determines what constitutes the just, faithful, and self-caring way of life for an individual.

Our relationality generally is always directed by an ordered appreciation for the common good, in which we treat all people as equal. As members of the human race, we are expected to respond to all members in general equally and impartially.

If justice urges us to treat all people equally, then fidelity makes distinctively different claims. Fidelity is the virtue that nurtures and sustains the bonds of those special relationships that humans enjoy, whether by blood, marriage, love, citizenship, or sacrament. If justice rests on impartiality and universality, then fidelity rests on partiality and particularity.

Fidelity here is like love in the "love-justice" dialectic. It is also like the claim that Carol Gilligan made in her important work *In a Different Voice*. Gilligan criticized Lawrence Kohlberg for arguing that full moral development is found in the person who can reason well about justice as impartial and universal. She countered that the human must aim both for the impartiality of justice and for the development of particular bonds. Her claims parallel my own: Justice and fidelity represent the two different voices.

Neither of these virtues, however, addresses the unique relationship that each person has with oneself. Care for self enjoys a considered role in our tradition, as for instance, the command to love God and love one's neighbor as oneself. In his writings on the order of charity, Thomas Aquinas developed this love at length (as have others).

Finally, prudence has the task of integrating the three virtues into our relationships, just as it did when it was among the classical list of the cardinal virtues. Thus, prudence is always vigilant—looking to the future, trying not only to realize the claims of justice, fidelity, and self-care in the here and now, but also calling us to anticipate occasions when each of these virtues can be more fully acquired. In this way, prudence is clearly a virtue that pursues ends and effectively establishes the moral agenda for the person growing in these virtues. But these ends are neither in opposition to nor in isolation from one another. Rather, prudence helps each virtue shape its end as more inclusive of the other two.

Inasmuch as all persons in every culture are constituted by these three ways of being related, by naming these virtues as cardinal, we have a device for talking cross-culturally. This device is based, however, on modest claims. The cardinal virtues do not purport to offer a picture of the ideal person nor to exhaust the entire domain of virtue. Rather than being the last word on virtue, they are among the first, providing the bare essentials for right human living and specific action. As hinges (*cardo* means "hinge"), the cardinal virtues provide a skeleton of both what human persons should basically be and at what human action should basically aim. All other issues of virtue hang on the skeletal structures of both rightly integrated dispositions and right moral action.

Human identity is worked out in a variety of contexts, but virtue ethicists, in particular, have the task of elucidating that identity by providing practical guides. Sensitive to the fact that religious, cultural, and personal communities are especially interested in thickening virtues, virtue ethicists offer these guides only heuristically to help in furthering the historically progressive task of expressing the human.

By seeing the virtues perfecting the ways we are related, we can now turn to the three other common objections raised about virtue ethics. First, by speaking about perfection, virtue ethicists appear to promote a near-Pelagian lifestyle. This claim is without merit. As Gerard Gilleman taught us, Christian virtues flow from charity—the virtue that, like faith and hope, is infused as pure gift. The very possibility of a Christian moral life depends first on the initiative of God, who through charity gives us grace. In the light of that perfection, the perfection by which we come into union with God, a union that is the foundation of all subsequent relationships, we are able to pursue the virtues.

Furthermore, we need to see that the term *perfection* in the moral and ascetical manuals was always more a verb than a noun. The virtues perfect our powers, Thomas repeatedly writes. Similarly, I suggest that the virtues perfect the way we are related. But that *perfect* is not any different from *develop* or *rightly realize*. Simply put, the language of perfection is the pursuit of an end in which our ways of being related are placed on a trajectory that reflects the virtues.

Moreover, as David Solomon showed us, whatever complaints we have against virtue ethics we can equally have against other systems like deontological or responsibility ethics. Many a Kantian has been a Pelagian, and similarly many responsibility ethicists have believed that a person on his or her own could become morally upright. The charge of being Pelagian applies to any ethical system. By pointing to the virtue of charity, virtue ethicists reject the complaint.

The second objection concerns the provision of normative guidance. Like others, I have argued that prudence provides for us normative guidance. The foundation of our own norms results from the prudential judgments of those who have gone before us. Daniel Mark Nelson has argued this philosophically, and the great casuists Albert Jonsen and Stephen Toulmin have argued this historically.

Moreover, by referring to prudence, virtue ethicists have a way for re-visiting social norms to ask whether they need to be reexamined and/or reformulated. That is, the virtue of prudence recognizes the historicity of a norm and contributes to a norm's ability to further the values that it pro-tects and promotes. For this reason, moralists rightly revisit the claims of an articulated moral norm. Furthermore, we have an obligation to listen to the prudential judgments and experiences of others and in light of these to revisit norms to see how experience helps us better express the normative guidance for all.

Finally, still we wisely cast suspicions on virtue ethics' own compatibility with fascism and other groups that oppress and promote intolerance. In the United States, for instance, the religious right has begun to use virtue lan-guage not to promote human flourishing but rather to enjoin a harshly con-servative agenda that ostracizes its opponents as vicious. Loyalty, not justice, dominates these ideological platforms.

Virtues offer an anthropological identity. Since Plato we have recognized that by recommending particular virtues to particular communities, we can shape in part the identity of these particular cultures. For those who wish to control communities and to promote exclusion, certain virtues are rather helpful: Certain interpretations of loyalty, obedience, and humility all temper a society's ability to recognize the equality of others.

For this reason we need to recognize that it is not virtue ethics that sup-presses justice, for justice is a virtue itself, but rather it is the promotion of a particular hierarchy or constellation of virtues that really endangers the integ-rity and humanity of a society. A society that privileges loyalty above justice, for instance, thwarts equality and casts suspicion on the alien.

Notice, here, however, that by actually attending to the agenda of virtue, virtue ethics provides us with a vehicle for critiquing and challenging those fundamentalist movements that use particular virtues to subordinate the stranger and marginalize the nonconformist. As a matter of fact, we cannot address the many fundamentalist movements today unless we both acknowl-edge how they manipulate the masses by the espousal of particular virtues and offer in their stead a newer and more inclusive vision of the type of people we ought to become.

VIRTUE ETHICS ON TOMORROW'S LANDSCAPE

Let me conclude with a brief litany of the dissertations that my students have done on the topic of virtue ethics. I do this to demonstrate how virtue ethics is being developed in part by the next generation of moral theologians.

One man wrote on the need for a new *Ars moriendi* (manual for dying). Through the lens of the virtues of patience, compassion, and hope, he reads different sources (manuals by Erasmus, Robert Bellarmine, William Perkins, and Jeremy Taylor; contemporary secular and theological literature; and the death of Jesus in the Gospel of Luke) for developing a contemporary manual for dying. A woman writes on the virtue of mercy, comparing the works of Jean Vanier, the founder of L'Arche, and Jon Sobrino, the important liberation theologian. Another studied Thomas Aquinas on prudence and compared him to contemporary proportionalists and deontologists as well as feminists to see whether their notions of moral reasoning approached any degree of Thomas's sophistication. She found the feminists' descriptions of moral reasoning very close to Thomas's approach. One studied the Belgian Dom Odon Lottin's historical research and fundamental moral theology in order to develop his developmental notion of the person in the context of an ethics of virtue. A Mennonite offered a Christian apology for virtue ethics, and this text has subsequently become an important introduction to Christian virtue ethics. A Greek Orthodox priest studied early Eastern Fathers' writings on the virtues and applied them to church teaching on marriage. Another explored the function of humility in the field of epistemology by studying its appearance in the writings of Augustine, Bernard, and Thomas Aquinas.

Several turned to the role virtue ethics could play in providing a theological anthropology. Three different students were interested in the impact of developing a theological anthropology in the key of virtue: An Italian priest and physician applied his anthropological vision to the study of genetics; a Brazilian priest developed his for sexual education programs; and an American nun explored the type of anthropology we need for a time of AIDS. These doctoral dissertations give us an idea of how the next generation of scholars will promote the virtues. It also substantiates the claim that an ethics of virtue offers us a vast and original array of insights.

SELECT BIBLIOGRAPHY

Boff, Clodovis. "The Poor of Latin America and Their New Ways of Liberation." In *Changing Values and Virtues*, edited by Dietmar Mieth and Jacques Pohier, 33–45. Edinburgh, Scotland: T&T Clark, 1987.

Gilligan, Carol. *In a Different Voice: Psychological Theory and Women's Development.* Cambridge, MA: Harvard University Press, 1982.

Herdt, Jennifer. *Putting on Virtue: The Legacy of the Splendid Vices.* Chicago: University of Chicago Press, 2008.

Jonsen, Albert, and Stephen Toulmin. *The Abuse of Casuistry.* Berkeley: University of California Press, 1988.

Keenan, James. "Proposing Cardinal Virtues." *Theological Studies* 56, no. 4 (1995): 709–29.

———. "Virtue and Identity." In *Creating Identity: Biographical, Moral, Religious*, edited by Hermann Häring, Maureen Junker-Kenny, and Dietmar Mieth, 69–77. London: SCM Press, 2000.

———. "Virtue Ethics: Making a Case as It Comes of Age." *Thought* 67 (1992): 115–27.

Klubertanz, George. *Habits and Virtue.* New York: Appleton-Century-Crofts, 1965.

Kotva, Joseph, Jr. *The Christian Case for Virtue Ethics.* Washington, DC: Georgetown University Press, 1996.

Lebacqz, Karen, and Shirley Macemon. "Vicious Virtue? Patience, Justice and Salaries in the Church." In *Practice What You Preach: Virtues, Ethics, and Power in the Lives of Church Ministers and Their Congregations*, edited by James F. Keenan and Joseph J. Kotva Jr., 290–92. Franklin, WI: Sheed & Ward, 1999.

MacIntyre, Alasdair. *After Virtue: A Study in Moral Theory.* Notre Dame, IN: University of Notre Dame Press, 1981.

Meilaender, Gilbert. *The Theory and Practice of Virtue.* Notre Dame, IN: University of Notre Dame Press, 1984.

Mieth, Dietmar. "Continuity and Change in Value Orientations." In *Changing Values and Virtues*, edited by Dietmar Mieth and Jacques Pohier, 47–59. Edinburgh, Scotland: T&T Clark, 1987.

Nelson, Daniel Mark. *The Priority of Prudence.* University Park: Pennsylvania State University Press, 1992.

Patrick, Anne. "Narrative and the Social Dynamics of Virtue." In *Changing Values and Virtues*, edited by Dietmar Mieth and Jacques Pohier, 69–80. Edinburgh, Scotland: T&T Clark, 1987.

Pieper, Josef. *The Four Cardinal Virtues.* Notre Dame, IN: University of Notre Dame Press, 1966.

Porter, Jean. *The Recovery of Virtue: The Relevance of Aquinas for Virtue Ethics.* Louisville, KY: Westminster, 1990.

Ricoeur, Paul. "Love and Justice." In *Radical Pluralism and Truth: David Tracy and the Hermeneutics of Religion*, edited by Werner G. Jeanrond and Jennifer L. Rike, 187–202. New York: Crossroad, 1991.

Solomon, David. "Internal Objections to Virtue Ethics." In *Midwest Studies in Philosophy 13: Ethical Theory; Character and Virtue*, edited by Peter A. French et al., 428–41. Notre Dame, IN: University of Notre Dame Press, 1988.

Chapter Two

The Shape of Paul's Christian Virtue Ethics

PAUL'S CHRISTIAN VIRTUE ETHICS: PHILIPPIANS 3:10–11

The first city in Europe to which Paul brought Christianity was Philippi in Macedonia (see Acts 16:11–15). When Paul had moved on to other apostolic activities, he kept in contact with what has been described as his favorite community through the series of letters that now constitute the Letter to the Philippians. What now appears in Philippians 3:1a–4:1 was a warning to the Gentile Christians at Philippi not to be seduced by other Jewish Christian missionaries into becoming Jews and accepting circumcision ("Beware of those who mutilate the flesh," 3:2) and other observances such as Sabbath-keeping and the Jewish food and ritual purity rules. To do so would be in contradiction to Paul's gospel, according to which non-Jews could become full members of God's people through their faith and baptism in Christ without going through Judaism (see Galatians 3:6–29).

Paul's strategy in Philippians 3 is first to appeal to his own credentials as a Jew and then to affirm the overriding significance of his experience of the risen Christ. In doing so, Paul tells us who he was and who he is, who and what he wants to become, and how he hopes to get there. Thus in Philippians 3:10–11, he outlines the shape of his Christian virtue ethics.

> 10. I want to know Christ and the power of the resurrection and the sharing of his sufferings by becoming like him in his death, 11. if somehow I may attain the resurrection from the dead.

In describing who he was before his experience of the risen Christ, Paul had explained himself in 3:5–6 in terms of his life as a member of the Jewish people: "circumcised on the eighth day, a member of the people of Israel, of the tribe of Benjamin, a Hebrew born of Hebrews; as to the Law, a Pharisee; as to zeal a persecutor of the church; as to righteousness under the law, blameless." In other words, Paul was born into an observant Jewish family, became a member of the pious fraternity of Pharisees, perceived the nascent Christian movement as a dangerous aberration, and was exemplary in observing the Torah. There is no hint here of deep psychological conflicts or a tender conscience on Paul's part. Rather, he was the best Jew imaginable.

Nevertheless, Paul's experience of the risen Christ (narrated most fully by Luke in Acts 9, 22, and 26, as well as by Paul himself in Galatians 1:13–17) led him to recast his identity in a dramatically different way. And so he writes: "I regard everything as loss because of the surpassing value of knowing Christ Jesus my Lord" (3:8). In the context of his warning to the Philippians, Paul describes his exemplary credentials as a Jew now to be "loss" and even "rubbish" (3:8). What made them such was the surpassing value of knowing Christ Jesus as his Lord. And what Paul learned from his experience was that his "righteousness" or right relationship with God (justification) did not come from his own perfect observance of the Jewish Law. Rather, it was a gift from God that came with and through faith. While a proud member of Israel as the people of God, Paul unexpectedly came to recognize that knowing Christ Jesus as Lord had become the new center and dynamism of his life.

How then did Paul come to answer the question "Who am I?" His dramatic encounter with the risen Christ rendered by comparison his impeccable credentials as a Jew to be "loss" and even "rubbish" (3:8). What really counted now was knowing Christ Jesus and recognizing that God's grace and faith constitute the way to right relationship with God. The core of Paul's existence was no longer his Jewish identity or the Torah but his new life in Christ. Elsewhere, Paul represents himself as living out a kind of "Christ mysticism": "it is no longer I who live, but it is Christ who lives in me" (Galatians 2:20).

Who or what does Paul want to become? What is his goal (*telos* in Greek, *finis* in Latin)? As Philippians 3:10–11 indicates, what Paul wants is even greater knowledge of Christ and even greater identification with Christ's death and resurrection. Moreover, Paul wants in the end to "attain resurrection from the dead"—another way of referring to fullness of life with Christ in the eternal kingdom of God. Thus Paul's identification with Jesus' life, death, and resurrection (the paschal mystery) constitutes both the beginning and the end (in the sense of "goal") of his life project.

How does Paul intend to achieve his goal? In one sense his redefining encounter with the risen Christ had already shown Paul who he was, what his goal was, and what he needed to do to attain it. That initial experience of knowing Christ Jesus as Lord and recognizing the power of God's grace and the centrality of faith in response had moved Paul considerably on the way toward his goal of deeper knowledge of Christ and resurrection from the dead.

In Philippians 3:12–16, however, Paul goes on to insist that he still has a long and difficult road to travel on the way to fullness of life with Christ: "Not that I have already obtained this or have already reached the goal; but I press on to make it my own, because Christ Jesus has made me his own" (3:12). Paul's statement here acknowledges both the power of his experience of the risen Christ ("Christ Jesus has made me his own") and the struggle that he must undergo to reach his goal fully.

The struggle that Paul faced was the challenge of living a life that flowed from and was appropriate to his new identification with Christ. The struggle was not merely a matter of saying the right words or holding the right doctrines. It also (and especially) involved living and acting in a way that accorded with knowing Christ Jesus as Lord. That Paul perceived the difficulty of this challenge is manifest from his description of it in terms of a race or an athletic contest: "Straining forward to what lies ahead, I press on toward the goal for the prize of the heavenly call of God in Christ Jesus" (3:13–14).

When set in its historical and literary context, Paul's statement in Philippians 3:10–11 illustrates the basic concerns and contours of Christian virtue ethics. From his experience of the risen Christ, Paul was convinced that he finally knew better than he had ever before who he really was: a child of God through Christ. He also knew his goal or "end" in life: perfect participation in Christ's death and resurrection, and eternal life with Christ in God's kingdom. And he recognized that between perceiving his present identity in Christ and attaining his goal there was the challenge and even the struggle of living an authentic Christian life by acting in ways that fit with his identity and his goal.

WHO WAS PAUL?

The major sources of information about Paul's life are statements in his own letters and in the Acts of the Apostles. The critical problem with his letters is that he provides autobiographical information only sparingly and in the service of an argument on some other matter. And with Acts it is always difficult to know whether the information came directly from Paul or was developed by Luke for his own theological purposes. Nevertheless, it is possible to discern from Paul's letters and Acts at least an outline of Paul's life.

According to Acts 22:3–5, Paul was born in Tarsus of Cilicia, most likely in the first decade of the Christian era. His Hebrew name was Saul, while his "secular" name was Paul. He may well have been exposed to the rudiments

of Greek education in general and rhetoric in particular. However, in Acts he
is said also to have been educated in Jerusalem under the tutelage of Gama-
liel (a famous Jewish teacher). As noted in Philippians 3:5 ("as to the law, a
Pharisee"), Paul became a Pharisee, a member of a Jewish religious movement famous for celebrating their fellowship expressed in common meals and
for surrounding and adapting the Torah with their traditions.

Around 33 (or 36) CE, Paul the Pharisee became a Christian as the result
of his dramatic experience of the risen Christ on the road to Damascus (see
Acts 22:5). At Damascus he was taken in by the local Christians amid great
suspicion on their part because Paul had set out to persecute the new Christian
movement. In 36 (or 39) Paul made his first visit to Jerusalem as a Christian
rather than as a Pharisee, and there he conferred with Cephas (Peter) and
James, the Lord's brother (Galatians 1:18–19). Then after several years in
"the regions of Syria and Cilicia" (1:21), Paul again went up to Jerusalem
"after fourteen years" (50 CE, counting from 36) to confer with the Christian leaders there about the validity of his mission to non-Jews. According
to Paul's own account in Galatians 2:1–10 (see also Acts 15), the "pillars"
of the church there—James, Cephas, and John—approved the mission to the
Gentiles undertaken by Paul and Barnabas on the condition that the Gentile
churches would contribute to the support of the Christians at Jerusalem:
"They asked only one thing, that we remember the poor" (2:10). We know
also that at Antioch Paul confronted Peter and accused him of inconsistency
and even hypocrisy for failing to eat with Gentile Christians and thus refus-
ing to treat them as full Christians on the same level as Jewish Christians like
Peter and Paul (see Galatians 2:11–14).

Where Paul was and what exactly he was doing between his Damascus
Road experience (Acts 9) and the missionary journeys that are described in
Acts 13—28, is hard to know. Scholars are divided between viewing this
period as a quiet time of spiritual formation or as the occasion of vigorous
apostolic activity for which we have no record. At any rate, we do know
from Acts 13 onward that between 46 and 58 CE Paul conducted missionary
campaigns in various cities in Asia Minor and Greece; he had his greatest
successes among non-Jews. Paul's strategy was to found a new Christian
community and to move on when a certain level of stability had been reached
(see Romans 15:18–21).

Paul's seven undisputed letters—1 Thessalonians, Galatians, 1 Corinthians,
2 Corinthians, Philippians, Philemon, and Romans—were written between 51
and 58 CE. They were one of his ways of answering questions and resolving
disputes that arose in his absence. The remaining Pauline epistles—2 Thessalonians, Colossians, Ephesians, 1 Timothy, 2 Timothy, and Titus—are
generally regarded as having been composed after Paul's death in his name

and spirit to address new problems and conditions that arose in the churches. It is customary to refer to them as the Deuteropauline letters (from *deutero-*, meaning "secondary").

At the end of his longest and last letter—to the Romans—written in 58 CE, Paul outlined his plans to bring the proceeds of the collection to Jerusalem and then to visit the church at Rome (which he had not founded) on his way to further missionary activity in Spain (15:22–29). But matters turned out differently for Paul from what he had expected. When he arrived in Jerusalem with the collection, he was arrested, imprisoned, and put on trial at Caesarea Maritima. When Paul appealed to his status as a Roman citizen (Acts 22:22–29), it was decided among the various Roman officials that he should be sent to Rome and put on trial there: "You have appealed to the emperor; to the emperor you will go" (Acts 25:12).

After a dangerous sea journey from Palestine to Italy, Paul the prisoner came to Rome around 60 CE. There he continued to exercise his ministry as an apostle under a kind of house arrest (see Acts 28:16–31). According to early Christian tradition, Paul died a martyr's death at Rome around 64 CE in the persecution of Christians under the emperor Nero.

PAUL'S CONVERSION AND CALL

Paul's experience of the risen Christ on the road to Damascus was clearly the turning point in his life. It was the defining moment in which he came to know his true identity and to clarify who and what he wanted to be. All the ancient sources—Paul's own letters, Acts, and the Deuteropaulines—agree that before this life-changing experience Paul had been a fierce persecutor of the Christian movement. After it, Paul became Christianity's most energetic proponent.

What happened? The Acts of the Apostles offers three lengthy and dramatic narratives of Paul's "conversion" (Acts 9, 22, and 26). In his own autobiographical statement, Paul gives a short and simple version: "God, who had set me apart before I was born and called me through his grace, was pleased to reveal his Son to me, so that I may proclaim him among the Gentiles" (Galatians 1:15–16). Thus Paul describes the "conversion" event in terms of divine calling or vocation ("God . . . called me"), divine revelation ("to reveal his Son to me"), and mission ("so that I may proclaim him among the Gentiles").

In what sense was Paul a "convert?" If conversion means changing from one religion (Judaism) to another (Christianity), it is anachronistic to apply the label of convert to Paul. At the time of Paul's experience of the risen

Christ on the Damascus Road, it is very doubtful that anyone had yet classified Christianity as a different religion from Judaism. Rather, the Christian "way" would have been regarded as a sect or party within Judaism comparable to the Pharisees, Sadducees, and Essenes. And from Paul's own writings (see Romans 9–11), it is clear that Paul never viewed Christianity as entirely separate from Judaism and that he considered Jewish Christians like himself ("the rich root of the olive tree," Romans 11:17) to be the principle of continuity between Israel as the historic people of God and the church. And so it is more accurate historically and theologically to say that Paul "converted" from one form of Judaism (Pharisaism) to another form of Judaism (Christianity).

Many interpreters have tried to explain Paul's "conversion" in psychological terms. However intriguing and even irresistible this topic may be, the pertinent New Testament texts do not provide sufficient psychological data to gain any certainty on the matter. The appeal to the "I" statements in Romans 7:7–25 (e.g., "I see in my members another law at war with the law of my mind," 7:23) runs up against the current exegetical consensus that Paul in this passage was really concerned not simply with his own psychological and religious conflicts but rather with human existence viewed theologically before and apart from Christ. It may well mirror Paul's personal sentiments. But Paul's interests were theological rather than psychological. It cannot be cited as persuasive evidence for a uniquely conflicted or tender conscience on Paul's part, a theory contradicted by Paul's own statement in Philippians 3:6: "as to righteousness under the law, blameless."

In describing his own conversion, Paul used biblical-theological language to the point that many biblical scholars today prefer the language of vocation or calling (instead of conversion) to describe what happened to Paul on the Damascus Road. The vocabulary that Paul chose in Galatians 1:15–16 placed him in line with the "call" stories of great Old Testament figures like Moses, Gideon, Isaiah, and Jeremiah. Like them, Paul was an unlikely instrument to carry forward God's program. Like them, Paul was granted a divine revelation, in his case a revelation of Jesus as the Son of God ("God was pleased to reveal his Son to me"). Like them, Paul was given a mission that would affect the history and life of God's people, in his case the mission to proclaim Jesus Christ among the Gentiles and thus to open up membership in God's people to non-Jews.

From all accounts, Paul spent his life in responding to his call from God and in carrying out his mission to bring the gospel ("good news") of Jesus to as much of the Mediterranean world as he could. Paul proudly referred to himself as an apostle (literally, "one who is sent") and regarded himself as having been commissioned directly by God and God's Son to fulfill his mission: "sent neither by human commission nor from human authorities, but through Jesus Christ and God the Father" (Galatians 1:1). The special mission that Paul understood to be his was to proclaim the gospel to non-Jews: "I had been entrusted with the gospel for the uncircumcised" (2:7). This mission was in turn recognized and approved by the "pillar" apostles—Peter, James, and John—at Jerusalem (2:9).

It is important to recognize that Paul carried out his apostolic mission in collaboration with a team of coworkers (see Romans 16:1–16). Paul was not a solitary hero acting entirely on his own. Nor was he was a theology professor writing systematic descriptions of Christian doctrine. Paul was primarily an apostle who founded churches. His letters were concrete ways of extending his ministry when he was no longer present physically in the cities where he had founded churches. As such, they were exercises in pastoral theology, and so it is most appropriate to call Paul a pastoral theologian.

It is impossible to separate Paul's personal identity and self-consciousness from his conversion from Pharisaic Judaism to Christian Judaism and from his apostolic mission and activity in bringing the gospel to non-Jews and offering them membership in God's people through Jesus Christ. Paul's personal identity, "conversion," and mission all were integral parts in his answer to the fundamental question of virtue ethics: "Who am I?"

PAUL'S JEWISH ESCHATOLOGICAL CONSCIOUSNESS

The second great question of virtue ethics is, "Who or what do I want to become?" In the Christian tradition in general and in Paul's case in particular, the answer to this question is shaped in large part by hope for the fullness of eternal life with God as the goal or *telos* of human existence. Like Jesus and many of his Jewish contemporaries, Paul thought about his goal or end (*telos*) in eschatological or apocalyptic terms: "if somehow I may attain the resurrection from the dead" (Philippians 3:11). Like them, Paul regarded resurrection as part of the scenario of future events culminating in the full manifestation of God's rule and justice in the kingdom of God ("Thy kingdom come," Matthew 6:10).

In the preaching of Jesus and in other Jewish religious circles of his time, the kingdom of God was a major theological concept. It refers to God's future display of power and the acknowledgment of God's rule over all creation. When God's kingdom is made fully manifest, all creation will declare God's name "holy" ("Hallowed be thy name").

Rooted in the Old Testament doctrine of God's kingship and in ancient Israel's mixed experience of monarchy, the kingdom of God in Jesus' day had come to be regarded as a future ("Thy kingdom come") and transcendent (it is God's kingdom) entity. In their hope for the coming kingdom of God, Jews expected to experience the definitive display of God's justice in which the wicked would be punished and the righteous vindicated. The full coming of God's kingdom involves the end of the present evil age, the resurrection of the dead, the last judgment, appropriate rewards and punishments, and a new heaven and new earth. In some scenarios, the Messiah plays a pivotal role in gathering those to be judged and even in doing the judging. In other scenarios, the Messiah is absent or plays only a minor role.

The kingdom of God in this setting was an eschatological concept. The term *eschatology* derives from the Greek word for "end" or "last thing." When applied to the Judaism of Jesus' day, it refers to the events of the "last day" as listed in the preceding paragraph. The word *apocalyptic* is often used in connection with and even as a synonym for eschatology. The term *apocalypse* technically refers to a literary genre. An apocalypse is a revelation about the future and/or the heavenly realm (as in the biblical books of Daniel and Revelation). But since apocalypses are mainly concerned with the events leading up to the last day or with the heavenly court, the word *apocalyptic* is also used frequently to describe the content of the revelation.

The major biblical sources for Jewish eschatology or apocalyptic are Daniel and Revelation, as well as the extrabiblical books known as 1 Enoch, Assumption (or Testament) of Moses, 4 Ezra (2 Esdras 3–14), and 2 Baruch. While there was no uniform scenario for the last day, each of these books purports to describe a dramatic intervention on God's part that will disrupt the present evil course of history, will bring about a final and definitive judgment upon the righteous and the wicked, and usher in a new or purified heaven and earth. Because Jewish apocalyptic deals necessarily with events that are future (eschatological) and transcendent (belonging to God), it must resort to imaginative or symbolic language. It drew heavily on Old Testament and ancient Near Eastern motifs such as the Divine Warrior, the decisive Day of the Lord, cosmic signs and portents, and so on. But it reused them in describing what the future will be like when God fulfills his promises to Israel and establishes his kingdom for all to see and acknowledge.

The clearest presentation of Jewish eschatological or apocalyptic consciousness appears in the *Rule of the Community* (designated as 1QS), discovered among the Dead Sea scrolls at Qumran. The Dead Sea scrolls have been described as the greatest archaeological discovery of the twentieth century. The *Rule of the Community* (also known as the *Manual of Discipline*) was among the very first manuscripts to be discovered and deciphered in the late 1940s and early 1950s, and it remains one of the most important of the various texts that were previously unknown. Many scholars believe that the Jewish religious community that lived at the site of Qumran near the Dead

Sea followed this rule in its everyday life. Intended as a handbook for the community's spiritual leader or guide, it contains descriptions of life in a Jewish religious group (probably Essenes). It describes entry into the covenant of the group, their beliefs, purpose and way of life, punishments for inappropriate behavior, theology, and prayer. It was composed most likely in the second century BCE.

The presentation of the community's beliefs in 1QS 3:13–4:25 concerns the different kinds of persons and their spirits, the signs identifying their works during their lifetimes, and what they can expect at the last judgment. While not strictly an apocalypse by genre, the instruction provides an excellent example of eschatological or apocalyptic thinking. Thus it can help us grasp some of the presuppositions that New Testament writers like Paul (and John) brought to their theological reflections on the significance of Jesus' life, death, and resurrection.

The instruction proposes a modified apocalyptic dualism. Written by and for Jewish monotheists, the instruction takes as its starting point the affirmation of the absolute sovereignty of the one God of Israel: "From the God of knowledge comes all that is and shall be. . . . The laws of all things are in His hand, and He provides them with all their needs." In the Jewish context there can be only one God, the God of Israel who is the Creator and Lord of all things.

How then can there be evil in the world? And why do righteous and innocent persons suffer in the present time? This is where the dualism, though modified in keeping with the confession of God's absolute sovereignty, comes in. According to this instruction, God created humans to govern the world but appointed for them "two spirits in which to walk until the time of His visitation: the spirits of truth and falsehood." The term "walk" is a common biblical way of referring to ethical (or unethical) behavior. The "visitation" here refers to the last judgment. The idea is that between the creation and the definitive (eschatological) visitation, God has ceded some of his divine sovereignty to the two "spirits."

The dualism operates at three levels. There are two spirits: the Prince of Light (Michael the Archangel) versus the Prince of Darkness (Satan). There are two kinds of people: the children of light versus the children of darkness. And there are two kinds of actions: the deeds of light versus the deeds of darkness. The whole dualistic schema is summarized in the following sentence: "All the children of righteousness are ruled by the Prince of Light and walk in the ways of light, but all the children of falsehood are ruled by the Angel of Darkness and walk in the ways of darkness." On which side of these dualisms any individual may stand depends on whether one's "portion in the two divisions is great or small."

These dualisms, however, do not last forever: "But in the mysteries of His understanding, and in His glorious wisdom, God has ordained an end for falsehood, and at the time of the visitation he will destroy it forever." At the final visitation truth will arise forever, and all the works of falsehood will be put to shame. Then there will be a final judgment "according to the spirit within them at the time of the visitation." And God will definitively reaffirm his sovereignty over all creation, and the righteous will enjoy "every ever-lasting blessing and eternal joy in life without end," while the wicked will be destroyed "without remnant or survivor."

According to the schema of modified apocalyptic dualism in the Qumran *Rule of the Community* 3:13–4:25, God created everything; everything is proceeding according to God's plan; there are two spirits; humans are partici-pants in a cosmic struggle between good and evil; on which side they belong is decided by their actions; and at the final judgment they will be rewarded or punished accordingly.

Jewish apocalypticism is concerned with three questions: "Who is in charge?" "Why is there evil in the world?" and "What time is it?" Accord-ing to this schema of modified apocalyptic dualism, God is in charge but for a time has ceded his authority to the two spirits. There is evil in the world because God allows the evil spirit to be active and humans to follow that evil spirit. And in God's own time (which should be soon), God will intervene to vindicate the righteous and punish the wicked, to annihilate the Prince of Darkness and his followers, and to bring about a new heaven and a new earth where there will be no evil or suffering for the righteous.

WHAT DID PAUL HOPE FOR?

Something like the schema of modified apocalyptic dualism as illustrated by the Qumran text in 1QS 3:13–4:25 seems to have been the framework pre-supposed for much of Paul's thinking about Christ, the present existence of Christians, and their ethical self-consciousness and behavior. Written in the fifties of the first century, Paul's letters are the earliest complete documents preserved in the New Testament canon. As such they bear witness not only to the presence of modified apocalyptic dualism very early in the history of the Christian movement but also (and even more importantly) to how early Christians changed it in light of their convictions about Jesus' life, death, and resurrection.

Paul's letters contain several quotations that summarize early Christian beliefs about Jesus. For example, at the beginning of his long reflection on the resurrection in 1 Corinthians 15, Paul cites the tradition that he had handed on to the Corinthian Christians and notes that he himself had received this same tradition: "that Christ died for our sins in accordance with the scriptures, and that he was buried, and that he was raised on the third day in accordance with the scriptures, and that he appeared to Cephas, then to the twelve" (15:3b–5). Like other pre-Pauline confessions of faith (see Romans 1:3–4; 3:25–26) and the great hymn celebrating Jesus as the Servant of God (Philippians 2:6–11), this passage places the life, death, and resurrection of Jesus at the center of salvation history and Christian faith.

What Paul hoped for was to share in the power of Jesus' resurrection and to enjoy eternal life with God and Christ: "I want to know Christ and the power of his resurrection . . . if somehow I may attain the resurrection from the dead" (Philippians 3:10–11). Paul was convinced that the goal of his Christian life was being with God in the fullness of God's kingdom: "We will be with the Lord forever" (1 Thessalonians 4:17). And he was equally convinced that Jesus' life, death, and resurrection (the paschal mystery) had made the fulfillment of this hope into a reality.

Belief in the central significance of Jesus' death and resurrection led early Christians like Paul to adapt the Jewish schema of modified apocalyptic dualism. The clearest evidence for such adaptation comes in Romans 1–8, though traces of it appear throughout Paul's letters. The starting point in the adaptation was the Jewish belief that resurrection was to be an event in the scenario of end-time or eschatological events.

Paul agreed with the Jewish schema of modified apocalyptic dualism in affirming both the absolute sovereignty of God and the inevitability of the final judgment or visitation. So he asserted that since the beginning of creation God's "eternal power and divine nature, invisible though they are, have been understood and seen through the things that he has made" (Romans 1:20). And he also insisted that "on the day of wrath, when God's righteous judgment will be revealed . . . he will repay according to each one's deeds" (2:5–6). What got changed in the Jewish schema was the interpretation of the dynamics of history between Jesus' resurrection and the last judgment. This shift meant that all of Paul's ethical instructions are set in the context of "walking" between the times of Jesus' resurrection and the last judgment.

The most dramatic changes in Paul's Christian adaptation of the schema of modified apocalyptic dualism came in the protagonists and the timing. The role of the Angel of Light was given over first to Jesus and then to the Holy Spirit (the Spirit of Christ). Those who follow their leadership (Christians) are the children of light, and they do the deeds of light.

On the other side of the dualism, the role of the Prince of Darkness is attributed by Paul to an "unholy trinity" consisting of Sin, Death, and the Law. Paul rarely used "Satan" language. Especially in his letter to the Romans,

Paul preferred to describe the forces of evil in terms of personified "powers" set loose with Adam's sin. Sin and Death, of course, were among the consequences of Adam's sin (see Genesis 3). And when the Law was given to Moses, one of its functions (according to a rather peculiar position adopted by Paul) was to define sin more precisely and so (rather perversely) to serve as a stimulus to sin. Those who follow the leadership of Sin, Death, and the Law are the children of darkness, and they do the deeds of darkness.

An even more striking Pauline innovation came in the area of timing. This change came as a consequence of belief in the resurrection of Jesus from the dead. Among Jews of Jesus' time, the resurrection of the dead was expected to be a collective and eschatological event. The clearest Old Testament text is Daniel 12:2. It affirms that at the time of the decisive battle between Michael and the enemies of the righteous in Israel (the "great tribulation"), "many of those who sleep in the dust of the earth shall awake, some to everlasting life, and some to shame and everlasting contempt."

In its Jewish context, the early Christian proclamation that God had raised Jesus from the dead was doubly surprising. It was surprising because it asserted that one individual—Jesus of Nazareth—had been raised before and apart from anyone else. And it is also surprising because it implied that one great eschatological event (Jesus' resurrection) had happened without all the others (general resurrection, last judgment, rewards and punishments, and new heaven and new earth) having yet occurred around the same time.

Paul and other early Christians, however, put these matters in a different framework. For Paul (see Romans 1:18–3:20), the state of humankind was even more dire than it appears in Jewish modified apocalyptic dualism. Before and apart from Christ, all humans—Gentiles and Jews alike—were children of darkness because they all were under the power of Sin, Death, and the Law. All humans needed the revelation of God's righteousness in Christ (see Romans 1:16–17). With the appearance of Christ Jesus and especially through his death and resurrection, everything changed. Then it became possible for all humans—Gentiles and Jews alike—to become the children of light and to do the deeds of light insofar as they followed the leadership of Christ and his Holy Spirit.

Moreover, with the resurrection of Jesus the end-time or *eschaton* had already broken into human history. From the early Christian perspective, the "age to come" in Jewish apocalyptic speculation already replaced "this age," and so it had become possible for all persons to enjoy the benefits of God's kingdom and the age to come before the final visitation by God. Nevertheless, Paul retained the Jewish apocalyptic expectation that an even better way of life would appear in the future with the full coming of God's kingdom.

All of Paul's ethical teachings in his letters are directed to those who are "in Christ"—to members of Christian communities, to people who had responded to the proclamation of the crucified and risen Christ in faith and in baptism. Such persons were regarded as "walking between the times." They were already in the age to come by virtue of Jesus' death and resurrection. But they did not yet enjoy the fullness of God's kingdom that is still to be unveiled and toward which they strive as their end or goal (*telos*).

While taking over much in the Jewish schema of modified apocalyptic dualism, Paul transformed it in view of Jesus' death and resurrection. The goal of Paul's ethical striving was fullness of life with Christ. His ethical teachings were intended to show Christians, who through Christ were already living in the age to come, how they might attain an even more wonderful and lasting goal.

SELECT BIBLIOGRAPHY

Becker, Jurgen. *Paul: Apostle to the Gentiles.* Louisville, KY: Westminster/John Knox, 1994.

Fitzmyer, Joseph A. *Paul and His Theology.* Englewood Cliffs, NJ: Prentice-Hall, 1989.

Furnish, Victor Paul. *The Moral Teaching of Paul: Selected Issues.* Nashville, TN: Abingdon, 1985.

———. *Theology and Ethics in Paul.* Nashville, TN: Abingdon, 1968.

Gaventa, Beverly Roberts. *From Darkness to Light: Aspects of Conversion in the New Testament.* Philadelphia: Fortress, 1986.

Gorman, Michael J. *Reading Paul.* Eugene, OR: Cascade Books, 2008.

Harrington, Daniel J. *Meeting St. Paul Today.* Chicago: Loyola Press, 2008.

Murphy-O'Connor, Jerome. *Paul: A Critical Life.* Oxford, England: Clarendon Press, 1996.

Nock, Arthur D. *Conversion: The Old and the New in Religion from Alexander the Great to Augustine of Hippo.* Oxford, England: Oxford University Press, 1961.

Rosner, Brian S., ed. *Understanding Paul's Ethics: Twentieth-Century Approaches.* Grand Rapids, MI: Eerdmans, 1995.

Sampley, J. Paul. *Walking between the Times: Paul's Moral Reasoning.* Minneapolis, MN: Fortress, 1991.

Wright, N. T. *Paul in Fresh Perspective.* Minneapolis, MN: Fortress, 2005.

Chapter Three

The Human Condition before and after Christ: Pauline Perspectives

LIFE BEFORE AND AFTER CHRIST: ROMANS 7:24–8:2

Paul's letter to the Romans is arguably the most theologically important book in the Christian Bible. In this biblical chapter (and most others), we will focus first on the specific Pauline passage (here on Romans 7:24–8:2) and use it as a means of opening up a discussion of the wider literary, historical, and theological horizon in which it is set. Paul presents extended reflections on the human condition and Christian freedom in Romans 5–8. They constitute the theological heart of what is arguably the most important book in the New Testament. In Romans 5–7, Paul considers the powers (Sin, Death, and the Law) from which the Christian has been freed through Christ. And in Romans 8, Paul discusses life in the Holy Spirit, the life for which the Christian has been freed through Christ. For Paul, freedom is not simply personal autonomy (as in "Nobody's going to tell me what to do"). Rather, freedom is to be found in serving the proper master, and the only real master is Christ (and his Spirit).

Building on the Jewish framework of modified apocalyptic dualism, Paul constructed a schema of the human condition and of Christian existence that places God (Father, Son, and Holy Spirit) at the center and celebrates the significance of the Christ-event in the lives of those who are led by the Spirit of Christ.

At the core of Paul's analysis of the human condition (anthropology) are Greek terms that were by no means original with him: *soma* ("body"), *sarx* ("flesh"), *pneuma* ("spirit"), *psyche* ("soul"), *kardia* ("heart"), *nous* ("mind"), and *syneidesis* ("conscience"). Paul's originality lay with his use of these terms on the theological level to designate aspects (not parts) of the human person.

29

The word *soma* ("body") is often used to refer to the person qua human person in a neutral way, while *sarx* ("flesh") may describe the aspect of the person under the dominion of Sin, Death, and the Law.

The term *pneuma* is generally positive and appears frequently in contexts that describe the person's openness to being led by the Holy Spirit. In other words, the "spirit" (*pneuma*) of the person is open to the Holy "Spirit" (*pneuma*). In leading "spiritual" persons, the Spirit also rescues those "neutral" aspects of the person (*soma*) designated as soul, heart, mind, and conscience from the dominion of Sin, Death, and the Law. Life in the Spirit/spirit makes possible for human persons the freedom to serve God and to enjoy the saving effects of Jesus' life, death, and resurrection: justification, sanctification, reconciliation, salvation, and so forth.

At the transition or intersection between Paul's reflection on the negative state of humans under the rule of Sin, Death, and the Law (Romans 5–7) and the positive way of life under the Spirit (8), there are some statements that neatly express Paul's views on the two contrasting dimensions of the human condition. In various ways, Romans 7:24–8:2 provides a good introduction to how Paul regarded the human condition, first before and apart from Christ and then "in Christ Jesus" and in the Spirit.

> 24. Wretched man that I am! Who will rescue me from this body of death? 25. Thanks be to God through Jesus Christ our Lord. So then, with my mind I am a slave to the law of God, but with my flesh I am a slave to the law of sin. 8:1. There is therefore now no condemnation for those who are in Christ Jesus. 2. For the law of the Spirit of life in Christ Jesus has set you free from the law of sin and death.

The pitiful cry "Wretched man that I am!" in 7:24a summarizes Paul's lament about human existence in the state of enslavement to Sin, Death, and the Law. The adjective *talaiporos* ("miserable, wretched, distressed") appears elsewhere in the New Testament only in Revelation 3:17. It is the opposite of *makarios* ("blessed, privileged, happy, fortunate") found in the beatitudes (see Matthew 5:3–12; Luke 6:20–23). Here it expresses the cry of one who recognizes that he cannot save himself, one who needs help from God, one who can find relief only by acknowledging the need for salvation and by turning to God.

"Who will rescue me from this body of death?" The cry for help is accompanied in Romans 7:24b by a frank description of the human condition when Sin and Death reign. The phrase "body of death" is not so much a negative evaluation of the human body or the flesh. Rather, Paul frequently uses the word "body" (*soma*) in a neutral way to refer to the human person or the human condition. One who lives under the rule of Sin is at the same time under the sway of Death, which is the consequence of Sin. That person is effectively dead on the spiritual level and inevitably dead on the physical level. The question "Who will rescue me . . . ?" expresses the human recognition of a person's slavery apart from Christ and the longing for right relationship with God, which according to Paul only Christ could provide.

Paul answers his own question immediately in Romans 7:25a: "Thanks be to God through Jesus Christ our Lord." Adopting the language of prayer, Paul confesses that God has made it possible for humans to change masters, to put off the "body of death," and to be animated by the Holy Spirit. Writing some twenty-five years after Jesus' death, Paul attributes to Jesus the titles "Messiah" (Christ) and "Lord" without hesitation, thus suggesting that they had been part of the Christian theological vocabulary for some time already. In developing his own Christology, Paul was primarily concerned with the effects or results of Jesus' life, death, and resurrection. One of the results is salvation—the possibility that a human person living in the "body of death" may be rescued or "saved" from this pitiable state and be transferred to the lordship of Christ and the Spirit.

Romans 7:25b is sometimes regarded as a gloss or later scribal addition to the text. That may be so. But in any case it does provide a neat summary of Paul's lament over the conflicted and miserable state of human existence before and apart from Christ. It takes for granted that humans must always have a master: "I am a slave to . . . . I am a slave to . . . ." The choice is between God and Sin as one's master or lord. Yet this choice is not entirely an intellectual decision. Rather, there is a conflict between one's mind or intellect (here *nous* is understood as an aspect of the person that is open to God and to God's Spirit) and the "flesh" (here *sarx* is the aspect of the person under the rule of Sin and Death). This plight is sometimes compared to the situation of an alcoholic or drug addict who knows the harmful effects of the addiction and wants to stop but fails to do so repeatedly. Whatever the origin of Romans 7:25b, it does summarize Paul's lament for enslaved humankind in Romans 7:14–25 and his reflections in Romans 5–7 as a whole.

According to Romans 8:1, "there is therefore now no condemnation for those who are in Christ Jesus." The context for this statement is the last judgment. The word *katakrima* ("condemnation") could even be translated as "death sentence." The idea is that those who are "in Christ Jesus" by faith and baptism have already by anticipation been subjected to the last judgment and in principle at least have been declared acquitted and so "righteous" by God (justification). Romans 8:1 is sometimes also taken to be a textual gloss. Again as in 7:25b, whatever its origin may have been, it is an accurate summary of Paul's understanding of the present condition of those who are in Christ.

According to Paul, the "age to come" began with the resurrection of Jesus, and so those who are "in Christ Jesus" have in a sense experienced the last judgment. It is, of course, possible to fall away. The acts of faith and baptism are not magical guarantees of salvation. But for those who abide "in Christ Jesus" and act in a way that is appropriate to that identity, there is every reason to view the last judgment as the ratification of a decision that God has already rendered and as a moment in the process of eternal life that began with the transfer of lords from Sin, Death, and the Law to Christ Jesus and his Spirit in baptism.

Romans 8:2 offers still another summary of Paul's teaching about the human condition. Here he contrasts the "law" of the Spirit and the "law" of Sin and Death. Whereas Paul generally uses the Greek term *nomos* to refer to the Mosaic or Jewish law (the Torah), here he seems to take it to mean the "principle" or (even better) the "system." Once more there is a contrast between masters or lords: Spirit/Christ versus Sin and Death. And once more the claim is that the "system" represented by Christ and his Spirit can bring freedom from the enslaving "system" presided over by Sin and Death. Freedom is not the absence of any lord or master. Rather, genuine freedom means living under the true lordship of Christ and his Spirit.

These short sentences in Romans 7:24–8:2 appear at the transition between Paul's lament over the human condition before and apart from Christ (life under the system of Sin, Death, and the Law) in 7:14–25 and his description of life under the system of Christ and his Spirit in 8:1–39. With passages from Paul's letter to the Romans as a guide, we will now look at life under Sin, Death, and the Law. Then we will treat Paul's lament, and finally we will consider his meditation on Christian life in the Spirit.

SIN, DEATH, AND THE LAW

Paul's picture of human existence before and apart from Christ is starkly negative. Humans live under the dominion of Sin, Death, and the Law. Whereas other Jewish and New Testament writings depict evil in personal terms (Satan, the Devil, the Prince of Darkness, Belial, etc.), Paul generally represents evil somewhat more abstractly in a kind of "unholy trinity" or "gang of three"—as powers or forces able to influence and even dominate human beings. At the same time, these powers retain enough personal characteristics to be described at the very least as personifications. In the history of theology there has always been a tension between picturing evil as an individual, personal figure (Satan) or as a collective, metaphorical entity (Evil). Paul is at the root of this tension because both aspects appear in his analysis of the source and place of evil in human existence.

The purpose of Romans 1:18–3:20 is to show the need for the revelation of God's righteousness in Jesus Christ. To do so, Paul insists that all human beings—non-Jews and Jews alike—needed help from God in order to enjoy right relationship with God (justification). That help took definitive form in the person of Jesus.

In Romans 1:18–32, Paul traces the downward spiral of Gentiles apart from Christ. The root of their plight, according to Paul, was their failure to recognize God in and through creation: "Ever since the creation of the world his eternal power and divine nature, invisible though they are, have been understood and seen through the things he has made" (1:20). This initial failure led the Gentiles downward into idolatry, various forms of sexual misconduct, and all kinds of vices (1:21–32; see Wisdom 13–14). In Paul's view, the Gentiles before and apart from Christ were enmeshed in evil and evildoing under the power of Sin.

Even Jews, who presumably should have known better because they had the Torah, also found themselves under the power of Sin. Their problem, according to Paul in Romans 2:1–3:20, was that they failed to do what the Law commanded (see Romans 2:13). The point of Paul's argument is to show that "all, both Jews and Greeks, are under the power of sin" (3:9). This conclusion is repeated as a presupposition when Paul begins to develop the more positive part of his argument: "All have sinned and fall short of the glory of God" (3:23).

The connection or alliance between Sin and Death is as old as Genesis 3. Whereas the serpent (a Satan figure) promises Eve that "you will not die" (Genesis 3:4), one of the consequences of disobedience to the divine command on the part of Adam and Eve is death: "You are dust, and to dust you shall return" (Genesis 3:19).

Paul makes the narrative of Genesis 3 into part of his analysis of the human condition before and apart from Christ: "Therefore, just as sin came into the world through one man, and death came through sin, and so death spread to all because all have sinned" (Romans 5:12). Where Sin is, Death is also present: "Death exercised dominion from Adam to Moses" (5:14). Left to their own resources, humans apart from Christ repeat the experience of Adam. On the contrary, those who are alive to God in Christ Jesus are "dead to sin" (6:10).

The role of the Law or Torah in this unholy alliance is more complex. On the one hand, Paul insists that "we uphold the law" (3:31) and that "the law is holy, and the commandment is holy and just and good" (7:12). On the other hand, Paul portrays the Law as a source for knowledge about Sin and even a stimulus toward sins: "For through the law comes the knowledge of sin" (3:20). For Jews, the Law then becomes a criterion by which they will be judged when God repays each according to one's deeds at the last judgment (see 2:7, 12).

In proving his thesis that all humans—Jews and Gentiles alike—lived under the dominion of Sin and Death, Paul calls upon the Torah itself (here understood widely to include all parts of the Old Testament) to show that every person and every part of every person (throats, tongues, lips, mouths, feet, eyes) stood under the power of Sin and Death (see the anthology of quotations in Romans 3:10–18). Without Christ, in Paul's perspective, humans are "slaves to sin" (6:20) and "the wages of sin is death" (6:23).

In Paul's schema, the Law also functioned as the instrument of Sin and Death. Having claimed that "now we are discharged from the law" (7:6), Paul reflects on the role that the Law played in the alliance between Sin and Death. He repeats the charge that the Law provided knowledge about Sin: "if it had not been for the law, I would not have known sin" (7:7). He goes on to suggest that the Law with its many commandments against sin revived Sin as a power, and so ironically "the very commandment that promised life proved to be death to me" (7:10).

How the three powers worked together in humankind before and apart from Christ is expressed dramatically by Paul in Romans 7:13: "It was sin, working death in me through what is good [= the Law], in order that sin might be shown to be sin, and through the commandment might become sinful beyond measure." In his letter to the Romans, Paul paints a dismal picture of human existence under the dominion of Sin, Death, and the Law.

THE LAMENT OF THE ENSLAVED

Most of Romans 5–7 concerns the state of humankind under the dominion of Sin, Death, and the Law, while Romans 8 portrays life under the guidance of the Holy Spirit, a life made possible through Jesus' death and resurrection. Romans 7:14–25 serves as Paul's summary of what it felt like to be under the dominion of the three hostile powers. It is the cry or lament of someone who knows and wants to do what is right and good but cannot do so because that dominion seems to be so powerful.

Much of the discourse in Romans 7:14–25 is presented in the first-person singular (I, me). There is a longstanding debate about the identity of the speaker in Romans 7. The most obvious candidate, of course, is Paul himself, the writer of the letter as a whole. One problem with that theory is that it seems to conflict with Paul's own statements about himself before his "conversion." For example, in Galatians 1:14 Paul claims: "I advanced in Judaism beyond many among my people." And in Philippians 3:6 he contends: "as to righteousness under the law, blameless." One can explain this conflict to some extent in terms of the different rhetorical situations. In Galatians and Philippians Paul was establishing his credentials as an observant Jew, whereas in Romans his goal was to show that the Jewish Law on its own could not bring about right relationship with God (justification). But taking Romans 7 as strictly autobiographical and applicable to Paul alone is probably too narrow a reading.

Most interpreters today regard Romans 7 as the cry of all humankind before and apart from Christ. Insofar as Paul once shared that condition, it is his cry too. But it is also the cry of all humans since Adam, and so in that sense Paul uses first-person language to speak on behalf of them. It is wrong to take Romans 7 simply as the cry of one conflicted and tortured soul (that is, of Paul alone). Paul intends to speak for a much larger constituency.

In Romans 7:14, Paul brings together many of his key terms and ideas used thus far in this letter. While acknowledging that the Law is spiritual, Paul as a representative human before and apart from Christ and living under the shadow of Adam describes his condition as "of the flesh, sold into slavery under sin." Here to be "of the flesh" (*sarx*) refers to the person as open to and led by the promptings of Sin, Death, and the Law. It is synonymous with being fallen and totally self-oriented. To be "sold into slavery under sin" means to be under the dominion of Sin (and Death), much like those who follow the Prince of Darkness in the Qumran *Rule of the Community*. In this condition the Law, while good in itself, becomes a stimulus or provocation to further sins.

The conflict that plagues persons in this condition is sketched in Romans 7:15–20. Admitting that he is a puzzle even to himself ("I do not understand my own actions"), Paul as a representative human complains that "I do not do what I want, but I do the very thing I hate" (7:15). The closest ancient parallel is from the Roman poet Ovid, who in his *Metamorphoses* 8.19–20 states: *video meliora proboque, deteriora sequor* ("I see the better things and approve them, but I follow the worse").

However, here Paul is talking about something far more powerful and encompassing than weakness of will. Rather, he is describing the human condition as "sold into slavery under sin" (7:15). He twice describes this state as a kind of possession by Sin: "It is no longer I that do it, but sin that dwells within me" (7:17, 20). Before and apart from Christ, says Paul, human beings are so enslaved under Sin, Death, and the Law that they cannot even do the good deeds that they want to do. Such persons neither understand themselves nor will the effects of their actions.

In the second part of his lament (7:21–25) Paul contrasts his experience of the "law of God" and "the law of sin." While approving and delighting in the Law of God, he nevertheless finds himself in a war between the two laws or "systems" and discovers that too often the law of sin wins out. This realization is the context for his cry and his question in 7:24: "Wretched man that I am! Who will rescue me from this body of death?"

Is Paul's analysis too pessimistic? Certainly his picture of the human condition before and apart from Christ in Romans 7 is very bleak. Some scholars (notably E. P. Sanders) suggest that Paul was arguing backward from solution to plight. In other words, Paul was so convinced and enthusiastic about what he believed had happened to him through Jesus' life, death, and resurrection (the solution) that he tended to exaggerate the negative features of the human condition under the dominion of Sin, Death, and the Law (the plight). The theological strategy of denigrating the human condition as a way of increasing and celebrating the power and glory of God appears in the Old Testament and various Jewish texts (most prominently in the Qumran Thanksgiving Hymns). In the context of Romans then, so the argument goes, Paul's description of the dismal condition of humans before and apart from Christ would be part of his positive theological program of highlighting the salutary effects of the Christ-event and so glorifying God.

Is Paul too optimistic? This charge is raised against Paul by those who contend that he thought the Christ-event did too much. But Paul was not naive. He recognized that even after baptism Christians could and did sin. His earlier letters—1 Thessalonians, Galatians, 1 and 2 Corinthians, Philippians, and Philemon—provide abundant evidence of Paul's recognition of sins committed by Christians. Indeed, the reason for his ethical instructions was to keep Christians from falling back into Sin. However, in Romans 1–8, Paul was more interested in Sin than in sins—in Sin as a force in salvation history, as the cause of Death, and as capable of enlisting God's Law in the battle against God, Christ, and the Holy Spirit. In that cosmic context, Paul's optimism about Christ overruled his pessimism about the human condition.

NEW LIFE IN CHRIST JESUS AND IN THE HOLY SPIRIT

Paul was convinced that a new era in salvation history had begun with Jesus' death and resurrection. This conviction seems to have been the primary result of his own experience of the risen Christ on the Damascus Road: "God . . . was pleased to reveal his Son to me" (Galatians 1:15–16). The focus of Paul's theology is sometimes described as christological soteriology; that is, it focuses on the saving effects or significance of Jesus' death and resurrection. Paul describes these effects in many ways: justification, sanctification, reconciliation, atonement, salvation, peace with God, access to God, and so on. These effects, Paul believed, not only pertain to the end-time but also shape Christian life in the present.

According to Romans 5:12–21, Sin and Death came into the world through Adam's sin, described in Genesis 3. As a result, all humans repeated the experience of Adam: "All have sinned" (5:12). But Christ, according to Paul, was more powerful than Adam, and likewise life in Christ is far better than life in Adam. Adam and Christ represent two ways of thinking about the human condition, two bearers of very different destinies, and two options placed before humans.

For his contrast between Adam and Christ in Romans 5:12–21, Paul takes as his starting point the account of Adam's sin in Genesis 3. There his sin is one of disobedience to God's commandment not to eat of the fruit of the tree of the knowledge of good and evil. Adam's one sin then unleashed a whole series of sins, to the point that there seems to be something terribly wrong about humans. Capable of so much good, they are also capable of great evil. Adam's sin brought condemnation from God not only upon Adam and Eve but also upon all their descendants. And one of the consequences of Adam's sin, according to Genesis 3:19, was death. In summary, then, Adam's sin brought disobedience, sin, condemnation, and death.

According to Paul, Adam and Christ represent two aspects or dimensions of the human condition. But Paul wants even more to emphasize that the gift (which is Christ) is not like the transgression (which is Adam and his sin). The gift has come to us in and through Jesus' life, death, and resurrection. While the result of Adam's sin was the reign of Sin and Death for all humans, the result of Jesus' sacrificial fidelity is the reign of grace and life for all humankind.

Where Adam was disobedient toward God's commandment, Christ was obedient to his Father's will even to the point of death. Whereas Adam sinned, Christ remained perfectly righteous and without sin. Whereas Adam brought condemnation upon himself and upon all humans, Christ brought acquittal from condemnation at the judgment and the possibility of a new relationship with God (justification). And whereas Adam brought death upon us all, Christ brings to us all the possibility of eternal life with God. In summary, then, Christ's sacrificial fidelity brought obedience, righteousness, acquittal or justification, and life.

Since the resurrection of Jesus, life in Christ Jesus is effectively life in the Holy Spirit, who carries on the work of Jesus. In Romans 8:5, Paul recapitulates the dualistic schema that has been the framework for much of his letter thus far: "For those who live according to the flesh set their minds on the things of the flesh, but those who live according to the Spirit set their minds on the things of the Spirit." In the present time between the resurrection of Jesus and the last judgment, the Spirit takes on the role of Christ/the angel of Light as the champion and guide of those who seek spiritual things and do good works.

Paul reminds the Roman Christians about where they now stand before God: "But you are not in the flesh; you are in the Spirit" (8:9). The varied terms that Paul uses to describe the Holy Spirit in 8:9–11 serve to remind the readers of the Spirit's close connections with Christ and God the Father. Paul refers in turn to "the Spirit of God . . . the Spirit of Christ . . . Christ in you . . . the Spirit . . . the Spirit of him who raised Jesus from the dead." And just as Paul before and apart from Christ lamented about "sin that dwells within me" (7:20, 23), now he celebrates the Spirit "that dwells in you" (8:11). The essence of Christian life in the present is to be led by the Holy Spirit: "For all who are led by the Spirit of God are children of God" (8:14). Being led or drawn on by the Spirit means being able to call upon God as "Abba! Father!" as Jesus did, and to be glorified with him "if, in fact, we suffer with him" (8:17).

The proviso about suffering with Christ is a reminder that Christians do not yet share in the fullness of God's kingdom. In fact, in Romans 8:18–25, Paul paints a vivid picture of all creation eagerly awaiting "the revealing of the children of God" (8:19). He describes the present state of Christians both as having "the first fruits of the Spirit" (through faith and baptism) and as groaning inwardly "while we wait for adoption, the redemption of our bodies" (8:23). Meanwhile, it is the Spirit who "helps us in our weakness" (8:26), even to the point of aiding us in prayer and interceding for us with God (8:27).

If God is for us, who can be against us? This rhetorical question, treated in Romans 8:31–39, expresses Paul's basic conviction about life in Christ and in the Spirit. No one and no thing can separate those who are in the Spirit "from the love of God in Christ Jesus our Lord" (8:39).

Perhaps Paul is too pessimistic about life before and apart from Christ. And perhaps he is too optimistic about the radical change that faith and baptism could bring in the present lives of Christians.There is nonetheless a realism and a balance about Paul's theological interpretation of the human condition.

Paul saw clearly that all people—Jews and Gentiles both—needed God's intervention to overcome the dominion of Sin and Death. He found in Jesus' death and resurrection the possibility of freedom from those powers and the opportunity to serve God as the only true master. He acknowledged the reality of suffering, the commission of sins by believers, and the eager longing (even groaning) for the fullness of God's kingdom on the part of those who are in the Spirit. At the same time, he regarded those who are led by the Spirit as loved by God, as free to serve God, as able to do good deeds, and as moving toward fullness of life with God.

SELECT BIBLIOGRAPHY

Bultmann, Rudolf. *Theology of the New Testament.* New York: Scribner, 1955.
Byrne, Brendan. *Romans.* Collegeville, MN: Liturgical Press, 1996.

Deidun, Thomas J. *New Covenant Morality in Paul.* Rome: Pontifical Biblical Institute, 1981.

Fitzmyer, Joseph A. *Romans.* New York: Doubleday, 1993.

Gundry, Robert H. *Soma in Biblical Theology with Emphasis on Pauline Anthropology.* Cambridge, England: Cambridge University Press, 1976.

Jewett, Robert. *Paul's Anthropological Terms: A Study of Their Use in Conflict Settings.* Leiden, the Netherlands: Brill, 1971.

Lambrecht, Jan. *The Wretched "I" and Its Liberation: Paul in Romans 7 and 8.* Leuven, Belgium: Peeters, 1992.

Longenecker, Richard N., ed. *The Road from Damascus: The Impact of Paul's Conversion on His Life, Thought, and Ministry.* Grand Rapids, MI: Eerdmans, 1997.

Sanders, E. P. *Paul and Palestinian Judaism.* Philadelphia: Fortress, 1977.

Wright, N. T. *The Climax of the Covenant: Christ and the Law in Pauline Theology.* Edinburgh, Scotland: T&T Clark, 1991.

Chapter Four

Conversion and the Human Condition: Theological Perspectives

ARTISTIC REPRESENTATIONS

I want us to consider two painters, Michelangelo and Caravaggio, who each depicted the conversion of St. Paul. Each also accompanied their Pauline conversion painting with a rendition of the crucifixion of St. Peter.

Michelangelo's painting *Conversion of St. Paul* (1542–1545) hangs in the Pauline chapel of the papal apartments. It is on a massive canvas at one end of an enormous hall, with the Peter painting at the other end. Together they mark the last paintings of Michelangelo. In the Paul painting, God, accompanied by angels and saints, sails majestically and powerfully from heaven onto the human terrain to claim Paul. God dominates the upper half of the canvas and dramatically enters history by parting the sky and allowing heaven's light to aim tornado-like on the person of Paul. God intervenes directly onto a plain, scattering fifteen others who are terrified by the display of sheer heavenly force. Paul's horse gallops away. As everyone else flees, an elderly, white-bearded, stunned, fallen, and blinded Paul shields his face, as he is compelled by the light and helped by his companion to sit up. The light from God shining on Paul connects the painting's upper half with its lower half, joining God's kingdom and the Palestinian terrain.

Michelangelo's *Crucifixion of Peter* captures the moment that Peter is being raised upside down on the cross. A large crowd is there watching the activity. No one is fleeing; in fact, several are standing there in discussion about the matter they are beholding. Peter is old and wearing a loincloth, clearly not interested in any of the thirty persons witnessing the event. In fact, no one is there accompanying him. This lonely death, however, is shaped by Peter staring intently at the viewer. The viewer is brought into the narrative

41

as the sympathetic witness of Peter, who seems to have great resolve in facing his death.

At the center of the painting is Peter's very large cross, which gives the appearance of considerable weight. Peter's crucifixion will be the center of the human landscape.

Caravaggio's *Conversion of St. Paul* (1600) hangs in a small chapel at the Roman church of Maria del Popolo. Not ten feet across from it is the *Crucifixion of St. Peter* (1604). As opposed to the vastness of the Pauline chapel, this chapel is small, hardly able to hold fifteen viewers.

In the conversion of Paul, there are only three figures: Paul, an idle horse, and Paul's companion tending to the horse; neither is aware of what is happening to Paul. The horse stands there, not fleeing. Only Paul in his deep interiority is receiving the Lord. Paul is young, wearing armor, very handsome on his back, legs open, eyes closed. The conversion is an ecstatic moment in which Paul is purely the recipient of God's grace. It has a deeply erotic tone to it. Paul's muscled body is aching for its transformation. He's in union with the Lord. This deeply, internalized conversion clearly conveys that God is doing something to Paul.

It also conveys the difference from the Pauline letters between the body as *sarx* and as *soma*. There is not a jot of *sarx* in Paul's conversion. His body is being absolutely claimed by God. It is *soma*, radiantly so.

God is not, as in the Michelangelo painting, visible. God is present nonetheless, but in Paul, because someone is doing something to Paul. Caravaggio capture's Paul's experience, making sure that the agent we see active is not actually Paul but God. Even though you see God in Michelangelo, still your eyes move to Paul. In Caravaggio, you see Paul, but you look for God.

This move by Caravaggio is insightful. The event is not Paul being turned around. The event is Paul deeply attuned to the presence of God in his life. Rather than a (literally) striking approach to Paul's conversion (à la Michelangelo), Caravaggio's Paul seems like he is being seduced willingly into a new relationship.

In Caravaggio's *Crucifixion of St. Peter,* Peter is old, nearly naked, on his back, too. Though there is a similarity to the "pose" of Paul, there is nothing erotic about this moment. Peter's legs are bound closed and as in Michelangelo's painting, Peter's cross is about to be raised with his head downward. Though three faceless figures are erecting the cross with Peter's body on it, they are unaware of the significance of the moment. There is no discussion; they are just the workers carrying out the execution. Peter looks tired and resigned, focusing almost meditatively on his left hand, which has been nailed to the cross. He seems captured by the act that is unfolding. He's at the end of the conversion narrative: Just as the call of Paul would lead to death, so here ends the call of Peter. The fisherman is about to be executed, dying the death of the one whom he denied. These are worthy meditations for Christian conversion.

THE ABSOLUTE PRIORITY OF GOD'S LOVE AND ACTION

In both conversions we see the absolute priority of God's activity. God enters exteriorly or interiorly into our world on God's own initiative. The definitive beginning of Paul's call is in God's hands and is part of God's providential plan. Paul, in both paintings, seems to be familiar with God—surprised, of course, by God's action, but not alienated from it. Paul is receiving revelation from God. The narrative of his journey is coming together.

The Australian Redemptorist Brian Johnstone wisely wants us to appreciate that there is a before, during, and after of conversion. He argues that most conversion accounts occur in the form of a narrative. Narrative is not simply a story but rather a way of connecting sequences in belief and attitude, in the lives of persons and in the traditions of communities.

Here we can ask a question about the "moment" of conversion. If one has been baptized as an infant and raised in the faith, is there a conversion to be expected or needed? Surely Paul was converted, but was Peter? For that matter, were John the Baptizer, Mary, the Mother of Jesus, or any of the other followers of Jesus converted? The language of conversion that locates the depth of one's relationship with God in a dramatic, specific salutary event strikes many as foreign to their experience.

Isn't there a way when we talk of conversion that we are really talking about the deepening awareness of the presence of God in our lives accompanied by an awareness of a specific call from God? When does that call occur?

St. Ignatius of Loyola speaks less of conversion and more of an election. He refers to three ways of making an election, recognizing that the call of Paul was fairly rare. He writes in the *Spiritual Exercises*:

> First Time: The first time is, when God our Lord so moves and attracts the will, that without doubting, or being able to doubt, such devout soul follows what is shown it, as St. Paul and St. Matthew did in following Christ our Lord.
>
> Second Time: The second, when enough light and knowledge is received by experience of consolations and desolations, and by the experience of the discernment of various spirits.
>
> Third Time: The third time is quiet, when one considers, first, for what man is born—namely, to praise God our Lord and save his soul—and desiring this chooses as means a life or state within the limits of the Church, in order that he may be helped in the service of his Lord and the salvation of his soul.

> I said time of quiet, when the soul is not acted on by various spirits, and uses its natural powers freely and tranquilly.
> If election is not made in the first or the second time, two ways follow as to this third time for making it.

Ignatius then outlines a series of six insights for one perspective on the third way and another set of insights to guide us in making that election, presuming that most of us are somehow located around this third (reflective) form of election. Ignatius realizes that we may not be converted, but we do need to be attentive to experience a sense of a particular call and that we need to be responsive to it.

Is that call a moment? Certainly there is some point when we realize that we responded to the call, but isn't even that response something we recognize often years after we did make that response?

In some instances, like Paul's, it clearly is a recognizable moment; a moment of conversion or call connects the past with the future. In others it is part of a trajectory in which we realize how deeply God has called us. Neither of these ways is superior to the other. Each of us is offered a call according to our histories: Some may have frequent illuminating experiences of God and name that array as the call; others may have a Pauline-like experience; and still others may simply assess God's will for them.

Whether it is momentary or a trajectory, the call, says Johnstone, is a breaking in to the conscious mind of connections that have long been forming in the unconscious. Long before the call, God is already at work in us, though often we do not yet recognize God's powerful presence in our lives. At some point, we are able to identify the call or conversion, as we see and understand the long-standing involvement of God in our lives. It is that recognition of the working of God that becomes so key, and we need a narrative in order to locate the call. Still, does that discovery of the call mean that we are actually aware and present to the moment of conversion or call?

Here I think of the call of Moses. When did Moses actually associate the burning bush with the definitive nature of his call? Was it actually as he heard the bush call to him? Or could it have been while he was wandering the desert with his entire tribe in tow that he asked himself, "How did I get here?" He tries to find out. He recalls the burning bush, and it becomes for him the centerpiece of his account. But when did he realize that it was?

The narrative of Moses highlights the agency of God, from his birth and the protection during his infancy, to his lethal combat with the Egyptian, to his encounters with Pharaoh, to the dying days. But when did the narrative of God's movements become irrevocably known to Moses? Certainly many call and conversion "moments" are part of an extended narrative, in which at some point we realize that the history of the narrative comes together. That is, often we do not even know the moment, but rather look back at our lives and see that God has been calling us.

Often we do not know when God's call first occurs. Think of the account of the disciples on the road to Emmaus. At the end of their encounter with Jesus, they recount that they recognized him in the breaking of the bread. But in their walk, the risen Jesus has already unfolded for them the meaning of the Scriptures. Later when they realize the moment has come, they look back: Were not our hearts on fire?

Part of the reason for raising the question of the moment of conversion is that in the narrative we acknowledge that long before we respond to or even recognize the call, God is working within us.

Psalm 139:1–9 tells us this:

> O Lord, you have probed me, you know me:
> you know when I sit and stand; you understand my thoughts from afar.
> My travels and my rest you mark; with all my ways you are familiar.
> Even before a word is on my tongue, LORD, you know it all.
> Behind and before you encircle me and rest your hand upon me.
> Such knowledge is beyond me, far too lofty for me to reach.
> Where can I hide from your spirit? From your presence, where can I flee?
> If I ascend to the heavens, you are there; if I lie down in Sheol, you are there too.

In *The Confessions* (10.27), Augustine captures the beauty of God's enduring pursuit of us. That God is constant in pursuing us. Augustine recounts God's work in his life *and* his delay in recognizing that work:

> Late have I loved you, O Beauty ever ancient, ever new, late have I loved you!
> You were within me, but I was outside, and it was there that I searched for you.
> In my unloveliness I plunged into the lovely things which you created. You
> were with me, but I was not with you. Created things kept me from you; yet
> if they had not been in you they would have not been at all. You called, you
> shouted, and you broke through my deafness. You flashed, you shone, and you
> dispelled my blindness. You breathed your fragrance on me; I drew in breath
> and now I pant for you. I have tasted you, now I hunger and thirst for more. You
> touched me, and I burned for your peace.

This passage from Augustine ought to remind us that even though our call, our salvation and redemption is inaugurated exclusively by God, still God waits for our response. God's call requires our assent. God, who created us in our freedom, does not possess us unwillingly; God may seduce us, but God still leaves us free to accept the call.

This work of God has great ramifications for moral theology. Not only does it affirm the absolute priority of God, not only does it convey God's loving and unrelenting pursuit of us, but it also instructs us in the order of love. Earlier in the *Confessions* (3.6), Augustine acknowledges that God is closer to us than we are to ourselves: "You were inside me deeper than the deepest recesses of my heart." Because of God's proximity, Augustine argues for the order of love to be love of God, love of self, love of neighbor.

This is not a hierarchical order but an order of relatedness or intimacy. We love God because God is more intimate to us than we are to ourselves, and we love ourselves before our neighbor because in us God is closer to us than the presence of God in our neighbors. This is not then an order based on some command; rather it is a deepening of our relationship with God and through it a deepening of our relationships with self and others.

THE ABSOLUTE PRIORITY OF JESUS CHRIST

Just as all initiatives come first from God, so too the person of Jesus Christ precedes all others. Adam is made in the image of Jesus. In a manner of speaking, there is no human condition before Christ. Indeed, Christ is the alpha and the omega of human existence.

Michelangelo captures this in the Sistine Chapel. If we look up at the central ceiling panel, we see the person of Adam in the creation by God. We look at his face and then look at the face of the figure of the risen Jesus on the front wall, depicting the last judgment. Sooner or later we see the similarity. Adam created in the image of God bears the imprint of Jesus, who is the firstborn of all creation. Before Adam, there was the Word.

Think of the remarkable testimony of John in the opening of his Gospel:

> In the beginning was the Word, and the Word was with God, and the Word was God.
> He was in the beginning with God.
> All things came to be through him, and without him nothing came to be. What came to be through him was life, and this life was the light of the human race; the light shines in the darkness, and the darkness has not overcome it.

Jesus has always been at work in us. Our whole history is caught up in his, and we are united to God through him. In the tenth book of *Paradise Lost*, John Milton describes the wonderful passage from Genesis in which our first parents, Adam and Eve, realize their nakedness. His interpretation is remarkable. The one who clothes us in the garden is the one who disrobes himself at the Last Supper. In both, Jesus assumes the position of a servant, who dresses humanity and who later washes their feet as well.

Milton writes:

then pittying how they stood
Before him naked to the aire, that now
Must suffer change, disdain'd not to begin
Thenceforth the form of servant to assume,
As when he wash'd his servants feet so now
As Father of his Familie he clad
Thir nakedness with Skins of Beasts

Conversion then is an awakening to the movements of God and Jesus Christ. It is a reminder of God's creation as a continuous unfolding of what God has begun. It is then an unfolding narrative, and like the call of Paul leading to the crucifixion of Peter, the narrative is all-embracing. Like the paintings, the narrative is personal, historical, and concrete.

The naming of the conversion or call is only possible after we have become awakened and aware and responsive. Naming it, then, is an act of gratitude, whether for Moses, Peter, Paul, or Augustine. But the act of naming it allows us to see more and more about the nature of our lives. We become like Paul, acknowledging that the way we live now is distinctively different from the way we once lived.

Like the song "Amazing Grace," acknowledging God's intimate work in our history prompts us to be thankful. We become surprised by what God has accomplished in us. The theologian James Alison notes that we recognize the identifying mark of conversion when we experience a subverted, inclusive gratitude. When we experience gratitude we might ask ourselves, "Why are we grateful?" (other than gratitude's being a sign of the Holy Spirit!).

Alison marks conversion as the bringing down of one's own righteousness and the ineffable encounter with the unambiguous love of God. He recounts his own experience over some time, when in the context of great negativity surrounding his life and after some time with these experiences of rejection and alienation, he began to realize that he was being "caught and held through the depths in which the utterly terrifying and yet completely gentle, unambiguous 'yes' of God started to suggest into being the consciousness of a son, to bring forth the terrifying novelty of an unbound conscience" (p. 95). In that conscientiousness, unbound and not exclusive, we learned to call on the name of the Lord.

THE RESPONSE TO LOVE

Paul responded to his own conversion in a way that ought to help us all. First, Paul disowned the righteousness he enjoyed. In Galatians (1:13–14) Paul wrote about his zeal for advancement in Judaism, and in Philippians (3:4–6) of his "blameless righteousness." But in light of his encounter with the glory of the Lord (1 Corinthians 15:8), he called his past "loss" and "rubbish" (Philippians 3:8).

Whereas before his conversion, Paul basically lived for his own advancement, now he pursues a completely other-directed mission, preaching the gospel. Here he serves Christ the Lord, but he also seeks to summon others to the glory of God. They become his work in the Lord (1 Corinthians 9:1). For them he becomes all things: His own self becomes malleable so that he can make in various forms the type of appeals to others so as to welcome them into Christ.

In looking at the absolute priority of God and Jesus Christ, we see these priorities in Paul after his conversion: Nothing means anything to him but Jesus Christ. However, rather than withdrawing, he evangelizes. Rather than remaining in prayer where he would be in singular discourse between him and God, Paul preaches the word of God. Paul's caring service and mindfulness of the well-being of others is constitutive of his answer to the call. Not only is he changed in his relationship to God, he has changed in his stance toward humanity: He has now become servant of all.

We will see later how faith, hope, and charity shape the lives of every Christian, and we will look at the virtues that Paul promotes. But here we should acknowledge that for Paul, the conversion makes possible a new direction in his life, not only for God but also for the entire Mediterranean population.

SELECT BIBLIOGRAPHY

Alison, James. *Faith beyond Resentment: Fragments Catholic and Gay.* New York: Crossroad, 2001.

Conn, Walter. *Christian Conversion: A Developmental Interpretation of Autonomy and Surrender.* New York: Paulist Press, 1986.

Happel, Stephen, and James J. Walter. *Conversion and Discipleship: A Christian Foundation for Ethics and Doctrine.* Philadelphia: Augsburg/Fortress, 1986.

Johnstone, Brian. "The Dynamics of Conversion." In *Spirituality and Morality: Integrating Prayer and Action*, edited by Dennis Billy and Donna Orsuto, 32–48. New York: Paulist Press, 1996.

Rahner, Karl. "Conversion." In *Encyclopedia of Theology: The Concise Sacramentum Mundi*, edited by Karl Rahner, V. 291–94. New York: Seabury Press, 1975.

Schindler, David. "History, Objectivity, and Moral Conversion." *Thomist* 37 (1973): 569–88.

Chapter Five

The Many Contexts of Paul's Ethical Teachings

THE CHRISTIAN THEOLOGICAL CONTEXT: ROMANS 12:9–16

A fundamental principle in understanding the "ethical" teachings contained in the New Testament in general and in Paul's letters in particular can be expressed in this way: Context is almost everything. Content counts, too. In Romans 12–13, Paul supplies a large amount of what can be called "ethical" teaching. Taken out of its present context, much of it sounds like what appears in the Old Testament wisdom books or in the writings of Greco-Roman moralists. But in the theological context of Paul's letter to the Romans, it becomes Christian moral teaching.

The grand story of salvation mapped out by Paul in Romans 1–11 provides the larger context for the ethical teachings presented in Romans 12–13. In those chapters, Paul established that all people (Jews and Gentiles alike) needed the revelation of God's righteousness in Christ; that Christ has liberated believers after the pattern of Abraham from the dominion of the three powers (Sin, Death, and the Law) and for life in the Spirit; and that God has a plan for salvation history that involves Christian Jews like Paul, Gentile Christians, and non-Christian Jews. It is against this broad theological background that we need to read Romans 12–13 and other "ethical" sections in his letters.

The ethical teachings in Romans 12–13 are introduced by a preface in 12:1–8 that places them in a Christian theological setting. With his opening word *parakalo* ("I appeal"), Paul characterizes what follows as advice or exhortation rather than as rules and regulations. He professes to give advice about the worship in everyday life that constitutes the spiritual "sacrifice" of the Christian, and he urges his readers to act as citizens of the new creation by discerning God's will and acting upon it (12:1–2). Then he reminds the

49

readers that they constitute "one body in Christ, and individually we are members of one another" (12:5) and so have responsibilities for and to each other. Finally he insists that each Christian is a gifted or charismatic person ("We have gifts that differ according to the grace given to us," 12:6a), and goes on to show how those gifts might be used to build up the church as the body of Christ (12:6b–8).

If context is almost everything for understanding Paul's ethical teachings, then Romans 1–11 in general and 12:1–8 in particular provide ample theological context: the need for Christ, the history of salvation, Christian freedom, eschatology, worship, the body of Christ, and the charismatic community. With all these great themes in mind, we can focus on the following sample of Paul's "ethical" teaching found in Romans 12:9–16:

> 9. Let love be genuine; hate what is evil, hold fast to what is good; 10. love one another with mutual affection; outdo one another in showing honor. 11. Do not lag in zeal, be ardent in spirit, serve the Lord. 12. Rejoice in hope, be patient in suffering, persevere in prayer. 13. Contribute to the needs of the saints; extend hospitality to strangers. 14. Bless those who persecute you; bless and do not curse them. 15. Rejoice with those who rejoice, weep with those who weep. 16. Live in harmony with one another; do not be haughty, but associate with the lowly; do not claim to be wiser than you are.

The passage takes the form of a gnomic discourse; that is, it is an epitome or collection of short maxims or aphorisms that are presented in a rapid-fire style and in the form of imperatives or their grammatical equivalents. In fact, many of the commands take the grammatical forms of infinitives and participles ("hating . . . holding fast"), which according to some commentators suggest a Semitic (Hebrew or Aramaic) background. (For another Pauline example of such a gnomic discourse, see 1 Thessalonians 5:12–22.)

The block of ethical teachings in Romans 12:9–16 lists the virtues, attitudes, and actions that are most appropriate for Christian life within the body of Christ and the charismatic community. The opening phrase in Romans 12:9a ("Let love be genuine") sets the tone for what follows. Whereas thus far in Romans, Paul had focused mainly on God's love for us made manifest in Christ, now he considers how mutual love might be made manifest within the Christian community. A "genuine" or unfeigned (literally, "not hypocritical") love is one that is practical and issues in good actions; it is not merely a matter of words.

What follows in Romans 12:9b–13 is a series of short sayings arranged in pairs and with similar content: 9b and 9c, 10a and 10b, 11a and 11b, 11c and 12a, 12b and 12c, and 13a and 13b. Most of these sayings use participles to express their orders or commands.

The strong language in the first pair of sayings ("Hate what is evil, hold fast to what is good," 12:9b–c) fits well in the framework of modified apocalyptic dualism that was established earlier in Paul's letter to the Romans. The second pair (12:10) transfers to the community the spirit that should prevail in the household at its best: "Love one another with mutual affection; outdo one another in showing honor." The third pair ("Do not lag in zeal, be ardent in spirit," 12:11a–b) flows from the Christian community's identity as the body of Christ and the assembly of those who have been gifted by the Holy Spirit.

The fourth and fifth pairs seem to insert an eschatological horizon, with their mentions of serving the Lord and rejoicing in hope (12:11c and 12:12a), and of being patient in suffering and persevering in prayer (12:12b and 12:12c). The sixth pair (12:13) calls for generosity in contributing to the collection for "the saints" (the poor Christians in Jerusalem) and in showing hospitality to strangers. Thus these six pairs of short sayings illustrate how genuine love can be practiced within Christian community life.

The literary pattern changes somewhat in Romans 12:14–16 where the "commands" are expressed in turn by imperatives (12:14), infinitives (12:15), and participles (12:16). The double command to "bless those who persecute you" in 12:14 echoes Jesus' teaching in Matthew 5:44 (see Luke 6:27–28). The call to show compassion in all circumstances of both joy and sorrow (12:15) echoes in part Sirach 7:34: "Do not avoid those who weep, but mourn with those who mourn." And the call to make a realistic reckoning of oneself in 12:16 ("Do not claim to be wiser than you are") features the verb *phronein* and so recalls 12:3 ("Think with sober judgment"), thus rounding off the unit and linking the content (12:9–16) with the context (12:3–8).

Where did these ethical teachings come from? Some may have come from Paul himself, as the verbal links (*phronein* and related terms) in Romans 12:3 and 12:16 suggest. At least one teaching here may have come from a saying attributed to Jesus in the Synoptic tradition: "Bless those who persecute you" (12:14; see Matthew 5:44). Some might have come from the Old Testament, if it could be proved that Paul knew the book of Sirach (12:15); see Romans 12:19–20, where Paul explicitly bases his ethical teachings on Deuteronomy 32:35 and Proverbs 25:21–22. The sharp division implied in 12:9b–c is reminiscent of the Jewish apocalyptic dualism witnessed in the Qumran *Rule of the Community*. And the use of pairs and the tight structure (which would facilitate memorization) suggest that here Paul may have been using an early Christian catechetical piece. The possibility of very different sources contributing to the moral teachings conveyed by Paul in Romans 12:9–16 confirms the point with which this exposition began: Context is almost everything.

An important part of context is the kind of motivation provided for acting in the ways sketched by the various short sayings. In this passage, perhaps the most obvious reason for appropriate ethical behavior is the assumption that personal integrity, altruism, generosity, and the related virtues and actions can and do contribute to individual and communal happiness. On a more theological level, these instructions illustrate the attitudes and actions that would enable the church at Rome to be the body of Christ and the charismatic community described in 12:3–8. These ethical teachings also spell out what it means to be ardent or glowing in spirit/the Spirit and to serve the Lord (12:11). And the hints at eschatology in 12:12 link the practice of these teachings to the last judgment, when "God, through Jesus Christ, will judge the secret thoughts of all" (Romans 2:16).

INDICATIVE AND IMPERATIVE

Another way of saying that "Context is almost everything" in Pauline ethical teaching is to invoke the grammatical terms "indicative" and "imperative." A sentence in the indicative mood states a fact ("The dog is barking"), whereas a sentence with the verb in the imperative mood gives a command ("Be quiet, Fido"). The point of applying these terms to Pauline ethics is to emphasize that what we have become through Jesus' life, death, and resurrection should shape and direct what we do. Another (Thomistic) way to make the same point is to say: *agere sequitur esse* ("action follows being").

The basic insight that what Christians do should flow from who they are in Christ provides the key to understanding Paul's virtue ethics and indeed all of Paul's "ethical" teachings. Christian being and Christian action go together. They are neither totally separate categories, nor should they be reduced to one category. Rather, what Christians have become in and through the Christ-event should express itself in actions that are appropriate to their state of being in Christ. Who we are in Christ (our identity) and what we wish to become (our goal) should determine what we do as the means toward achieving that goal (our actions).

This basic principle of virtue ethics (*agere sequitur esse*) is stated in various ways throughout Paul's letters. For example, in Galatians 5:25, Paul writes: "If we live by the Spirit, let us also be guided by the Spirit." Here Paul reminds the Galatians that they had already received the Holy Spirit and were living their Christian existence through the Spirit (see 3:2–4). The main purpose of his letter is to urge the Galatians to continue to live by the power of the Holy Spirit. He wants them to resist the promptings of other Jewish Christian missionaries who were trying to convince Gentile Christians to become Jews and to take upon themselves all the obligations of the Jewish Law. Having described the nature of Christian freedom (5:1–15) and having listed the "works of the flesh" (5:16–21) and the "fruit of the Spirit" (5:22–23), Paul insisted that the Galatian Christians should let their actions be guided by the Holy Spirit, who makes them who they are. The Spirit remains their life force and their dynamism. And what Christians do should be empowered and directed by the same Spirit. Or in other words, who we are (the indicative) ought to flow into and express itself in what we should do (the imperative).

Another example of the confluence between the indicative and the imperative in Pauline ethics occurs in an initially unlikely passage, where Paul tells the Philippians: "Work out your own salvation with fear and trembling" (2:12b). Read out of context, this instruction seems to place the terrible burden of saving oneself totally upon the individual Christian. And the phrase "with fear and trembling" certainly may raise the level of anxiety. However, the following verse (2:13) provides a balance and illustrates the importance of context in Pauline ethics. In 2:13, Paul adds: "For it is God who is at work in you, enabling you both to will and to work for his good pleasure." The quest for salvation, according to Paul, is not a lonely human pursuit. Rather, God is always working in us, by telling us who we are and showing us ways in which we might act in a manner appropriate to our identity in Christ. Both Galatians 5:25 and Philippians 2:12–13 insist that it is not simply a matter of God first supplying our identity in Christ and then our obeying God's commands all on our own. Rather, God in the Holy Spirit is with us, empowering and working with us, and helping us recognize both who we are in Christ and what we ought to do.

Paul also uses Christian identity as part of an argument about ethical conduct. In explaining why the Corinthians should avoid sexual immorality (*porneia*) in general and consorting with prostitutes in particular in 1 Corinthians 6:12–20, Paul argues that such immoral behavior is simply inappropriate in light of their identity in Christ: "The body is meant not for fornication but for the Lord, and the Lord for the body" (6:13).

When addressing the issue of visiting prostitutes, Paul becomes quite graphic in developing his case that such behavior is inconsistent with Christian identity. With an obvious reference to sexual intercourse, Paul asks rhetorically: "Should I therefore take the members of Christ and make them members of a prostitute?" (6:15). He goes on to remind them that through Jesus' life, death, and resurrection they "were bought with a price" (6:20), thus alluding to the exchange of money involved in prostitution. In developing his argument Paul reminds the Corinthian Christians "that your body is a temple of the Holy Spirit within you, which you have from God, and that you are not your own" (6:19). In this case Paul appeals to the dignity of Christians as members of the body of Christ and as temples of the Holy Spirit, in order to show them that certain kinds of conduct are not appropriate for them.

Paul's entire letter to the Romans can be viewed as an essay designed to establish that through the Christ-event persons of faith can participate in the new creation, which is the breaking in of the kingdom of God in the present. In Romans 12:1–2, Paul summarizes the whole process of redemption through Christ as the manifestation of "the mercies of God." The initiative of divine mercy has made it possible for Christians to be freed from the power of Sin, Death, and the Law and to be freed for life in the Holy Spirit.

In response to "the mercies of God," Christians should try to make their entire lives into an act of worship: "Present your bodies as a living sacrifice, holy and acceptable to God, which is your spiritual worship" (12:1). Furthermore, since through God's grace they now live not in "this world" but in the world (or age) to come, their task is to apply themselves to "discern what is the will of God—what is good and acceptable and perfect" (12:2). As redeemed persons touched by the grace of God, Christians have the obligation to conform their lives to what is their new identity in Christ. It is in the context of Christian identity (the indicative) that Paul presents his ethical directives (the imperatives) in Romans 12–13 and elsewhere in his letters.

THE LAST JUDGMENT

Acting in a manner that is appropriate to one's Christian identity is a major motivation in Paul's ethical teaching. But it is not the only motivation. For all his emphasis on realized or anticipated eschatology, Paul never loses sight of the future manifestation of the fullness of God's kingdom and the final judgment that will accompany it. On the one hand, Paul stresses that salvation is offered in the present to all who come to believe in Christ and that condemnation comes upon those who reject it. On the other hand, he is convinced that all who live "between the times"—between the Christ-event and the last judgment—will still have to face a future judgment. And the criterion by which all will be judged and then rewarded or punished involves the rightness and goodness of their actions: "For he will repay according to each one's deeds" (Romans 2:6).

The idea of a final judgment according to one's deeds was deeply rooted in Jewish apocalyptic thinking. It emerged in large part from Israel's traumatic experience of exile in the sixth century BCE and flourished from the second century BCE onward in light of the crisis brought about in Jerusalem by the Syrian king Antiochus IV Epiphanes and his Jewish collaborators. What was at stake in these events were the omnipotence and the justice of God, as well as Israel's hope in God's promises in the midst of its sufferings. As seen in the book of Daniel (composed around 165 BCE), Jewish apocalyptic thinking looked toward a final judgment before God when the righteous would be vindicated and the wicked punished. This judgment was regarded as the moment when God's omnipotence and justice would at last be fully manifest.

Jewish apocalypticism has been called "the mother of Christian theology" (by Ernst Käsemann). Jesus' preaching had as its main theme an apocalyptic concept: the kingdom of God. Likewise, Paul's theology is largely shaped by modified apocalyptic dualism, though modified by his Christian convictions about Jesus and his resurrection (another apocalyptic concept!). It is not surprising then that the apocalyptic concept of the last judgment should be a prominent element in Paul's ethical vision.

Jewish and Christian apocalyptic writings provide various scenarios for the last judgment. For example, in Daniel 7, with the "Ancient One" presiding, we are given a vision in which "the court sat in judgment, and the books were opened" (7:10). According to 4 Ezra (= 2 Esdras 3–14) 7:33–34, at the resurrection of the dead "the Most High shall be revealed on the seat of judgment, and compassion shall pass away, and patience shall be withdrawn. Only judgment shall remain, truth shall stand, and faithfulness shall grow strong." The most famous New Testament judgment scene appears in Matthew 25:31–46 where the glorious Son of Man rewards the just and punishes the wicked according to their deeds done (or not done) on behalf of "the least of these." And the last great apocalyptic scenario in the book of Revelation reaches its climax with the opening of the book of life, when the dead are "judged according to their works, as recorded in the books" (20:12). In Jewish and Christian apocalypticism, the last judgment is the definitive manifestation of the justice of God and the occasion for God to punish the wicked and to reward (and so vindicate) the righteous.

There are many allusions in Paul's letters to the last judgment and even references to the risen Christ as the judge (see 1 Thessalonians 5:2; 1 Corinthians 5:5; 2 Corinthians 1:14; Philippians 1:6, 10). The last judgment is clearly a presupposition of Paul's theology, not something that he felt he needed to explain or defend.

Paul's most extensive treatment of the topic appears in Romans 2:6–11. In the context of explaining why all people—Jews and Gentiles alike—needed the revelation of God's justice or righteousness in Christ, Paul warns that on "the day of wrath, when God's righteous judgment will be revealed" (2:5), God "will repay according to each one's deeds" (2:6). In 2:7–8 Paul contrasts the reward ("eternal life") for the righteous and the punishment of the wicked ("wrath and fury"). Then in a play on his own schema of salvation history ("to the Jew first and also to the Greek," 1:16), he asserts that in the giving of eschatological punishments and rewards that same order will be in force: "the Jew first and also the Greek" (2:9, 10).

Paul closes his presentation of the last judgment by stating another principle: "For God shows no partiality" (2:11). Just as all—Jews and Gentiles alike—needed the revelation of God's justice or righteousness in Christ, so all—Jews and Gentiles alike—will witness the justice of God at the last judgment. Then one's ethnicity will not count. What will count most are God's justice and "each one's deeds" (2:6). Whereas "the mercies of God" (12:1) have been on display throughout salvation history and especially in the Christ-event, at the last judgment the justice of God (with no partiality) will be manifest to all.

The prospect of a definitive divine judgment according to each one's deeds is a powerful motivation for proper ethical behavior in Paul's letters and almost everywhere else in the New Testament. Its presence in Scripture and in the Christian tradition should not be ignored or played down. Paul's warnings that we all will be judged according to our actions and that God will show no partiality serve to produce a healthy respect before the justice of God (the biblical meaning of "fear of the Lord") and a powerful motive for conduct that is appropriate for those who are "in Christ." For Paul (as for other Jews of his time), there was no contradiction between God's mercy and God's justice, or between faith and works (despite James 2). What counts before God is "faith working through love" (Galatians 5:6).

OTHER INFLUENCES

While Paul's own experience of the risen Christ and his belief in the last judgment were very important influences on his ethical teachings, the world in which Paul grew up—as a Jew in the Roman Empire—was also part of the context for his efforts at guiding his fellow Christians toward recognizing and living out the implications of their vocations as Christians in the present.

The most obvious influence on Paul was the Old Testament. In Philippians 3:5, Paul claims to have been "a Hebrew born of Hebrews; as to the law, a Pharisee." In various key passages in his letters (e.g., Galatians 3; Romans 4 and 9–11), Paul quotes many Old Testament texts (usually in their Greek Septuagint form) and weaves them into complex theological arguments. It is safe to say that a great many of Paul's theological terms, concepts, and assumptions came from the Jewish Scriptures, which constituted his "Bible."

Nevertheless, it is rare that Paul uses Old Testament texts as an explicit authority in making a practical or "ethical" argument (as opposed to a doctrinal one). One exception is his quoting Deuteronomy 25:4 ("You shall not muzzle an ox while it is treading grain") in 1 Corinthians 9:9, where he defends the practice of community support for apostles—something that Paul refused to accept for himself. Also in 1 Corinthians 10:6 and 11, Paul cites the negative example of ancient Israel's rebellious behavior in the wilderness as a warning to the Christians at Corinth. And in Romans 15:4, he observes regarding the Old Testament that "whatever was written in former days was written for our instruction."

Paul's attitude toward the Old Testament Law is one of the most difficult problems in New Testament scholarship. Indeed, it appears that Paul himself may have been somewhat confused on the matter and addressed it from several different perspectives. On the one hand, Paul claims that "the law is holy, and the commandment is holy and just and good" (Romans 7:12). On the other hand, according to Paul, before and apart from Christ, the Law became an ally of Sin and Death, and held people like Paul in a kind of spiritual slavery. Likewise, Paul says that "the one who loves another has fulfilled the law" (Romans 13:8) and that "the whole law is summed up in a single commandment, `You shall love your neighbor as yourself'" (Galatians 5:14). However, Paul also denies that he was overthrowing the Law by insisting on faith, and he affirms that "we uphold the law" (Romans 3:31). There is little or no evidence in Paul's letters for the later Christian theological distinction between the ethical (to be followed) and the cultic (to be disregarded) precepts of the Old Testament.

In Galatians 3:19, Paul raises the question "Why then the law?" And immediately he gives three answers: "because of transgressions" (that is, to specify sins and make people know what is a sin); "until the offspring would come to whom the promise had been made" (that is, to prepare for the coming of the Messiah); and "it was ordained through angels by a mediator" (that is, to provide a preparatory but inferior mode of divine revelation to ancient Israel). In 3:24, Paul goes on to describe the Law as "our disciplinarian" (*paidagogos*) until Christ came." The *paidagogos* was a servant or slave who cared for the children of wealthy families and accompanied them to and from school. While acknowledging the value of the *paidagogos,* Paul affirms "now that faith has come, we are no longer subject to a disciplinarian" (3:25).

It appears that on ethical matters Paul's attitude toward the Old Testament Law was pragmatic. Where a biblical text or precept (e.g., regarding incest in 1 Corinthians 5:1–5) strengthened or illustrated Paul's position, he used it. But as a moral authority the Law was clearly subordinate to the gospel (that is, the saving significance of Jesus' death and resurrection).

It is possible to discern other influences on Paul's ethical teachings besides the Old Testament. As a citizen of the Greco-Roman world and the recipient of a rhetorical education, Paul used the literary forms employed also by Greco-Roman moralists such as the epitome (see 1 Thessalonians 4:3–8; Romans 12:9–21) and the list of vices (Galatians 5:19–21; 1 Corinthians 6:9–10; Romans 1:29–31). For an anthology of key texts from the writings of the Greco-Roman moralists and suggestions about their relevance for New Testament studies, see Abraham J. Malherbe's *Moral Exhortation*. In his introduction, Malherbe makes an important point that pertains to the matter of context: "The major differences between the philosophers and Christians therefore reside in the way religion was thought to be related to ethics and in the different views of human nature that they held" (15). For example, the Stoic teacher Musonius Rufus proposed a very strict sexual ethic, like that of Paul: "All intercourse with women which is without lawful character is shameful and is practiced from lack of self-restraint. So no one with any self-control would think of having relations with a courtesan or a free woman apart from marriage, no, not even his own maid-servant" (Malherbe, 153). But the theological context in which Paul places his teachings about sexual ethics is very different and really most important (see chapter 21).

The warning against associating with unbelievers in 2 Corinthians 6:14–7:1 is so close to the ethical dualism recommended in the Dead Sea scrolls (especially the *Rule of the Community*) that some scholars have interpreted it as a textual interpolation from an Essene source. In 1 Corinthians 7:10–11, Paul claims to be quoting Jesus' own teaching about marriage and divorce ("not I but the Lord"). And there is at least some evidence for a body of Christian ethical instruction already in place before Paul wrote his letters: "the teaching you have learned" (Romans 16:17).

Paul is aptly described as a pastoral theologian, and his letters were pastoral communications rather than works of biblical exegesis, philosophy, systematic theology, or Christian ethics. Whatever ethical advice that he provides in these letters appears in a pastoral context. He never offers a treatise on method or a comprehensive presentation about the foundations of Christian ethics. His pastoral context determined to a large extent what he may have taken from his sources: the Old Testament, the Greco-Roman moralists, contemporary Judaism, Jesus, or Christian tradition. The center of Paul's theological vision remained "the surpassing value of knowing Christ Jesus my Lord" (Philippians 3:8). That experience was always the core context for Paul's ethical teachings.

SELECT BIBLIOGRAPHY

Bultmann, Rudolf. "The Problem of Ethics in Paul." In *Understanding Paul's Ethics: Twentieth-Century Approaches,* edited by Brian S. Rosner, 195–216. Grand Rapids, MI: Eerdmans, 1995.

Malherbe, Abraham J. *Moral Exhortation: A Greco-Roman Sourcebook.* Philadelphia: Westminster, 1986.

———. *Paul and the Popular Philosophers.* Philadelphia: Fortress, 1989.

Meeks, Wayne A. *The First Urban Christians: The Social World of the Apostle Paul.* New Haven, CT: Yale University Press, 1983.

———. *The Moral World of the First Christians.* Philadelphia: Westminster, 1986.

———. *The Origins of Christian Morality: The First Two Centuries.* New Haven, CT: Yale University Press, 1993.

Parsons, Michael. "Being Precedes Act: Indicative and Imperative in Paul's Writing." In *Understanding Paul's Ethics: Twentieth-Century Approaches,* edited by Brian S. Rosner, 217–47. Grand Rapids, MI: Eerdmans, 1995.

Plevnik, Joseph. *Paul and the Parousia: An Exegetical and Theological Investigation.* Peabody, MA: Hendrickson, 1997.

Raisanen, Heikki. *Paul and the Law.* Tübingen, Germany: Mohr Siebeck, 1987.

Sampley, J. Paul. *Walking between the Times: Paul's Moral Reasoning.* Minneapolis: Fortress, 1991.

Theissen, Gerd. *The Social Setting of Pauline Christianity: Essays on Corinth.* Philadelphia: Fortress, 1982.

Wilson, W. T. *Love without Pretense: Romans 12.9–21 and Hellenistic-Jewish Wisdom Literature.* Tübingen, Germany: Mohr, 1991.

Chapter Six

Experience and Conscience in Theology Today

Paul's experience of conversion not only transformed him but gave him an authority to preach the gospel without any endorsement. Christ himself has summoned Paul, and Paul knows that and insists on the task entrusted to him.

But what is experience? Isn't it one of the most fluid concepts of our age? One would think that the texts of Scripture emphasize God's word and God's teaching. But Paul receives that word through his own experience: He knows in the fibers of his being the call of Christ. For Paul, his experience is undeniable and becomes a model of Christian confidence in the providence of our God.

I begin by considering the stances of three theologians. First, Margaret Farley writes about experience as having a role in moral reasoning. She comments that experience

> is the actual living of the events and relationships along with the sensations, feelings, images, emotions, insights, and understandings that are a part of this lived reality. Experience in this sense is a given, something providing data to be interpreted; but also it is something already interpreted, its content shaped by previous understandings in a context of multiple influences. Moreover, experience . . . can belong both to the self and to others; it can be both personal and social. Experience is a private individual, unique to the one who experiences; but there are shared experiences, communicated as well as formed within communities and societies. Experience in each of these senses—given but not primitive, immediate but not innocent of interpretation, personal but not isolated, unique but not without a social matrix—plays an important role in moral discernment. It is a source of moral insight, a factor in moral judgment, a test of the rightness, goodness, and wisdom of moral decision. (135)

We should not miss the singularity of experience here, because in any given context no one else has ever lived and expressed the particularity of a specific situation before. Yet, often we want to communicate that experience. Whether solitary or shared, experience seeks to be reported, made known, and revealed. While unique and not repeatable, we are able to communicate its relevance and newness through language. We do not need to reinvent language; through language we express a new encounter.

Let's go to this restaurant. See this movie. Visit this gallery. The experience of these activities is precisely what we are looking for. There is a directness or immediacy to experience: It is not simply something we watch or read, but something we enter or participate in.

In one sense, experience is what we seek. We recall, for instance, the 1923 interview with George Leigh Mallory, who was asked why climb Mount Everest and simply responded, "Because it's there." Mallory, who died the following year in an expedition climbing the mountain, was climbing for, yes, the experience.

The late André Guindon wrote a work called *The Sexual Language*. In it he explored one of the most intimate experiential practices of the human being, our sexuality, which is important precisely because it is shared. If you think about it, few intimate practices are shared; on the contrary, they are often solitary. From our dreams to our prayers, our more intimate experiences are our own. Not so with sexuality, which is expressed by shared intimate experiences.

Guindon argued that sexual activity should be understood as language. This is a fascinating claim: It is not that sex is something we talk about; it is in itself an experiential mode of communication. Guindon saw sex as a human gesture by which one person expresses to another one's self, with emotion and meaning. In sexual activity that singular experience is shared with another. Guindon prompts us to see how often, say in sexual expression, someone is trying to communicate the desire for experience and the communication itself becomes the experience. But the experience is always about a sense of being connected.

And it captures again how there is a certain way that experiences between people have a certain intelligibility about them. We don't often use experience as a last, dismissive word ("Well, that was your experience!"); rather, we use it as a first word to explore our interior reception ("Tell me what your experience was"). Experience searches for communication.

We want to bring our experience into the world of others. Isn't that what evangelizers do? So we make appeals to experience. It serves as a standard to measure the claims of others. We use experience as a way of asking ourselves individually or collectively whether what is posited resonates with our own internal reception and assessment of reality.

Cristina Traina notes that experience is "perhaps both the most-cited factor and wildest variable in debates over methods and questions in ethics" (270). She wonders whether experience is always a true indicator. Does it sometimes validate another's experience when that experience has not yet matured? She reflects on hers and other's marital experiences and concludes "that norms limiting sex to marriage may be informed by a doctrine of procreative complementarity that reflects incomplete, immature experience" (284).

Traina's useful admonitions aside, let me offer an illustration of experience as a source of wisdom. Here, experience serves as a filter through which we weigh or discern interiorly our recognition of the true.

AN ILLUSTRATION

In February 2003, right after the shuttle disaster, I preached at St. Peter's Church in Cambridge where I have been working for more than fifteen years. It was the feast of the Presentation. I gave my homily on the Gospel reflecting on the characters of Simeon and Anna and their expectations and sense of vigilance, waiting to see what was on the horizon. I thought more and more of how their expectations were like those of the astronauts on the shuttle, filled with great expectations and a great sense of vigilance. I thought of the families of the astronauts and how they were, too. But then I thought how sometimes people with great expectations pay high prices and sometimes end up paying the ultimate price. I thought of similar people with great expectations: from Marie Curie to Amelia Earhart. I asked the congregation finally whether they had great enough expectations.

As I was doing this, I noticed that unlike other times, I was not connecting with the congregation. In my own experience, I found a rapport with the congregation developing as I preached, but this Sunday I wasn't doing that. Afterward I asked someone, and she said, "Oh, the sermon was fine—I liked it." I said, "But I didn't feel like I was speaking to people," and she replied, "I think they may just be sad over the tragedy." What she said struck me as true. They *were* sad. I saw it on their faces as they came for communion. They felt beaten down. They also felt the "inevitability" of the White House moving to war in Iraq; they were looking at another tragedy unfolding. The economy was beginning to show major signs of stress as well. They were down, and I was confronting them with whether their expectations were high enough!

My experience in giving the homily told me that something was not happening that usually did: I was not tapping into their experience. They came sad. That awareness struck me as true, once my friend suggested it to me. And instead of reflecting on the sadness, I was giving it a nice context: "Rise high.

You can fall hard, but that's what those with great expectations do." Here they were, and their expectations were now quite low. Have higher expectations, I was saying. Was what I was saying resonating with their experience?

The next day, I looked at the newspapers and found articles about how consoling the Sunday liturgies were. One pastor said, "They embodied our high hopes, and with their tragedy, we lost a little of our own expectations." He was acknowledging their loss, recognizing and acknowledging their experience. I was not. I was saying to them, "Why don't you have high expectations as the astronauts did?" I was giving a challenging pep talk, but these mature, hard-working, competent adults were not looking for that. When I came to this insight, my own experience of years of preaching there validated this assessment. Usually I ask myself what the congregation needs from the readings. I realized that I hadn't considered that. My experience made that clear to me.

Experience told me, first, that I was not connecting. Later I realized, second, that I had not adequately anticipated their experience of the weekend. Third, when I made the assessment that they deserved and needed to be consoled rather than challenged, the insight rang true to my experience. Experience became the backdrop against which I measured the rightness of my own exercise of pastoral ministry.

Experience is dependent on reflection and communication. I needed to learn what went wrong. Why the disconnect? I've seen experience work in a variety of ways, but one moral theologian helps me understand how communication serves as a way to connect experiences.

Not everyone agrees: The moral philosopher Immanuel Kant wrote on the first page of *The Critique of Pure Reason* that he saw no value in human experience: "Nothing, indeed, can be more harmful or more unworthy of the philosopher, than the vulgar appeal to so-called experience."

But the philosopher Martha Nussbaum thinks differently. In an essay on Aristotle, she helps us see that Aristotle is constantly appealing to an internal recognition of what it means to be a human being—that is, to some experiential affirmation that what he proposes is necessarily true. What Aristotle declares to be human nature begs for affirmation; it is not a simple stand-alone statement of fact.

Aristotle is constantly forging a consensual insight between himself and the reader. He is always asking us, "Ain't that so?" He is not appealing to a detached, impersonal, inexperienced reader, nor is he therefore presenting ethical knowledge, like other forms of scientific investigation, as given. Rather, his proposals are always that, proposals, submitted for validation to the reader: Their validation, the true meaning of his proposals, is not found independent from the reader. Rather, Aristotle appeals for agreement from the reader.

He also proposes contrasts, inviting us to see whether with or without certain elements human life could be possible. Thus he never presents any dimension of human nature as a statement of fact. It is all dependent on human judgment, though never ignoring empirical data or the tests of critical reflection.

Questions of personal identity are not matters of fact with no connection to human judgment, evaluation, or choice. Nussbaum argues: "Human nature cannot, and need not, be validated from the outside, because human nature just is an inside perspective, not a thing at all, but rather the most fundamental and broadly shared experiences of human beings living and reasoning together" (121).

Nussbaum is therefore denying that there is a divide between describing what is human nature and who we ought to become. When we begin to say that the human is social, then in affirming that, we are going to see the virtues of friendship and mutual respect as natural extensions of our identity needing to be affirmed.

There is no gulf between who we are and who we ought to become. For the descriptive answer to the first demands an affirmation from our own experience: Is this an accurate description of our humanity? Whatever we affirm conceptually carries within it the burden to realize ethically. Assenting to the descriptive, we have allowed our own internal selves to affirm something deeper than a fact, something that resonates with our internal appreciation of matters.

AN APPLICATION

In 1890 Joseph Merrick died from complications resulting from Proteus syndrome. His life was brought to the screen by the noteworthy work by David Lynch *The Elephant Man*.

In the movie, the hideousness of Merrick's body is striking: We are viscerally upset, in part because we cannot imagine Merrick as a human being. How could this be? How could anyone be born whose appearance violates our sense of what it means to be human? When we see him, we are visually repulsed; children were naturally terrified at seeing him; the appalling foreignness of his body was powerful. How could this be a human being? If this were a human being, it could happen again. My child or someone else's could be born like this. We would rather have the comfort of knowing no human being could be like this.

As the movie develops, we begin to recognize that Merrick is a human being. We become sympathetic to him. We resonate with him. We translate his experiences of rejection into what a human being would feel when being rejected. But our viewpoint as viewers is privileged in a way that those who have only occasional distant glimpses of Merrick is. Merrick hides himself from those on the screen; he covers his body so as to prevent anyone from recognizing him. It is only at night as he retires, as he takes off the layers of clothing, that we begin to see an outline of his many compromised features.

Still, he cannot hide himself from the cast. Fortunately, some are convinced of his humanity and try to bring Merrick into their company. But others continue to be frightened of his deformities: He can't possibly be a human being, they claim.

The climax happens as a group of bullies (whose experience of humanity is indeed coarse) chase him like an animal down streets and alleys until he is finally cornered, without any power and in complete humiliation, in a public toilet. He turns to them as they begin to herd around him and then start to rush at him and shouts out, "I am a human being!"

Is this a statement of fact or is this a demand for a recognition from the depths of the onlookers? I thought the first; I now recognize the second. When I first saw the scene, I thought: It is a statement of fact, albeit a compelling statement of fact, not one contrived. He is making a clear statement, and regardless of what they think, he is a human being.

Now I realize that he is not simply trying to impose a fact; he wants a response. He is not detached from their consideration of him. On the contrary, he wants an acknowledgment of his assertion. He wants—no, *demands*—that his claim be affirmed. He *is* a human being. The lyricism of the movie is that in the audience, we have come tearfully to the awareness of his claim as truthful. We want very much to affirm it, and we stand there expecting those on the screen to act similarly. We want to be in solidarity with him because he out of his humanity summons us to stand with him.

Some people think that making his statement depend on our acceptance of it undermines the validity of the claim to truth. But I think that the affirmation is the effective acknowledgment in me of another's claim. When we talk of matters of faith and/or morality, these are not matters of fact. Rather, they are about internal matters, about inside perspectives, as Nussbaum calls them. We need to see whether our experience confirms these claims.

So it is with Paul, writing to all the saints. When he says that Jesus is Lord, he waits for us to respond to his question, "Isn't this so?" Do we not need to say "Amen"? Paul expects our response. His statement demands our affirmation. Once I give it, I become united not only to Paul's experience but to my own deep-down belief that Jesus is Lord, and more importantly, I become united to the one I recognize as Lord. I can't but say "Amen."

CONSCIENCE

When we say "Amen," we say it in conscience. There we testify to the Lord-ship of Jesus and there we stand in solidarity with him. For Paul, conscience is where experience and authority meet; from experience, we encounter the authority of conscience, not as a personal construction but as a way of recognizing and testifying to the truth in love. In fact, just as Paul waits for us to respond in conscience to his testimony that Jesus is Lord, analogously Merrick's insistence on his humanity is at once an appeal to our consciences to recognize the truth in love.

Later we will reflect on conscience, scandal, and the church, but here we do well to see how in Christian theology the conscience recognizes the call to understand and witness to the truth.

The centrality of the personal conscience as the place for hearing the call to respond has had a long history in the church: Whenever growth and virtue are especially promoted, the conscience is also defended and promoted. During these robust periods, notably the patristic period of the first five centuries and the charismatic, religious, and scholastic movements of the twelfth to fourteenth centuries, the primacy of the conscience is consistently articulated. Not surprisingly, then, in the light of the reforms of the Second Vatican Council, which called for morals to be more rooted in Scripture and discipleship, the conscience again makes a vigorous appearance in contemporary moral theology.

What does Vatican II say about conscience? The definitive presentation is paragraph 16 of *Gaudium et Spes*:

> In the depths of our conscience, we detect a law which does not impose, but which holds us to obedience. Always summoning us to love good and avoid evil, the voice of conscience when necessary speaks to our heart: do this, shun that. For we have in our heart a law written by God; to obey it is the very dignity of being human; according to it we will be judged (2 Cor. 6:10). Conscience is the most secret core and sanctuary of a person. There we are alone with God, Whose voice echoes in our depths (John 1:3, 14). In a wonderful manner conscience reveals that law which is fulfilled by love of God and neighbor (Eph. 1:10). In fidelity to conscience, Christians are joined with the rest of humanity in the search for truth, and for the genuine solution to the numerous problems which arise in the life of individuals from social relationships. Hence the more right conscience holds sway, the more persons and groups turn aside from blind choice and strive to be guided by the objective norms of morality. Conscience frequently errs from invincible ignorance without losing its dignity. The same cannot be said for those who care but little for truth and goodness, or for a conscience which by degrees grows practically sightless as a result of habitual sin.

There are many elements that we could pursue here—the inner sanctuary of a person, the call to do good and avoid evil, the law being fulfilled in the love of God and neighbor—but so as to explain conscience better I want to examine only the "voice" of conscience and the formation of conscience.

THE VOICE OF CONSCIENCE

In a seminal article forty years ago, John Glaser distinguished two very different voices that we hear as adults: the voice of the superego and the voice of the conscience. The term *superego* (meaning "that-which-is-over-the-I") is how psychologists name that voice living in us that, though a leftover from early childhood years, continues to assert itself throughout our lives.

When we were young children, those who cared for us instructed us on matters of safety and hygiene. Our parents through persistent guidance kept us from running in front of cars, putting our fingers into electrical outlets, playing with knives, or turning on the oven. Similarly, they taught us to keep clean, wash our hands, eat with utensils, and use the toilet. These instructions were given through voices of authorities and spoken with great concern—often, understandably, with tones of stress and frustration. Subsequently, these voices formed the voice of the superego.

Because they could not be omnipresent, parents and guardians needed to instill in us a voice that could supervise us in their absence. Through constant warnings, we eventually felt their inhibiting presence restraining us from pushing a playmate in front of traffic or from exploring the many dangerous appliances in the kitchen. As children we learned that parents were always nearby. In fact, nothing could make parental control more palpably visible than when that horrendous sibling threat was uttered, "Wait till I tell Mom!"

When we were punished, we were most often sent to our room (the original place of "time out"). Our punishment was a way of separating us from people who loved us. At first we delighted in being sent away; our rebellious streak was awakened by the punishment. As time would pass, we would feel, however, the intended isolation and would seek permission to return to wherever the family was gathered. We would negotiate with our parents, promising never to be bad again, and claiming to be contrite all along the way. Of course, we were not that upset about the wrong we had done; it was the isolation we wanted to overcome. We wanted to feel loved again.

Glaser calls this internalized supervising voice "a principle of pre-personal censorship and control." This voice inhibits us from performing certain types of actions; we believe that were we to perform those actions, others would disapprove of us.

The superego still lives in us today. Unfortunately, inasmuch as this voice came from people literally bigger and older than we children were, we still perceive this voice as more powerful and more authoritative than we are.

The superego was not, however, a moral guide. It was simply meant to restrain us, to keep us safe, healthy, and well. Despite whatever moral lessons parents may have given us during this time, the only thing we children really heard was that we would get punished. The threat—not nice moral explanations—is what we remember.

Today that same fairly standardized cyclic movement has been hardwired into our adult lives. From the superego we experience inhibition and restraint. But whenever we decide to ignore the superego, we often encounter reprimand, punishment, isolation, guilt, negotiation, repentance, and acceptance. Through the superego, the cycle repeats itself time and again.

FORMATION OF THE CONSCIENCE

Unlike the superego, which warns us to stay where we are, the conscience calls us to grow. One example of this might concern a person who lacks assertiveness and believes (rightly) that the call to grow entails a call to greater assertiveness. But as we heed that call, we may hear another voice warning us, "You'd better not do it or else you will feel guilty." That guilt-inducing, inhibiting, and restraining voice is usually the superego.

Often the conscience's calls to grow are met with threats of the superego. When the superego dominates us, it usually does so by threatening or punishing us, compelling us into prepubescent cyclic forms of living and acting.

Certainly this is not to say that whenever we "feel guilty," the superego and not the conscience is working. When we say things like "I feel so guilty," we should ask ourselves, "Did I do anything objectively wrong?" If the answer is yes, then the conscience is probably judging us, but when the answer is no, the superego is probably intimidating us. Consider the case at hand: We need to develop assertiveness toward someone who has repeatedly treated us poorly. Our friends suggest, "You should speak up and tell that person to stop taking advantage of you." In conscience, we recognize that this is what we should do, but the superego keeps saying, "You should be a nice person." Eventually we decide to speak up. Afterward, we may "feel guilty." This feeling is probably rooted in the superego: We went against its command to be nice and so it punished us.

Of course, the superego is not bad. After all, because of it we do not run in front of cars or play with electrical outlets, and we (thankfully) use the toilet and wash our hands. However, during our adult lives we have to live by a higher voice (the conscience), which discerns the standards of what is right and wrong. In short, we need to be vigilant about the superego so that it does not inhibit the conscience.

Moreover, by the superego we experience a certain form of social compliance. Because we are so interested in being loved, the superego threatens us with isolation and therefore calls us always to conformity. The superego might inhibit us from recognizing Merrick's summons or from affirming Paul's testimony.

Conscience, on the other hand, is suspicious of conformity, particularly when injustice is at stake. Because the conscience calls us to aim more at being the one who loves than at being the beloved, it prompts us often to reach out to the one whom the more conformist society rejects. Moral progress, therefore, always occurs when people heed their consciences, take steps of their own, and move forward, even at the risk of isolation and loss. Consider when Rosa Parks took her place on the bus in Montgomery, when Thomas More refused to take the Oath of Supremacy, when Martin Luther King Jr. wrote to white preachers on scraps of paper in a Birmingham jail, when Gdansk shipyard workers decided to strike for their rights, when the faceless Chinese student stepped forward to meet an oncoming tank in Tiananmen Square, or when Ninoy Aquino returned to his beloved Philippines. In each instance, a person moved history and humanity forward with a conscience that demanded stepping forward where others feared to go.

Here we should never forget that the language of conscience is the forceful language of being called, of being commanded. As Vatican II's *Gaudium et Spes* states, conscience "holds us in obedience," it "summons" us. True, conscience is often used with the word "freedom," but this is not a freedom to do whatever we want. Rather, the call for freedom of conscience is so that we are not constrained from heeding our conscience. For this reason, Christians refer to the "dictates" or the "demands" of conscience: Conscience "demands" that we love God, ourselves, and our neighbors. Conscience "dictates" that we pursue justice. In fact, *Gaudium et Spes* reminds us that by the conscience we will be "judged."

When we appreciate the call of conscience, the voice to hear God's demands of love and of justice, then we similarly recognize the formation of the conscience as itself a command. We need to remember, however, that forming our conscience is a lifetime process. We form it based on the wisdom of parents, elders, and teachers, as well as friends and mentors; based on the teachings and stories from the sacred Scriptures, the church's tradition, and our local culture; and finally, based on the lessons learned in our own life experience.

I think the formation of the conscience is really a development of our relatedness in virtue: Mentored practices of justice, temperance, fortitude, fidelity, and self-care through the ministration of conscience's own prudence allow us to learn more and more about how we are to respond to God, neighbor, and ourselves in love. Virtuous practices become the exercises for the formation of conscience.

By way of conclusion, we might remember how Mark Twain taught us how easy it is to confuse conscience and superego. He describes Huck Finn's conflict prompted by what he mistakenly called his conscience. Huck has been traveling with his friend Jim, the runaway slave. Formed by his local community, Huck's "conscience" (read: "superego") requires him under pain of damnation to respect God and neighbor, and for this reason, to write a letter to poor "Ole Miss Watson" to let her know the whereabouts of her runaway slave. Driven by feelings that he is not heeding the community's expectations, Twain writes in Huck's voice: "So I was full of trouble, full as I could be; and didn't know what to do. At last I had an idea; and I says, I'll go and write the letter—and then see if I can pray. Why, it was astonishing, the way I felt as light as a feather right straight off, and my troubles all gone. So I got a piece of paper." Huck composes the letter. "I felt good and all washed clean of sin for the first time I had ever felt so in my life, and I knowed I could pray now. But I didn't do it straight off, but laid the paper down and set there thinking—thinking how good it was all this happened so, and how near I come to being lost and going to hell. And went on thinking."

Huck begins to think of Jim not as Miss Watson's "property," but as his own companion. He remembers details of all that Jim has done for him and what he has done for Jim and how much the two of them have learned together about life and friendship. He continues:

> and at last I struck the time I saved him by telling the men we had small-pox aboard, and he was so grateful, and said I was the best friend old Jim ever had in the world, and the ONLY one he's got now; and then I happened to look around and see that paper.
>
> It was a close place. I took it up, and held it in my hand. I was a-trembling, because I'd got to decide, forever, betwixt two things, and I knowed it. I studied a minute, sort of holding my breath, and then says to myself:
>
> "All right, then, I'll GO to hell"—and tore it up.

SELECT BIBLIOGRAPHY

Callahan, Sidney. *In Good Conscience: Reason and Emotion in Moral Decision Making.* San Francisco: HarperSanFrancisco, 1991.

Dwyer, Judith. "Vatican II and the Dignity of Conscience." In *Vatican II: The Unfinished Agenda: A Look at the Future*, edited by Lucien Richard, Daniel J. Harrington, and John W. O'Malley, 160–73. New York: Paulist Press, 1987.

Farley, Margaret. "The Role of Experience in Moral Discernment." In *Christian Ethics: Problems and Prospects*, edited by James Childress and Lisa Sowle Cahill, 134–51. Cleveland, OH: Pilgrim Press, 1996.

Glaser, John. "Conscience and Superego: A Key Distinction." *Theological Studies* 32 (1971): 30–47.

Guindon, André. *The Sexual Language: An Essay in Moral Theology.* Ottawa, ON: University of Ottawa Press, 1976.

Hogan, Linda. *Confronting the Truth: Conscience in the Catholic Tradition.* New York: Paulist Press, 2001.

Niebuhr, Reinhold. *Moral Man and Immoral Society: A Study in Ethics and Politics.* New York: Scribner, 1960.

Nussbaum, Martha. "Aristotle on Human Nature and the Foundation of Ethics." In *World, Mind, and Ethics: Essays on the Ethical Philosophy of Bernard Williams*, edited by J. E. Altham and Ross Harrison, 86–131. Cambridge, England: Cambridge University Press, 1995.

Patrick, Anne. *Liberating Conscience.* New York: Continuum, 1996.

Traina, Cristina. "Papal Ideals, Marital Realities: One View from the Ground." In *Sexual Diversity and Catholicism: Toward the Development of Moral Theology*, edited by Patricia Beattie Jung with Joseph Andrew Coray, 269–88. Collegeville, MN: Liturgical Press, 2001.

Part Two

THE THEOLOGICAL VIRTUES: PAUL AND THOMAS AQUINAS

Chapter Seven

Faith: Pauline Perspectives

THE THREE THEOLOGICAL VIRTUES:
1 THESSALONIANS 1:2–4

Paul's First Letter to the Thessalonians is generally regarded as the earliest complete document preserved in the New Testament. Paul founded the Christian community at Thessalonica in northern Greece (see Acts 17:1–9). After further missionary activities in Beroea and Athens (Acts 17:1–34), Paul arrived in Corinth. There he received a report from Timothy about the spiritual progress of the Thessalonian Christians. This generally good report did note certain areas in which problems had arisen for these new Christians. In the hope of encouraging them and shedding light on their difficulties, Paul wrote the letter now known as 1 Thessalonians in 51 (or 52) CE.

Paul's letter to the Thessalonians follows a general outline or pattern that was familiar in the Greco-Roman world: salutation (1:1), thanksgiving (1:2–10), body (2:1–5:11), and closing material (5:12–28). In all his letters except the one to the Galatians (with whom he was angry), Paul included a thanksgiving immediately after the salutation (indicating the senders and the recipients, along with a greeting). In the Greco-Roman convention, the thanksgiving was the occasion for the sender to give thanks in advance for the good health and good fortune of the recipient(s). As he did with other epistolary conventions, Paul reshaped and expanded the formulas to reflect important elements in his Christian theological vision.

Paul frequently used the thanksgiving section in his letters not only to give thanks to God for the spiritual health and progress of his addressees but also to preview or anticipate major themes in the body of his letter. The thanksgiving in 1 Thessalonians 1:2–10 illustrates Paul's practice very well.

Among the very first words from Paul in the first letter preserved in the New Testament is a sentence that contains the triad of theological virtues— faith, love, and hope—that has become the foundation of Christian virtue ethics. As we will see, this triad is not simply formulaic language for Paul. Rather, these three virtues shape the content of Paul's entire letter to the Thessalonians and provide the basis for Paul's outlook on Christian life.

> 2. We always give thanks to God for all of you and mention you in our prayers, constantly 3. remembering before our God and Father your work of faith and labor of love and steadfastness of hope in our Lord Jesus Christ. 4. For we know, brothers and sisters beloved by God, that he has chosen you.

In Greek the passage consists of a main verb "we give thanks" (*eucharistoumen*) along with three clauses that begin with participles: "mentioning" (1:2), "remembering" (1:3), and "knowing" (1:4). The use of the first person plural forms ("we") reflects the salutation in which "Paul, Silvanus, and Timothy" are designated as joint authors of the letter (1:1). Unlike other letters in which Paul notes joint authorship but quickly abandons it in favor of "I" language, in 1 Thessalonians the "we" forms carry through the letter.

Instead of thanking God for the health and prosperity of the recipients (as the Greco-Roman thanksgiving formula dictates), here as elsewhere Paul gives thanks to God for the spiritual progress that the Thessalonians have made. In 1:2 he claims to include the whole community ("for all of you . . . always") in his thanksgiving. And in the first dependent participial clause ("mentioning . . ."), he alludes to his constant or unceasing prayer on their behalf.

The three great theological virtues are listed in the second dependent clause in 1:3: "remembering before our God and Father your work of faith and labor of love and steadfastness of hope in our Lord Jesus Christ." Mention of "our God and Father" places the three virtues in a theological (and not merely a natural) context. Each of the three virtues is introduced by a noun that qualifies the virtue. The blandness of the NRSV translation ("work . . . labor . . . steadfastness") mirrors the bland Greek text. However, Earl J. Richard (*First and Second Thessalonians*, 46–47) prefers a more lively rendering of these nouns: "the dynamism of your faith, the dedication of your love, and the constancy of your hope in our Lord Jesus Christ." In either version, the point is that the theological virtues, while they originate with God, demand the active involvement of every Christian. The order—faith, love, and hope—reflects the conviction that even though all three virtues are part of ongoing Christian life, faith looks first of all to the past experience of coming to believe in God and Jesus Christ, love should animate Christian life in the present, and hope looks forward to the future coming of our Lord Jesus Christ.

The third dependent clause ("knowing . . .") in 1:4 provides the basis for the thanksgiving and for the theological virtues: the love that God has shown in choosing the Thessalonian Christians as the objects of God's love ("beloved by God"), and their being chosen as part of God's people ("he has chosen you"). Like other New Testament writers, Paul emphasizes the primacy of God's love for us and applies the Old Testament concept of Israel's election to those who now constitute God's people in Christ.

As the opening part of the thanksgiving in the earliest extant document in the New Testament, 1 Thessalonians 1:2–4 establishes the importance of faith, love, and hope in Christian life. In this passage Paul emphasizes their origin with God ("before our God and Father . . . beloved by God . . . he has chosen you") as well as the human effort that they require ("work . . . labor . . . steadfastness"). The order in which Paul lists these three virtues (faith, love, and hope), while it may confound our expectations, says something important about their place in Christian life in general (as the rest of the chapter will show) and in 1 Thessalonians in particular.

It is possible to take the three theological virtues as the organizing principle for all of 1 Thessalonians: faith (1:1–2:16), love (2:17–4:12), and hope (4:13–5:28). It is striking how well such an outline reflects the content of Paul's oldest extant letter.

Faith is the focus of the first part (1:1–2:16) of 1 Thessalonians. After the opening sentence in the thanksgiving (1:2–4), Paul reminds the Thessalonians how they came to faith in 1:5–2:16. He notes that the message of the gospel reached them "not in word only, but also in power and in the Holy Spirit" (1:5). He describes their conversion from paganism to Christian faith in this way: "how you turned to God from idols, to serve a living and true God" (1:9). Then in defending his own ministry against various criticisms and slanders in 2:1–16, Paul contends that he has been for them a conduit for the word of God and that they have accepted it "not as a human word but as what it really is, God's word, which is also at work in you believers" (2:13).

Love provides the theme that unifies 2:17–4:12. In expressing his desire to visit the Thessalonians again in 2:17–3:13, Paul tells them that they are "our glory and joy" (2:20) and expresses how anxious he was to receive news about their spiritual progress. His prayer for them is that they might grow in love: "And may the Lord make you increase and abound in love for one another and for all, just as we abound in love for you" (3:12). When in 4:1–12 Paul begins his exhortation, he urges the Thessalonians to abstain from fornication and to live "in holiness and honor" (4:3–4), and he reminds them how they "have been taught by God to love one another" (4:9).

Hope dominates Paul's advice about the coming of the Lord (4:13–5:11) and his closing remarks (5:12–28). First he counsels the Thessalonians not to "grieve as others do who have no hope" (4:13) over those Christians who have died, and he reassures them that they all will be reunited in glory on the day of the Lord. Since that day "will come like a thief in the night" (5:2), the proper attitude for them is constant watchfulness. Nevertheless, Christians can and should live in confident hope, since "God has destined us not for wrath but for obtaining salvation through our Lord Jesus Christ" (5:9). Even the various exhortations near the end of the letter are set in the context of preparation for the last judgment. Paul's hope is that the Thessalonians may "be kept sound and blameless at the coming of our Lord Jesus Christ" (5:23).

FAITH AS A PAULINE VIRTUE

In general, the virtue of faith (*pistis*) refers to considering something to be true and therefore worthy of trust. In Christian theology, it is a "theological" virtue first of all because it has God (*theos*) as its object. It is faith in God ("I believe in God . . .").

While the Greek word for faith (*pistis*) was not originally used in a religious context, in the Old Testament the Hebrew root *'aman* (the origin of our "Amen") is the appropriate human response to God's saving action. The concept of covenant with its notion of God's fidelity to Israel and what was expected of Israel by way of response is fundamental for understanding the New Testament idea of faith. The objective component of faith in the New Testament is the saving work of God in and through Christ as proclaimed in the gospel. The proper response involves acceptance of the Christ-event as true and trustworthy (the subjective component of faith), which in turn is made actual or concrete by baptism and by a way of life that is consistent with the gospel.

In Paul's letters, faith is not merely a vague commitment to fidelity or trust. Rather, for Paul and the other New Testament writers, the Greek verb *pisteuo* and the noun *pistis* also have an objective component, and the primary object of that faith is Jesus' life, death, and resurrection as well as the saving effects of those events (also known as the Christ-event or the paschal mystery).

In 1 Corinthians 15:3a ("For I handed on to you as of first importance what I in turn had received"), Paul states that the tenets of Christian faith that he had taught the Corinthians in the early fifties of the first century were the very same ones that he had received when he became a Christian around 36 CE. This statement indicates the existence of creedal formulas or summaries of beliefs very early in the history of the Christian movement. What Paul and other Corinthian Christians placed their faith in was the saving significance of Jesus' life, death, and resurrection.

In 1 Corinthians 15:3b–5 Paul repeats the creedal formula that he had received and then had handed on to the Corinthians: "that Christ died for our sins in accordance with the scriptures, and that he was buried, and that he was raised on the third day in accordance with the scriptures, and that he appeared to Cephas, then to the twelve." This creed mixes basic facts ("Christ died . . . he was buried") with claims that go beyond ordinary human history ("he was raised on the third day . . . he appeared . . .") and with theological interpretations ("for our sins in accordance with the scriptures").

The first theological interpretation ("for our sins") is that Jesus' death had the effect of wiping away human sins (see the discussion of Romans 3:25 below) and making possible right relationship with God. The second theological interpretation ("in accordance with the scriptures") affirms that the Christ-event did not come out of nowhere but rather was the continuation and fulfillment of God's covenantal relationship with Israel as God's chosen people. However shocking and scandalous Jesus' crucifixion (a punishment applied usually to slaves and rebels) was, the early Christians found theological meaning in it through their reflection on the Scriptures of Israel, especially Psalm 22 and Isaiah 52:13–53:12.

Another very early summary of Christian faith appears in what seems to have been an early Christian hymn quoted by Paul in Philippians 2:6–11. Again, the significance of this text is that it provides us with access to a very early (pre-Pauline) witness to what early Christians believed about Jesus. Paul introduces it not to inform us about Christology but rather to exhort the Philippian Christians to be united in a spirit of humility and to serve one another. Its insertion in Paul's exhortation suggests that the hymn was familiar both to Paul and to the Philippians. As a tradition current in the early church it was "common ground," something that Paul and the Philippians knew and accepted as true.

Philippians 2:6–11 is generally regarded as a pre-Pauline hymn quoted by Paul because of its poetic style (using parallelism extensively), unusual vocabulary, Semitic flavor (easily translated back into Aramaic), and liturgical spirit. The content of the hymn concerns the abasement of Christ in his becoming human and in dying on the cross (2:6–8), and the resurrection and exaltation of Christ (2:9–11). There are several problematic expressions in the hymn, and it is clearly the product of a sophisticated theological reflection. But the basic faith-claims about Christ are clear enough.

The first stanza (2:6–8) focuses on the humbling of Christ, who even though he was "in the form of God" nevertheless "emptied" (*ekenosen*) himself by becoming human ("being found in human form") and going to his death ("even death on a cross"). The second stanza (2:9–11) interprets the resurrection of Jesus as his exaltation ("God also highly exalted him") and as the reason why all creation—in heaven and on earth—should acclaim Jesus Christ as "Lord." This poem contains the most important elements of what Christians believe about Jesus: his preexistence, incarnation, death, resurrection, and exaltation. The hymn bears witness to how quickly such exalted beliefs about Jesus had developed in the twenty-five years between Jesus' death and Paul's letter to the Philippians.

The death and resurrection of Jesus and their theological significance are at the heart of two early Christian creedal formulas quoted by Paul in his letter to the Romans. In 3:25 he cites a tradition that interprets Jesus' death in terms of a sacrifice offered for sins: "whom God put forward as a sacrifice of atonement by his blood." While the letter to the Hebrews can be regarded as an extended reflection on this motif (see Leviticus 16), Paul himself uses it here only in passing to explain why both Jews and Gentiles can enjoy right relationship with God (justification). The idea is that the death of Jesus on the cross was the one perfect sacrifice that wiped away the sins of the past and made it possible for all humans to stand as "just" or "righteous" before God.

And in the salutation to his letter to the Romans, Paul establishes common ground with a community that he had not founded and had not yet visited by citing a traditional definition of the gospel. The letter as a whole is a defense of Paul's gospel (the "good news" that he was teaching about Jesus) and the implications that Paul drew from it—that is, Gentiles do not have to become Jews in order to share in the benefits of Jesus' death and resurrection and to become part of the people of God. The common ground is established at the start of the letter by the quotation of the pre-Pauline creedal formula: "the gospel concerning his Son, who was descended from David according to the flesh and was declared to be Son of God with power according to the spirit of holiness by resurrection from the dead, Jesus Christ our Lord" (Romans 1:3–4). This formula interprets the resurrection of Jesus as his vindication by God and as the occasion for the official divine proclamation of his identity as Son of God, Messiah or Christ, and Lord.

From these precious witnesses to the development of Christian faith between the time of Jesus' death in 30 CE and the early fifties—before the New Testament books were written down—we learn that for the earliest Christians, faith had as its object Jesus' life, death, and resurrection, as well as (and especially) the saving effects of those events.

Paul's emphasis on the objective dimension of faith is complemented by his insistence on its subjective dimension. Faith is the way by which humans participate in the history of salvation in general and in the Christ-event in particular.

The central theme of Paul's letter to the Romans (the fullest presentation of his theology) is the gospel—the good news of Jesus' life, death, and resurrection (see 1:3–4). In the passage that presents the proposition or basic thesis of the entire letter (1:16–17), Paul first observes that faith is the way by which we become part of the gospel: "For I am not ashamed of the gospel: it is the power of God for salvation to everyone who has faith, to the Jew first and also to the Greek." Paul asserts that the gospel works its power in those who respond to it in faith. He also affirms the traditional order of salvation history ("to the Jew first and also to the Greek") but insists that faith is demanded from both Jews and Greeks as the necessary precondition for their salvation. Then in 1:17, Paul adds that God's righteousness is revealed "through faith for faith" (in other words, faith from beginning to end), and he grounds his position with a quotation from Habakkuk 2:4: "The one who is righteous will live by faith."

In citing what was an already traditional formulation about Jesus' death as a sacrifice for sins (Romans 3:25), Paul seems to have added the phrase "effective through faith." Thus Paul again insists on faith as the subjective appropriation of the Christ-event. Humans can and do participate in the Christ-event and enjoy its positive effects or benefits through their faith.

One of the most important theological statements in the New Testament appears in Romans 3:28: "For we hold that a person is justified by faith apart from works prescribed by the law." The term "justified" refers basically to right relationship with God. The works of the Law may refer to all 613 commandments in the Torah or to the more distinctively Jewish observances such as circumcision, the Sabbath, or purity and food regulations. Paul's point, made against his Jewish Christian rivals who wanted Gentile Christians to become Jews, was that the Law, however "holy and just and good" (Romans 7:12) it may be, was not capable of accomplishing what Christ did—to make possible right relationship with God (justification). And the way in which we can participate in what Christ accomplished is through faith.

Abraham is the Pauline model for the virtue of faith. In Galatians 3:6–29 Paul argues that "those who believe are the descendants of Abraham" (3:7). For Abraham, faith took the form of trusting in God's promise that he would have many descendants (see Genesis 15:5). Because Abraham believed in God's promise, we are told in Genesis 15:6 that "the Lord reckoned it to him as righteousness." Since God declared Abraham "righteous" (justification) before he was circumcised (Genesis 17) and before the gift of the Law to Moses (Exodus 19–24) some 430 years later, then the ground of God's declaration must have been the faith of Abraham rather than circumcision or observance of the Law.

What Abraham believed was the promise from God that he would have "offspring." According to Paul in Galatians 3:16, that promised offspring was Christ. And so in Galatians 3:29, Paul draws the conclusion: "And if you belong to Christ, then you are Abraham's offspring, heirs according to the promise." So the theological virtue of faith for Paul is trust in the promise of God, and the content of that promise is Christ and the saving effects of his life, death, and resurrection. Even in Abraham the objective and the subjective dimensions of faith came together.

A similar and even more profound meditation on Abraham as the model of faith appears in Romans 4. Again the key biblical text is Genesis 15:6: "Abraham believed God, and it was reckoned to him as righteousness" (Romans 4:3). From this text Paul draws the conclusion that Abraham is "the ancestor of all who believe" (4:11), whether they be Gentiles or Jews. He goes on to explore the nature of Abraham's trust in God's promise as "hoping against hope" (4:18) and affirms that "no distrust made him waver concerning the promise of God" (4:20). And Paul concludes that Genesis 15:6 was written "not for his sake alone but for ours also" (4:23–24), and promises that what had been the experience of Abraham the model of faith will be that of "us who believe in him who raised Jesus our Lord from the dead" (4:24).

For Paul, faith is both objective and subjective. Its object is the saving action of God made manifest especially in Jesus' death and resurrection. At the same time, faith requires a subject, a person who is willing and able to summon up the same kind of basic trust in God and God's word that Abraham and Jesus showed in response to God's promises. However brilliant Paul the pastoral theologian was, he did leave open many further questions. This is where the wisdom of Thomas Aquinas, one of Paul's most insightful theological interpreters, can help us formulate those questions and develop answers to them.

SELECT BIBLIOGRAPHY

Hays, Richard B. *The Faith of Jesus Christ*. Chico, CA: Scholars Press, 1983.

Murphy-O'Connor, Jerome. *Paul the Letter-Writer: His World, His Options, His Skills*. Collegeville, MN: Liturgical Press, 1995.

Richard, Earl J. *First and Second Thessalonians*. Collegeville, MN: Liturgical Press, 1995.

Chapter Eight

Faith: Theological Perspectives

There are two sides to the Pauline virtue of faith: the objective side, meaning that which faith reveals to us, and the subjective side, meaning how we actually do believe. I would like to pursue more the latter dimension, particularly what we mean by referring to faith as an assent, a concept central to scholastic theology.

In looking to the theological tradition to see how we have developed the virtue of faith, so eloquently championed by Paul, I maintain that we should turn to the thirteenth-century theologian Thomas Aquinas (1224–1274). Why?

Paul gave us faith, hope, and charity as the trio of virtues that define Christianity. We cannot underestimate the significance of that contribution. Not only that, but he implicitly pointed to an interconnectedness among these virtues, through which we would realize that in order to understand one, we need to understand the others. Three centuries later, Augustine recognized Paul's distinctive and integrated contribution. Still, while Augustine certainly builds on Paul to offer his own theological claims about faith, hope, and charity, it is Thomas Aquinas who offers us a sustained theological investigation into the nature of these three virtues and the grounds by which we recognize their intrinsic relationships.

Thomas is without doubt an Augustinian, but he is more than that. Thirteen hundred years after Paul, Thomas systematizes all of theology. In his masterpiece the *Summa Theologiae*, Thomas dedicates all his comments on morality exclusively to the seven virtues: faith, hope, charity, justice, temperance, fortitude, and prudence. He called the first three the theological virtues, and the others the acquired virtues. In these next three chapters we will examine the *Summa Theologiae* on the specific theological virtues, respectively.

It might be good, therefore, to understand something about Thomas, something about the *Summa Theologiae*, and something about Thomas on faith per se. In Catholic circles, Thomas is the reigning theologian of the second millennium. Knowing how Thomas reflected on the Pauline virtues of faith, hope, and charity can lead us, I think, to an appreciation of how these virtues have flourished in the theological tradition. I will conclude by reflecting on what we mean by faith today as a personal and communal assent.

THOMAS AQUINAS

Thomas was born in an Italian town known as Roccasecca ("dry rock"). Aquino was the general family name; they belonged to lower nobility. His parents had nine children: four boys and five girls. Thomas was the youngest and therefore was dedicated by his parents to the church. His brother Reginald was executed for the attempted assassination of Emperor Frederick II. Despite a somewhat politically driven family, Thomas seemed not to be disposed to such agendas. For instance, he shunned constant invitations to become abbot of Monte Cassino, archbishop of Naples, or later, a cardinal. Promoting the work of God through theology and living the simple Dominican life were his only interests.

Thomas entered the Benedictines at Monte Cassino when he was five years old and stayed there for nine years, from 1230 to 1239. Difficulties between pope and emperor put the abbey in the middle of a power struggle, and the emperor eventually dislodged many members of the community. Eventually, Thomas too left the abbey and went to Naples, where he did studies for five years and learned Aristotle. There he heard of a relatively new order, the Order of Preachers (or the Dominicans, as they became known, since St. Dominic was their founder), which he joined in 1244. He was attracted to four features of the Order. First, the order was new. Second, unlike the Benedictines, who spent their lives at the abbey they entered under their vow of stability, the new evangelical order sent members throughout Europe. The mendicancy of the Dominicans attracted him, too: It assured members that the order would have a simple form of religious life. Finally, they were known for preaching throughout the new cities and towns. Evangelical movement, a religious charism animated by the Gospels, and a simple lifestyle were the traits that caught the mind and heart of the young Thomas. Almost thirty years later, as he completed the second part of the *Summa,* he claimed that a religious order that proceeds from its contemplative foundations to the practice of teaching and preaching is the most excellent and perfect of all states in life (*Summa Theologiae* II.II. 188.6). As the Dominican Simon Tugwell writes, Thomas is simply asserting that his order is "the best religious order."

The leadership of the new order recognized Thomas's intellectual gifts and sought to get him away from his fairly manipulative family. The family clearly had designs that Thomas would become the abbot of Monte Cassino, a major ecclesiastical appointment. But by entering the Order of Preachers, Thomas was excluding any such appointment. The Aquinos were not happy. The Dominicans sent him first to Rome; from there he would be sent on to studies in Paris. On his way to Rome, Thomas was kidnapped by his family and held at Monte San Giovanni, near Roccasecca, for more than a year; eventually, his mother relinquished her claims on him.

In 1246 Thomas left for Paris, where the Dominicans had their own program of studies. There, he studied at least a year with Albert, whose two interests were Aristotle and Platonic views in Augustine. In 1248 Albert was sent to Cologne to open another Dominican house of studies, and Thomas accompanied his teacher. (Still, his family wanted an appointment for Thomas. At this time, the pope invited Thomas to become the abbot of Monte Cassino, while keeping his Dominican vows. Thomas declined the offer.)

After four years in Cologne, Thomas was appointed in 1252 to his first major assignment, lecturer on the *Sentences of Peter Lombard* at the University of Paris for four years. The *Sentences* was a systematic collection of patristic texts, whose organization by Peter allowed him to probe more deeply into the mysteries of faith. Between the rationalism of Abelard and the biblical positivism of the monks, the *Sentences* was a mix of Scripture and patristic writings, with an overarching rational foundation. It was divided into four volumes: *Creation, Christ, Virtues,* and *Sacraments.* In lecturing on the *Sentences,* Thomas emphasized the hidden, unknowable mystery and silence of God.

In 1256, he was appointed for three years as Regent Master at Paris. During this time, he began writing the *Summa Contra Gentiles,* his epistemological work *De Veritate,* and a series of lectures on the Gospel of Matthew. He also volunteered to champion the university event held during Advent and Lent every year, at which anyone could ask the presiding faculty member anything—an assembly cleverly called the "Whatevers" (the *Quodlibets*). During this time, he also became involved in controversial debates with critics of the Dominican order.

Eventually he was appointed the Dominican instructor at Orvieto (1261–1265), where he finished the *Summa Contra Gentiles* and wrote the *Compendium of Theology,* his *Commentary on Job,* and the *Office of the Feast of Corpus Christi.*

In 1265, he suggested to the Italian province an experiment. Young Dominicans were trained in one of two ways. The vast majority were simply given assignments after novitiate, and like all others in their convent, heard nightly lectures on how to hear a good confession and assign a fair penance. Fewer than 10 percent of the new Dominicans received theological training at one of the houses of study at the leading universities (Paris, Oxford, Cologne, and Bologna). These Dominicans, like Thomas himself, were designated to teach at the universities. As an alternative to both, Thomas proposed theologically training a small group of young Dominicans who eventually would become preachers, confessors, and pastors. His proposal was accepted and the experiment was established in Rome. After two years of teaching them commentaries on Peter's "Sentences," he designed for them a textbook: the *Summa Theologiae.*

SUMMA THEOLOGIAE

The *Summa Theologiae* is arguably the most accomplished theological work in the history of the church. Unlike the *Sentences* of Peter Lombard, Thomas tried to lead readers through, not a series of statements or judgments (sentences), but questions. An investigatory work, each of the three parts of the *Summa* is made up of a series of questions, in which we learn that there has been extensive discussion on *every* theological position. In light of those debates, Thomas gives his reply. Still, rather than answering a "big" question directly, Thomas descended into greater particularity and broke down the question into a set of articles; each of these articles is also written in the interrogative form and to these he makes his replies.

Part I, on God, is made up of 102 questions. The second part, on the moral life as a response to God, consists of two sections: The first has 108 questions on all the components of moral agency, and the second is made up of 170 questions on the seven virtues as the matter of the moral life. Thomas collapsed while doing the third part, on Christ and the sacraments, finishing the first 89 questions.

THOMAS IN THE *SUMMA* ON FAITH

We are reading the first virtue (faith) in the second section of the second part, particularly question 4, which asks whether faith is a virtue. In the question we find eight articles. The first one asks whether the definition from Hebrews 11:1 is right: "Faith is the substance of things to be hoped for, the evidence of things that appear not." Not surprisingly, Thomas writes that it is the working definition of faith, but he adds that the beginning of things to be hoped for is brought about by the assent of faith, which contains virtually all things to be hoped for. Yet he insists that faith is not a series of statements but a virtue, a key internal disposition that develops significantly the way we live: "Faith is a habit of the mind, whereby eternal life is begun in us, making the intellect assent to what is non-apparent."

In the second article, he asks where we locate in the believer the virtue of faith. Here he focuses on our intellectual capabilities: Faith informs and perfects but does not contradict our rationality. In the third article, he asks whether charity is formed by faith. This basically means, Does faith make charity possible? Does faith prompt us to be charitable? He responds that the goal or end of faith is charity, which he defines as union with God. In fact, it is only by faith that we can hope for charity: Without the grace to believe, we would not know nor long for the experience of charity. Conversely, when we have charity our faith is deepened, enlivened, and nurtured. While we need faith to receive charity, charity in turn sustains and animates faith.

In the fourth article, Thomas reflects on faith without charity, or what he calls lifeless faith. Faith is faith whether alive or lifeless, he argues, but charity makes lifeless faith real. We may believe in God but still be miserable; lifeless faith is the faith of a Christian without charity. Typically, after Thomas makes this affirmation, he examines the topic from another viewpoint: Is lifeless faith a virtue? No, he responds. A faith animated by charity is a true virtue, but lifeless faith, while informing us of who God is and what God wants of us, does nothing more than help us understand. It does not help us love God, self, and neighbor. Faith without union with God is not virtuous. Only a faith formed by charity is truly virtuous.

In the sixth article he claims that faith is one virtue, and in the seventh he asks if it is the first of the virtues. Faith teaches us that God is the object of heavenly bliss; it precedes charity and hope. Without faith, there is no hope or charity. Finally, in the eighth article, Thomas claims that faith is more certain than other virtues: It is founded on revealed, divine truth; it makes the believer more certain; and it is the foundation of all other grounds for hoping and loving God.

THE ASSENT OF FAITH

In his essay on faith, Stephen Brown argues that according to Thomas it is by faith and our assent that God moves us inwardly. But it is not an assent to what is known. "Revealed truth is not a self-evident message that forces assent. Faith is an assent to what is not self evident. It is an assent to what is beyond human invention and grasp" (224).

By our assent, we bind ourselves to these revealed teachings. By giving our "amen" to them, we are not enhancing the truth validity of the statements; rather, we are saying that we must now let ourselves be shaped by these truths—for instance, that we are made in God's image or that Jesus is Lord.

Revelation is for our benefit. Faith therefore has a transformative effect on us. We look at the world differently, under the light of faith. Faith does not remain in us as an idea over against others; rather it prompts us to constantly understand everything we know and learn. It shapes our worldview.

Faith nags at us. That's why so-called fallen-away Catholics often feel themselves uncomfortable with leaving. In the movie *Agnes of God,* a psychiatrist speaks with the mother superior of the convent in which the narrative occurs. The psychiatrist tries to explain to the mother superior that she can't rid herself of her former faith. The superior responds that faith grabs you by the throat and stays there.

Faith also nags at those of us who stay. I think, for instance, funerals are very challenging affairs for believers. Surely, we believe in the resurrection, but at funerals we feel the death, the loss. We believe that God is merciful, but we don't understand why our loved one died.

In the eyes of faith, living between the now and the not-yet means entering into a tension. An agnostic attends a funeral and mourns the dead; but the Christian wants to know "Where was the hand of God in this?" and "Why"? We leave ourselves in a very unsettling situation. In the 1970s, theologians asked, "Does faith add any normative content to Christian ethics?" Most answered no. But I thought that though faith might not give us new norms, it does change our entire notion of thinking.

For instance, we believe that God is creator: Do we look at the use of genes or stem cells differently? Does it make us feel and think differently about "creating" embryos for research purposes? Does not faith in God as creator have some impact in how we think and act?

When we hear that we are made in God's image or that God is Lord of Life, does that make us consider capital punishment in a new light? When we read that Christ has been reconciled to us while we were still sinners, does that not affect how we live and interact with others?

SELECT BIBLIOGRAPHY

Boyle, Leonard. *The Setting of the* Summa Theologiae *of Saint Thomas.* Toronto: Pontifical Institute, 1982.

Brown, Stephen. "The Theological Virtue of Faith: An Invitation to an Ecclesial Life of Truth." In *The Ethics of Aquinas*, edited by Stephen Pope, 221–31. Washington, DC: Georgetown University Press, 2002.

Keenan, James F. *Goodness and Rightness in Thomas Aquinas's* Summa Theologiae. Washington, DC: Georgetown University Press, 1992.

Kent, Bonnie. "Habits and Virtues." In *The Ethics of Aquinas*, edited by Stephen Pope, 116–30. Washington, DC: Georgetown University Press, 2002.

O'Meara, Thomas. *Thomas Aquinas, Theologian.* Notre Dame, IN: University of Notre Dame Press, 1997.

Pieper, Josef. *Faith, Hope, and Love.* San Francisco: Ignatius Press, 1997.

Pinckaers, Servais. "The Sources of the Ethics of St. Thomas Aquinas." In *The Ethics of Aquinas*, edited by Stephen Pope, 17–29. Washington, DC: Georgetown University Press, 2002.

Pope, Stephen, "Overview of the Ethics of St. Thomas Aquinas." In *The Ethics of Aquinas*, edited by Stephen Pope, 30–55. Washington, DC: Georgetown University Press, 2002.

Sherwin, Michael. *By Knowledge and Love: Charity and Knowledge in the Moral Theology of St. Thomas Aquinas.* Washington, DC: Catholic University of America Press, 2005.

Thomas Aquinas. *Summa Theologiae.* New York: Benziger Brothers, 1922.

Torrell, Jean-Pierre. *Saint Thomas Aquinas: The Person and His Work.* Washington, DC: Catholic University of America Press, 1996.

Tugwell, Simon. *Albert and Thomas: Selected Writings.* Mahwah, NJ: Paulist Press, 1988.

Chapter Nine

Love: Pauline Perspectives

FAITH WORKING THROUGH LOVE

For Paul, the primary object of love is God (who has loved us first) and other persons (for whom Christ died). An apt summary of Paul's ethical vision appears in Galatians 5:6b: "The only thing that counts is faith working through love." The idea is that faith (*pistis*) expresses itself in deeds motivated by love (*agape*). Another good summary that highlights the role of love occurs shortly afterward in Galatians 5:13, where Paul reflects on the meaning of Christian freedom. There he insists that Christian freedom is not simply an opportunity for self-indulgence. Rather, the Christian concept of freedom involves serving others: "Through love become slaves to one another."

LOVE IN BIBLICAL PERSPECTIVE

In general, the virtue of love involves having a warm regard for and an interest in another person, wishing only good for the other. In the Old Testament, the Hebrew verb for "love" (*'ahab*) may have many contexts and objects. But surely the most important context for our purposes is God's covenant with Israel. God initiates the covenant out of love for Israel, and one of Israel's covenant obligations is to love God in return. In Hosea, the theme of love provides the context in which the prophet explores God's covenant fidelity to Israel and Israel's infidelity to God and its covenant obligations.

In the Synoptic Gospels (see Matthew 22:34–40 and parallels), Jesus makes a link between love of God (see Deuteronomy 6:4–5) and love of neighbor (Leviticus 19:18), and he extends the scope of love of neighbor to include even enemies (see Matthew 5:43–48). Both teachings presuppose the prior experience of God's love for humankind. Indeed, the basis for loving enemies is the imitation of God's own love for all kinds of persons.

In John's Gospel, the sending of Jesus the Son and Word of God (that is, the revelation and revealer of God) is proof of God's love for us: "For God so loved the world that he gave his only Son, so that everyone who believes in him may not perish but may have eternal life" (John 3:16). The "new commandment" that Jesus gives to his disciples is that they should love one another (see John 13:34). There is a "chain" of love from God through Jesus to the followers of Jesus: "As the Father has loved me, so I have loved you; abide in my love" (John 15:9).

LOVE AS A PAULINE VIRTUE

The wider theological context for understanding the nature of love and its place in Pauline ethics is developed in the letter to the Romans. In Romans 5:5, Paul insists that love is a gift from God: "God's love has been poured into our hearts through the Holy Spirit that has been given to us." And the proof of God's love for us is the gift of Jesus' life, death, and resurrection: "But God proves his love for us that while we were still sinners Christ died for us" (5:8). The starting point and the dynamism for the Christian virtue of love is God's love for us, as it has been made manifest through the person of Jesus Christ and the Holy Spirit.

This point is underscored toward the end of Paul's meditation on life in the Holy Spirit in Romans 8. As that meditation draws to a close, Paul becomes increasingly emotional and rhetorical. In 8:31 he asks, "If God is for us, who is against us?" And the proof that God is for us is the fact that he "did not withhold his own Son but gave him up for all of us" (8:32). That having been said, Paul goes on to ask in 8:35: "Who will separate us from the love of Christ?" The answer, of course, is that nothing and no one "will be able to separate us from the love of God in Christ Jesus our Lord" (8:39).

God has loved us first, and God has shown this love in and through Jesus Christ and the Holy Spirit. The proper response to God's love for us is for us to love God and to love one another. At the very beginning of his practical ethical advice in Romans 12, Paul places instructions about love: "Let love be genuine. . . . Love one another with mutual affection" (Romans 12:9, 10). And in Romans 13:8–10, Paul puts forward the Old Testament commandment about loving one's neighbor (Leviticus 19:18) as the summary of the whole Law. He goes so far as to say that "the one who loves another has fulfilled the law" (13:8) and that "love is the fulfilling of the law" (13:10). Paul's reasoning seems to be that since love does no wrong to the neighbor, then one who loves the neighbor will naturally observe all the commandments that pertain to relationships and interactions with other persons. The positive ideal of Christian life is aptly described as "walking in love" (14:15). Love is the virtue that should animate all of Christian life in the present.

Perhaps the most famous text in Paul's letters is his description of the virtue of love in 1 Corinthians 13: "Love is patient; love is kind; love is not envious or boastful or arrogant or rude." Paul prefaces his description by asserting that even "if I have all faith, so as to remove mountains, but do not have love, I am nothing" (13:2). And he ends by singling out the three great theological virtues and ranking love as supreme among them: "And now faith, hope, and love abide, these three; and the greatest of these is love" (13:13). The post-Pauline description of love as the "bond of perfection" in Colossians 3:14 ("Above all, clothe yourselves with love, which binds everything together in perfect harmony") adds further substance to the centrality of love among the Christian virtues in Pauline ethics.

SELECT BIBLIOGRAPHY

Fuller, Reginald H., ed. *Essays on the Love Commandment.* Philadelphia: Fortress, 1978.

Furnish, Victor Paul. *The Love Command in the New Testament.* New York: Abingdon, 1972.

Perkins, Pheme. *Love Commands in the New Testament.* New York: Paulist Press, 1982.

Spicq, Ceslas. *Agape in the New Testament.* St. Louis: Herder, 1966.

Chapter Ten

Charity: Theological Perspectives

If faith is about being caught between the now and the not-yet, love or charity is about the already. What's outstanding in faith is the entire encounter with truth and with God who is truth. With charity we are already in union with God; the only thing missing for charity is its perfection. That is, the difference between faith in this life and what happens in the next is a difference in kind; the difference between charity here and in the next life is a difference in degree. Charity in the next life is but the perfection of what it is in this life, and that perfection is what makes charity permanent, immutable. But in the next life, in the kingdom of God, we will not need faith, because we will have truth. Still, we will have the one virtue that lasts, charity, because by it we will remain in union with God, with ourselves, and with one another.

THOMAS IN THE *SUMMA* ON CHARITY

We have seen how love/charity as a Pauline virtue is deeply connected to faith. Now I want to turn again to Thomas. I think invoking Thomas from the tradition offers us an enormous amount of material to flesh out how central charity has become in the tradition. We will look at two questions, one on charity in itself, or the objective side, the other on charity as it resides in the subject.

In the twenty-third question of the second part of the second part (the Secunda Secundae) of the *Summa Theologiae*, Thomas describes the virtue of charity "in itself" in eight articles. In the first article, he brilliantly asks whether charity is friendship. Before he begins his own reply, Thomas writes, "It is written (John 15:15) I will not now call you servants but friends. Now this was said to them by reason of nothing else than charity. Therefore friendship is charity."

In his reply he notes that Aristotle, through friendship, weds love to benevolence. He focuses, however, on the mutuality of friendship, in particular the communication between the human and God in charity.

In the next article, he asks whether charity is created in the soul. How is it that charity as the "Divine Essence Itself" is also an infused virtue that inclines us to act in charity? Here he follows up on his previous point on communication and adds that when we love our neighbor we participate in divine charity. Then he asks, "Is charity a virtue?" He notes that human virtue is the source or guide of all humans' good acts and that it consists in following the rule of acts: human reason and God. He distinguishes between moral virtues, which are defined as being in accord with reason (à la Aristotle), and another form of virtue he calls theological or infused, like charity, which consists in attaining God. He adds that by charity we are united to God. He concludes that unlike the moral virtues, the goodness of charity is not founded principally on the virtue of the human but on the goodness of God.

This leads him in the fourth article to ask whether charity is a special virtue. Answering in the affirmative, he notes the radical uniqueness of charity: in attaining God through union. After he affirms that charity is one virtue in the next article, he asks whether it is the most excellent of virtues. Here he explains how the two rules to be attained in virtue are human reason and God, which pertain to the acquired and theological virtues, respectively. Certainly, attaining God is greater than attaining reason, just as the theological virtues are greater than the acquired virtues. But among the theological virtues only charity attains God per se; faith and hope help us as only in our move to attaining God (by God's grace, of course!). In closing, he notes that charity implies union with the good, hope implies distance.

He then considers whether there is any true virtue without charity. This is an unthinkable position for Augustine, who tells us that the only true virtue is one performed out of charity. But Thomas distinguishes between a true imperfect virtue and a true perfect virtue. The former applies to an act of justice that conforms to the good of reason but is not done out of charity. Were it done out of charity, it would be perfect; for as justice, it conforms to the rule of reason, and as informed by charity, it conforms to the rule of God. One could lack charity by belonging to another faith or to no faith, for only by faith is there the possibility of charity. But the absence of charity does not vitiate the moral virtue. Still, it lacks perfection, in that by charity we are in union with God, the perfect end of all humanity. (Thomas quotes here his favorite sentence, Psalm 72:28: "It is good for me to adhere to God.") Thus if a virtue lacks charity, it is not perfectly good, because it lacks due order to the last end. Thomas completes the question by stating that charity is the form of virtue in that it directs everything to the last end.

Rather than entertain each of the twelve articles in the next question (on the subject of charity), it might help us if we consider the key elements relevant to our understanding of how we grow in charity. Thomas first notes that charity is caused in us by God's own and singular initiative. He adds, however, that charity increases along the way, not by more charity being added but by charity being more intensely in the subject. Charity increases in us not by one act of charity after another, but by our striving in charity. Since charity is about union with God, our participation in charity can increase indefinitely. Also, as charity increases in us, so does our ability to grow in charity increase.

What then is charity? It is to love God as much as one can. Still, only in the kingdom of God will we be able to love God with our whole heart always and actually. Yet the charity we have on earth, unstable as it is, is not different from the charity of heaven.

As Eberhard Schokenhoff notes, Thomas's assessment of charity is profoundly interpersonal: Our end is in being in union with God, and yet already we are in union with God. We bear within ourselves the seeds of beatitude. Moreover, this union is about communication, a mutual sharing, where we love our neighbor out of the love of God.

In conclusion, Thomas writes about several of the effects of charity. The interior effects are peace and mercy; the exterior ones are almsgiving, beneficence, and fraternal correction.

Since charity is union, peace is a sense of concord in relationship not only with God but also with ourselves and our neighbor. A serenity and a form of integration emerge from the union. Charity does not seek that serenity in itself; rather, by being directed to God, the true good, serenity is found as an effect of charity. Though mercy is an internal effect, it leads us toward acts of mercy. On being merciful, Thomas remarks that the sum total of the Christian religion consists in mercy, as regards external works, but as regards internal works, it consists in charity. He adds that charity likens us to God in love, while mercy likens us to God in a similarity of works.

Charity leads us to beneficence because charity binds us to be always willing to do good to all. Following from the order of love (a topic developed in the writings of Stephen Pope), Thomas holds that we are bound to be more beneficent to those closer to us. While almsgiving results, by extension, from mercy, the act of fraternal correction deserves comment. He highlights two different reasons why we correct one another. If we admonish someone so as to dissuade or prevent him or her from harming another or compromising the common good, then the action belongs to the virtue of justice. But if we admonish because we are concerned about the well-being of the sinner, then it is an act of charity. Here we are acting out of concern for the sinner's relationship with God.

In conclusion, charity is the presence of the Holy Spirit in us; it is union with God, and a union that is as real now as it will be later. In union with God, we become in union with ourselves and with our neighbor. It gives us, then, a principle of order. This union is an affective one, which prompts integration and peace in ourselves and with others. It makes us divine in our mercy. Finally, unlike all other virtues, charity is the only virtue that lasts. In attaining union with God, it attains the last end, and therefore is unique among the four cardinal and three theological virtues.

This examination of Thomas on charity illustrates, I think, how theology thinks through the Scriptures. While many think that the primary text in the study of theology in the medieval university was *The Sentences of Peter Lombard*, it was in fact the sacred Scriptures. Theology is what happens when faith seeks understanding and we seek understanding by studying revelation. Thus Thomas not only does not contradict Paul, but his writings expand on Paul, appreciating specifically why it is that, as Paul says, charity is the only virtue that lasts.

SELECT BIBLIOGRAPHY

Cates, Diana Fritz. *Aquinas on the Emotions: A Religious-Ethical Inquiry.* Washington, DC: Georgetown University, 2009.
———. *Choosing to Feel: Virtues, Friendship, and Compassion for Friends.* Notre Dame, IN: University of Notre Dame Press, 1997.
Gilleman, Gerard. *The Primacy of Charity in Moral Theology.* Westminster, MD: Newman Press, 1959.
Ouwerkerk, C. A. J. *Caritas et ratio: Études sur le double principe de la vie morale chrétienne d'après S. Thomas D'Aquin.* Nijmegen, the Netherlands: Gebr. Janssen, 1956.
Pope, Stephen. *The Evolution of Altruism and the Ordering of Love.* Washington, DC: Georgetown University Press, 1994.
———. "Expressive Individualism and True Self-Love: A Thomistic Perspective." *Journal of Religion* 71, no. 3 (1991): 384–99.
Schockenhoff, Eberhard. "The Theological Virtue of Charity." In *The Ethics of Aquinas*, edited by Stephen Pope, 244–58. Washington, DC: Georgetown University Press, 2002.
Vacek, Edward C. *Love, Human and Divine: The Heart of Christian Ethics.* Washington, DC: Georgetown University Press, 1994.

Chapter Eleven

Hope: Pauline Perspectives

WHAT PAUL HOPED FOR

In writing to the Philippians, Paul expresses his most basic hope as to "be with Christ" after his death (1:23) and to "attain the resurrection from the dead" (3:11). His hope for eternal life with Christ flowed from his faith in the saving power of Jesus' death and resurrection. This is the just reward for a life animated by love of God and love of neighbor. Hope for eternal life with Christ provides the goal (*telos*) and the horizon for his Christian life in the present: "I press on toward the goal for the prize of the heavenly call of God in Christ Jesus" (3:14).

HOPE IN BIBLICAL PERSPECTIVE

In general, the virtue of hope (*elpis*) refers to looking forward to something with some reason for confidence that it will come to fulfillment. What Paul looked forward to was eternal life with Christ in the kingdom of God, and he based his hope on the resurrection of Jesus and on his own experience of the Holy Spirit.

In Greek thought, the object of hope may be (among many other things) life after death based on the immortality of the soul (Plato) or happiness in this life (Aristotle). In the Hebrew Scriptures and in early Judaism, hope was based on the promises of God, whether for offspring in the case of Abraham, for Israel's goodness and greatness, for the ideal king (the Messiah), for its restoration as God's people living under a new covenant (Jeremiah 31:31–34), and for vindication of the righteous with the full coming of God's kingdom (Daniel).

For early Christians like Paul, the basis for their hope was Jesus' resurrection from the dead and the experience of the Holy Spirit. Christians took these events as past and present manifestations of the fullness of what was hoped for in the future: eternal life with God through Christ, and the definitive manifestation of God's kingdom. This hope in turn made it possible for Christians to live in confidence and patience, since eternal life has already begun through faith and baptism and makes possible a positive attitude toward God's future intervention. Two statements in Luke's eschatological discourse neatly summarize the subjective dimension of Christian hope: "By your endurance you will gain your souls" (Luke 21:19) and "Now when these things begin to take place, stand up and raise your heads, because your redemption is drawing near" (21:28).

HOPE AS A PAULINE VIRTUE

First Corinthians 15 is Paul's extended meditation on the relationship between Christ's resurrection and our resurrection. Paul makes Christ's resurrection pivotal for Christian faith: "If Christ has not been raised, your faith is futile and you are still in your sins" (15:17). Affirming his belief in Christ's resurrection, Paul describes Christ as "the first fruits of those who have died" (15:20). In other words, Christ is the first in a long series of resurrections: "For as all die in Adam, so all will be made alive in Christ" (15:22). As he develops his concept of the spiritual body, Paul considers what happened at Christ's resurrection and what he hopes will happen at ours: "For this perishable body must put on imperishability, and this mortal body must put on immortality" (15:53). The hope for resurrection and immortality is based on the resurrection and immortality of Christ. It is not the natural property of being human (the immortality of the soul). Rather, it is a gift from God, given in and through Jesus' death and resurrection.

According to 2 Corinthians 5:1–10, God has prepared for those who live in Christ "a house not made with hands, eternal in the heavens" (5:1). Eternal life with God is the destiny that God has established for those who are in Christ. Thus, life in the present can be regarded as a preparation for eternal life, and the experience of the Holy Spirit in the present is the pledge or down payment on eternal life: "He who has prepared us for this very thing is God, who has given us the Spirit as a guarantee" (5:5). However, in order to enjoy one's heavenly home, one must first "appear before the judgment seat of Christ" and "receive recompense for what has been done in the body, whether good or evil" (5:10). One must live in the present in such a way as to receive God's gift of eternal life with Christ.

According to Romans 8:18–23, the full coming of God's kingdom will be cosmic in scope. In 8:22, Paul compares the present state of creation to a pregnant woman "groaning in labor pains until now." He regards the day of the Lord as a glorious vindication of those who are in Christ. In fact, it is something that all creation looks forward to: "The creation awaits with eager longing for the revealing of the children of God" (8:19). There is a kind of sympathetic longing for fullness between the cosmos and those "who have the first fruits of the Spirit" (8:23).

Hope for the coming kingdom of God and for eternal life with Christ provides the goal and the horizon for Paul's ethical teachings. Those who have the first fruits of the Spirit must live in an appropriate manner so as to pass the judgment according to their deeds before Christ the judge. In the light of this ultimate hope, all other hopes find their place.

While in some respects Paul's hope is already fulfilled in the present (note the images of "guarantee" and "first fruits"), the fullness of his hope remains in the future. Paul expresses perfectly the nature of hope and its already/not-yet in dynamic in Romans 8:24–25: "For in hope we were saved. Now hope that is seen is not hope. For who hopes for what is seen? But if we hope for what we do not see, we wait for it with patience."

SELECT BIBLIOGRAPHY

Beker, Johan Christiaan. *Paul the Apostle: The Triumph of God in Life and Thought.* Philadelphia: Fortress, 1980.

———. *Suffering and Hope: The Biblical Vision and the Human Predicament.* Grand Rapids, MI: Eerdmans, 1994.

Harrington, Daniel J. *What Are We Hoping For? New Testament Images.* Collegeville, MN: Liturgical Press, 2006.

———. *Why Do We Hope? Images in the Psalms.* Collegeville, MN: Liturgical Press, 2008.

Lynch, William. *Images of Hope: Imagination as Healer of the Hopeless.* Baltimore: Helicon, 1965.

Chapter Twelve

Hope: Theological Perspectives

THOMAS IN THE *SUMMA* ON HOPE

In question 17 of the *Secunda Secundae*, Thomas asks about hope in itself—and naturally the first article is, "Is hope a virtue?" In a wonderful discussion on virtue he notes that virtue not only attains a rule, whether reason or God, but it attains the rule by the help of the rule. Thus by prudence the moral virtues (temperance, fortitude, and justice) attain the rule of reason, and by God, the theological virtues (faith, hope, and charity) bring us to God. For this reason we acknowledge that the theological virtues are infused by God; God makes us able to "reach" God. Here then, hope is a virtue because it attains God, by God's power.

In the next article, Thomas asks, "What then is the object of hope?" He answers: Eternal happiness is the proper object of hope. The good that hope seeks is eternal life, which consists in the enjoyment of God's self. We should hope for nothing less than God's self, since God's goodness, whereby God imparts good things to us, is no less than God's nature.

Here Thomas notes both the limit of hope and the breadth of hope. First, there is distance between us and God: that which we hope for is still veiled. But hope embraces all virtuous objects, to the extent that they are referred to as eternal happiness.

On these two points, Thomas turns in the third article to ask whether we may hope for another's happiness. Appreciating the distance of God, he writes that hope is always about something arduous, something not yet achieved. Hope differs from charity in this: Charity denotes union, while hope denotes movement or a stretching forth of the appetite toward an arduous good. So hope is about what is veiled and arduous to attain, but by extension it concerns not only our end, but others' last end. We can hope for another's eternal happiness.

Is it lawful to hope in fellow humans? Thomas asks in the next article. Yes, he writes, but only as a secondary cause. We hope in God, but we may hope to get the wisdom of others, who may guide us into better understanding God's gift of hope.

Is hope a theological virtue? Here he refers to two ways that we may see the particularity of hope as a theological virtue. First, when we say that hope is infused, we mean that God effectively causes hope in us; God is the efficient cause of hope. God is also the end or final cause of hope.

Is hope distinct from the other theological virtues? Here Thomas returns to Psalm 72:28, by which he claims that by charity we adhere to God but adds that through charity we adhere to God for God's own sake, uniting our minds to God by the emotion of love. Faith and hope make us adhere to God as to a principle by which we derive other understandings and gifts. Thus, by hope we trust in the divine assistance for obtaining happiness.

In the next two articles Thomas discusses the relationship among the three virtues: Do they have an order among them? Thomas proposes two orders. By the order of generation, faith precedes hope and together they precede charity; according to the order of perfection, however, charity precedes and perfects both faith and hope.

In the next question, Thomas turns to the subject of hope. Noteworthily, Thomas asks whether in the blessed in the kingdom of God there is hope. He writes that when happiness is finally attained, hope, like faith, will be voided in heaven. The blessed ones experience the end, God, which faith and hope helped them attain. Thus, as long as hope lasts, the last end is outstanding.

Just as there is no hope in heaven because there is no need for hope, similarly for those eternally damned, where there is no longer any possibility of attaining God, there is no possibility of hope. With no hope in hell and none in heaven, we appreciate why Thomas insists that hope is for the wayfarer.

What about the vices of hope? Augustine gives us (from Plato) the insight that for every virtue, there are two vices: one that is its contrary, the other that is its deceptive resemblance. Fortitude, for instance, has cowardliness as its contradictory, but foolhardiness as its deceptive resemblance. Both are vicious because both fail to adhere to the rule of reason. Likewise, hope has despair as its contradictory, but presumption as its deceptive resemblance. Both are vicious because both fail to adhere to the rule of God.

Despair means that the wayfarer no longer believes that the journey is doable. Presumption means that the journey is doable, but that we do not need to rely on God. In neither vice do we in fact rely on God. God is beyond our needs for the journey.

APPLYING THE INSIGHTS OF THOMAS (AND PAUL)

In closing this part on the three virtues, I would like here to review five insights pertaining to the virtue of hope (and the vices associated with it).

First, if the journey is not arduous, worry! If you do not rely on God, worry!

Second, hope is not first an action, but a virtue that keeps us in action. Hope is clearly interior. In fact, we see it in the face of despair. Have you seen the face of one in despair—say, one who has attempted suicide? There is no rootedness in the person; you see how his or her roots, his or her interiority, is exhausted.

Third, hope requires discipline. Paul talks about the race, the focus on the goal, the discipline. He uses athletic imagery. One exercise for hope is vigilance: looking out for the extremes—presumption and despair—and finding the middle way. Hope then is recognizing the signs of grace, where confidences are restored and consolation is experienced in knowing that loved ones who have died are well.

Fourth, prayer is the exercise for hope. By prayer we encounter God on the arduous journey of sanctification. Hope lets us stop on the journey. Hope helps us recognize that we are not alone on the journey; that God is with us and assists us; and that while we still have eternal life before us, we are accompanied on the journey.

A wonderful image for hope is the flight into Egypt. Here the holy family flees during this arduous journey, but they know they are not alone and that divine providence will bring them to where they need to be. Caravaggio conveys beautifully the notion of hope in his *Flight into Egypt*. An angel plays a violin for the mother and child as Joseph holds the musical score. The interlude is not only restful; it is restorative. Prayer then is a rest on the journey, an encounter with divine assistance, an appreciation of the ardor of the way but a confidence that one has not left the way.

Fifth, whereas prayer lets us know where we are, our imagination is necessary for anticipating where we are going. We need images of the kingdom. Here in particular, we have the communion of saints: those who have gone before us, enjoying the end that we are seeking, while interceding for us who are approaching them. This final exercise of hope invites us to allow our imaginations to consider the resurrection of the body, the communion of saints, life everlasting, meeting our loved ones, and encountering God.

SELECT BIBLIOGRAPHY

Cessario, Romanus. "The Theological Virtue of Charity." In *The Ethics of Aquinas*, edited by Stephen Pope, 232–43. Washington, DC: Georgetown University Press, 2002.

Kelly, Anthony. *Eschatology and Hope.* New York: Orbis, 2006.

Lear, Jonathan. *Radical Hope: Ethics in the Face of Cultural Devastation.* Cambridge, MA: Harvard University Press, 2008.

Moltmann, Jürgen. *The Coming of God: Christian Eschatology.* Philadelphia: Fortress, 2004.

——. *In the End—The Beginning: The Life of Hope.* Philadelphia: Fortress Press, 2004.

——. *Theology of Hope: On the Ground and the Implications of a Christian Eschatology.* Philadelphia: Fortress, 1993.

Pieper, Josef. *On Hope.* San Francisco: Ignatius Press, 1986.

Volf, Miroslav, and William Katerberg, eds. *The Future of Hope: Christian Tradition amid Modernity and Postmodernity.* Grand Rapids, MI: Eerdmans, 2004.

Wright, N. T. *Surprised by Hope: Rethinking Heaven, the Resurrection, and the Mission of the Church.* New York: Harper, 2008.

Part Three

OTHER VIRTUES
AND CHRISTIAN LIFE

Chapter Thirteen

Virtues and Vices:
Pauline Perspectives

LISTS OF VICES AND VIRTUES: GALATIANS 5:19–23

Paul brought the gospel of Jesus' life, death, and resurrection to Galatia in central Asia Minor (modern Turkey). He had special success in attracting non-Jews to his form of Christianity. He did not impose on them the obligation to become Jews and to observe the Jewish Law, especially those elements such as circumcision, Sabbath observance, and the food and purity rules that set Jews apart from their neighbors. After Paul moved on to further missionary activity elsewhere, other Jewish Christian missionaries came to Galatia and sought to convince the Gentile Christians at Galatia that they had to become Jews in order to be real Christians. Paul wrote his letter to the Galatians to persuade them to hold firm to the Law-free gospel that he had taught them.

Paul's primary argument was that the Gentile Christians in Galatia had already received the Holy Spirit apart from observing the Jewish Law. In 3:2, Paul asks them: "Did you receive the Spirit by doing the works of the law or by believing what you heard?" Through his long meditation on Abraham as the model of faith in Galatians 3 and his allegory on Hagar and Sarah in Galatians 4, Paul argued from the Jewish Scriptures that what counts most before God is faith and not "the works of the Law." What frightened Paul was that the Galatian Christians might give up their freedom as Gentile Christians and simply accede to the persuasion of the other Jewish Christian missionaries.

When Paul reached the hortatory or "ethical" part of his letter to the Galatians, he prefaced his instruction with a statement that summarized his own position: "For freedom Christ has set us free. Stand firm, therefore, and do not submit again to a yoke of slavery" (5:1). Of course, for Paul, freedom meant serving God alone as master. Freedom from the power of Sin, Death, and the Law makes possible freedom for serving God and for living under the guidance of the Holy Spirit.

In Galatians 5, Paul provides both a list of vices (5:19–21) and a list of virtues (5:22–23). He labels these lists "the works of the flesh" and "the fruit of the Spirit," respectively.

> 19. Now the works of the flesh are obvious: fornication, impurity, licentious-ness, 20. idolatry, sorcery, enmities, strife, jealousy, anger, quarrels, dissen-sions, factions, 21. envy, drunkenness, carousing, and things like these. I am warning you, as I warned you before: those who do such things will not inherit the kingdom of God. 22. By contrast, the fruit of the Spirit is love, joy, peace, patience, kindness, generosity, faithfulness, 23. gentleness, and self-control. There is no law against such things.

Here as elsewhere in Paul's letters, context is very important for understand-ing Paul's ethical teachings. The "ethical" teachings are always embedded in a theological context. Or rather, ethics flows from theology, just as action flows from being (*agere sequitur esse*). Paul is not interested in moral formation for its own sake. Rather, his concern is always how might Christians best express in action what they have become through their faith and baptism.

The theological context for these lists is the opposition between spirit/ Spirit and flesh. For Paul, the "flesh" is that aspect of the person that is open to domination by Sin, Death, and the Law. And the "spirit" is that aspect of the person that is open to domination by the Holy Spirit. Since the same Greek word *pneuma* can refer to both the "spirit" of the human person and the Holy Spirit, it is often difficult to determine which one Paul is talking about at any time.

Paul's modified apocalyptic dualism supplies the theological context for his lists of vices and virtues. Those who live in the "flesh" follow the lead of Sin, Death, and the Law. Those who live in the "spirit/Spirit" follow the lead of the risen Christ and the Holy Spirit. The vices are the behaviors charac-teristic of those who walk in the flesh, whereas the virtues are the behaviors characteristic of those who walk in the spirit/Spirit.

The two lists in Galatians 5:19–23 are sandwiched between passages (5:16–18 and 5:24–26) that place them in a highly theological context. By way of introduction in 5:16–18, Paul distinguishes sharply between the spirit/ Spirit and the flesh: "For what the flesh desires is opposed to the Spirit, and what the Spirit desires is opposed to the flesh" (5:17a). By way of conclusion in 5:24–26, Paul affirms that "those who belong to Christ Jesus have crucified the flesh" (5:24) and urges those who live by the Spirit to "be guided by the Spirit" (5:25). The list of vices illustrates the ways of the flesh, while the list of virtues is the "fruit" of the Holy Spirit.

In the list of the "works of the flesh" in Galatians 5:19–21 there are fifteen vices. The first three—fornication, impurity, and licentiousness—concern sexual immorality or misconduct. The terms are generic, and so it is hard to discern whether there is any exact differentiation among them. The next two vices—idolatry and sorcery—are connected with exercises of false religion. The largest category—enmities, strife, jealousy, anger, quarrels, dissensions, factions, and envy—contains eight words that pertain to problems likely to arise within a community or at a social level. The emphasis on this topic is reinforced by what follows, and suggests that Paul tailored his list of vices to respond to problems within the Galatian community. The last two items— drunkenness and carousing—fall under the general category of debauchery.

These "works of the flesh" are vices or behaviors to be avoided by those who are in the spirit/Spirit. Paul warns that those who do such things "will not inherit the kingdom of God" (5:21b). And he speaks as though such lists of vices were part of the teachings that he had imparted to the Galatians when he brought them to Christian faith and thus had been part of the early Christian tradition of preaching: "I am warning you, as I warned you before" (5:21).

In the list presented in 5:22–23 there are nine items. They are labeled as "the fruit of the Spirit," which is a way of acknowledging their origin and dynamism with the Holy Spirit. They are ways by which the Holy Spirit dwelling within the Christian empowers good and helpful actions. Here as elsewhere, the Christian "virtues" are not personal accomplishments or self-standing character attributes. Rather, their context is the Christ-event and the gift of the Holy Spirit. Like the charisms (see Romans 12:6–8; 1 Corinthians 12:8–10, 28), they are expressions of the Holy Spirit given for the common good.

The first three items on the list of "virtues" are terms that Paul in Romans also predicates of God: love (5:5, 8), joy (15:13), and peace (15:33; 16:20). The idea is that those who exhibit these virtues imitate the example set by God. The second group of three virtues—patience, kindness, and generosity—pertain to life in relationship to other persons, especially within a community. They are the positive virtues needed to offset the eight vices ranging from enmities to envy that tend to destroy the peace and harmony of a Christian community. In the third triad—faithfulness, gentleness, and self-control—there is again an emphasis on virtues that contribute to the smooth running of a Christian community. The appearance of self-control (*enkrateia*) as the final member of the list is notable as the only occurrence of this term in Paul's letters, even though it was a prominent word in Hellenistic ethical writings (where it often had the connotation of self-mastery in sexual matters) and later became very prominent in early eastern Christian circles.

The impression that Paul has tailored his lists of vices and virtues to respond to tensions within the Galatian Christian community is strengthened by

Paul's final words of advice in Galatians 5:26: "Let us not become conceited, competing against one another, envying one another." These lists are combinations of Paul's theology (the "virtues" of God, modified apocalyptic dualism, etc.), the vocabulary and conventions of Greco-Roman ethical teachings, and Paul's own pastoral concerns and sensitivity. Thus they are miniature presentations of Paul's general approach to ethics and the life of virtue.

MORE LISTS

Romans 5:3–5 contains a "chain" that at least approximates a list of virtues: "Suffering produces endurance, and endurance produces character, and character produces hope, and hope does not disappoint us." Whatever human wisdom may be contained in this sequence, it is immediately placed in a theological context by Paul's insistence that the force that makes possible this human growth is God's love: "because God's love has been poured into our hearts through the Holy Spirit that has been given to us." For another New Testament list of virtues in the form of a "chain," see 2 Peter 1:5–7: "You must make every effort to support your faith with goodness, and goodness with knowledge, and knowledge with self-control."

Lists of vices appear elsewhere in Paul's letters. In 1 Corinthians 6:9–10, he writes: "Fornicators, idolaters, adulterers, male prostitutes, sodomites, thieves, the greedy, drunkards, revilers, robbers—none of these will inherit the kingdom of God." And at the conclusion of his portrayal of the wretched moral state of Gentiles before and apart from Christ, Paul offers still another list of vices in Romans 1:29–31: "They were filled with every kind of wickedness, evil, covetousness, malice. Full of envy, murder, strife, deceit, craftiness, they are gossips, slanderers, God-haters, insolent, haughty, boastful, inventors of evil, rebellious toward parents, foolish, faithless, heartless, ruthless." For other Pauline lists of vices, see 1 Corinthians 5:10–11 ("sexually immoral or greedy . . . an idolater, reviler, drunkard, or robber") and 2 Corinthians 12:20 ("quarreling, jealousy, anger, selfishness, slander, gossip, conceit, and disorder"). For still another list of vices, see Mark 7:21b–22 (see also Matthew 15:19): "fornication, theft, murder, adultery, avarice, wickedness, deceit, licentiousness, envy, slander, pride, folly."

There is a good deal of overlap in these lists of vices. Nevertheless, no one of them is exhaustive or comprehensive. Rather, they are indicative of the behavior into which those who live in the flesh fall. Likewise, the virtues are the behavior made manifest in the lives of those who live in the spirit/Spirit. The lists of vices and virtues are integral parts of Paul's ethical teaching. That means that they appear in the wider context of Paul's theological vision and not simply as freestanding moral instructions.

EXTRABIBLICAL EXAMPLES

Lists of virtues and vices also occur in non-Christian writings outside the Bible. Indeed, it is generally held that Paul in Galatians 5:19–23 and his other lists followed a convention that was well established among Greco-Roman moralists. One example of this convention occurs in an epistle ascribed to the Cynic philosopher Crates (365–285 BCE) but more likely written by a pagan philosopher in Crates' name in the first or second century CE:

> Shun not only the worst of evils, injustice and self-indulgence, but also their causes, pleasures. For you will concentrate on these alone, both present and future, and on nothing else. And pursue not only the best of goods, self-control and perseverance, but also their causes, toils, and do not shun them on account of their harshness. For you would not exchange inferior things for something great? As you would receive gold in exchange for copper, so you would receive virtue in exchange for toils. (Pseudo-Crates, *Epistle* 15)

As in Galatians 5:19–23, this text first treats vices (injustice and self-indulgence) and then deals with virtues (self-control and perseverance). The order illustrates what one first needs to be freed from and then what one needs to pursue and live by. But unlike Paul, Pseudo-Crates wrote in the context of philosophy and moral development. There is no all-encompassing religious framework such as that supplied by the Christ-event according to Paul's theology. Nor is there from Pseudo-Crates any hint of divine grace helping one lead a virtuous life. The emphasis is on "self-help" entirely.

A more illuminating parallel (in terms of form, content, and context) comes from the *Rule of the Community* discovered among the Dead Sea scrolls found at Qumran. This work seems to have been composed as a handbook or rule for a Jewish religious sect (the Essenes) roughly contemporary with Jesus and Paul. In its "Instruction for the Master" (3:13–4:25), the Qumran *Rule* presents lists of vices and virtues that are similar to Paul's lists in context and context.

In the Qumran text the list of virtues comes first. They are the characteristic traits or behaviors of those who are the Children of Light and follow the leadership of the Prince of Light:

> These are their ways . . . a spirit of humility, patience, abundant charity, unending goodness, understanding, and intelligence; (a spirit of) mighty wisdom

which trusts in all the deeds of God and leans on His great loving-kindness; a spirit of discernment in every purpose, of zeal for just laws, of holy intent with steadfastness of heart, of great charity toward all the sons of truth, of admirable purity which detests all unclean idols, of humble conduct sprung from an understanding of all things, and of faithful concealment of the mysteries of truth. These are the counsels of the spirit to the sons of truth in this world. (Vermes, 102)

In this list there is a mixture of "natural" virtues (e.g., patience) and "theological" virtues (e.g., "mighty wisdom which trusts in all the deeds of God and leans on His great loving-kindness"). In fact, as in the Pauline lists, there is no real distinction between the categories of natural and theological virtues.

Likewise, the list of vices presents the characteristic behaviors of the Children of Darkness who follow the leadership of the Prince of Darkness:

But the ways of the spirit of falsehood are these: greed, and slackness in the search for righteousness, wickedness and lies, haughtiness and pride, falseness and deceit, cruelty and abundant evil, ill-temper and much folly and brazen insolence, abominable deeds (committed) in a spirit of lust, and ways of lewdness in the service of uncleanness, a blaspheming tongue, blindness of eye and dullness of ear, stiffness of neck and heaviness of heart, so that man walks in all the ways of darkness and guile. (Vermes, 104)

Here too there are "natural" vices (e.g., greed) as well as "theological" vices (e.g., "slackness in the search for righteousness"). Indeed, as in all of Paul's writings, the religious context is so all-embracing as to render useless the distinction between natural and theological vices.

Even more important than the links in form and content between the Qumran and the Pauline lists of vices and virtues are the similarities in the theological contexts in which they appear. Both the Essenes and the early Christian movement assumed the theological framework of modified apocalyptic dualism. The Qumran instruction takes as its theological assumption the absolute sovereignty of the one God: "From the God of Knowledge comes all that is and shall be." However, according to the Qumran instruction, God has left the present course of human history under the control of two powers—the Prince of Light and the Prince of Darkness. Those who follow the lead of the former constitute the Children of Light, while those who follow the latter are the Children of Darkness. In Paul's Christian adaptation of this schema of modified apocalyptic dualism, the role of the Prince of Light is taken by Jesus Christ and the Holy Spirit, while the role of the Prince of Darkness is taken by Sin, Death, and the Law.

In this dualistic context there are two kinds of persons: the Children of Light (those who live by the spirit/Spirit), and the Children of Darkness (those who live by the flesh). The deeds of the members of each group reflect their identity, so that the Children of Light do virtuous deeds and the Children of Darkness do evil deeds. And for their deeds there are rewards for the Children of Light ("healing, great peace in a long life, and fruitfulness, together with every everlasting blessing and eternal joy in life without end") and punishments for the Children of Darkness ("a multitude of plagues . . . eternal damnation . . . eternal torment and endless disgrace"). And as in Paul's letters, there is a strong sense of a final divine judgment ("the visitation") that will bring an end to the struggle between good and evil and provide full vindication for the Children of Light.

DEUTEROPAULINE LISTS OF VIRTUES

Following the convention already prominent in Paul's uncontested letters, the Pastoral Epistles (1 and 2 Timothy, Titus) present more lists in which vices and virtues appear. In explaining why the Mosaic Law is good if used legitimately, 1 Timothy 1:9–10 gives a list of persons for whom the Law was intended: "for the lawless and disobedient, for the godless and sinful, for the unholy and profane, for those who kill their father and mother, for murderers, fornicators, sodomites, slave traders, liars, perjurers, and whatever else is contrary to sound teaching." This list combines items with biblical roots and those of more general moral applicability. The inclusion of "slave traders" is unusual, since the economy of the Roman Empire was in large part dependent upon the institution of slavery. In the present context of the Pastorals, the idea is that the Mosaic Law is used legitimately as a way of identifying sins and warning people against doing such actions.

In warning against false teachers (one of the major themes in the Pastorals), 1 Timothy 6:3–5 describes them as conceited, stupid, and craving controversy. Then it makes a link between such teachers and certain vices that have the effect of corrupting life within a Christian community (see Galatians 5:19–21): "From these come envy, dissension, slander, base suspicions, and wrangling among those who are depraved in mind and bereft of the truth, imagining that godliness is a means of gain."

One of the standard features in Jewish and early Christian apocalyptic scenarios is the outbreak of wicked and sinful behavior. In 2 Timothy 3:2–5, there is a list of vices associated with "the last days": "For people will be lovers of themselves, lovers of money, boasters, arrogant, abusive, disobedient to their parents, ungrateful, unholy, inhuman, implacable, slanderers, profligates, brutes, haters of good, treacherous, reckless, swollen with conceit, lovers of pleasure rather than lovers of God." This list specifies what such wicked behaviors will be, again with the aid of items that evoke the biblical tradition (e.g., "disobedient to their parents") as well as the broader moral tradition of the Greco-Roman world.

It is noteworthy that all these lists of vices occur in wider Christian theological contexts: the role of the Mosaic Law (1 Timothy 1:9–10), community tensions (1 Timothy 6:3–5), and eschatology (2 Timothy 3:2–5). The lists are not ends in themselves but rather function in the service of clarifying more important topics.

The lists of qualifications for bishops and deacons in 1 Timothy 3:1–13 combine virtues and vices; they are clearly influenced by the "list" tradition. These lists are concerned not so much with matters of faith or even with practical skills and experience as they are with the moral qualities and character that persons should bring to these positions of leadership in local Christian communities.

Thus a bishop (*episkopos*) should be "above reproach, married only once, temperate, sensible, respectable, hospitable, an apt teacher, not a drunkard, not violent but gentle, not quarrelsome, and not a lover of money" (1 Timothy 3:2–3). The main test for the prospective bishop's administrative skill is his ability to manage his own household in a smooth way (3:4–5), thus linking the household tradition and tradition of the lists of vices and virtues. The importance of vices and virtues in the profile of the bishop is part of the early church's search for external respectability in the Greco-Roman world of the late first century CE. This emphasis is well expressed in 3:7: "He must be well thought of by outsiders."

Likewise, a deacon (*diakonos*) must be "serious, not double-tongued, not indulging in much wine, not greedy for money" (3:8). And "women" (female deacons, or the wives of deacons) should also be "serious, not slanderers, but temperate, faithful in all things" (3:11). The deacons too should be married only once (or a husband of one wife) and prove themselves capable of managing "their children and their household well" (3:12).

The letter to Titus directs that those who are appointed to be elders (*presbyteroi*) should be "blameless, married only once, whose children are believers, not accused of debauchery, and not rebellious" (1:6). Again there is a combination of personal qualities and the proven ability to direct a household. The insistence that bishops, deacons, and presbyters be married only once (or husbands of one wife) assumes that they will be married and heads of households. But what exactly this phrase forbids—polygamy, divorce and remarriage, or marriage after the wife's death—is not entirely clear. The bishop too must be "blameless," another indication of the importance of public respectability. The passage goes on to state that a bishop "must not be arrogant or quick-tempered or addicted to wine or violent or greedy for gain; but he must be hospitable, a lover of goodness, prudent, upright, devout, and self-controlled" (1:7–8).

These lists of qualifications for local church offices—bishops, deacons, and presbyters—illustrate certain moral ideals that early Christians expected from their leaders and presumably from themselves. They highlight the seriousness with which early Christians took the moral virtues and vices, the importance of external respectability, and the household as a social institution. The roots of these themes are in Paul's uncontested letters, but the Deuteropauline writings give them even more prominence. Readers today, however, should not isolate them from the theological framework of the Pauline corpus as a whole. What can result when the larger context is ignored is an appeal to the Pastorals as the biblical basis for a legalistic and "middle-class" brand of cultural Christianity without much theological depth or religious fervor.

A DEUTEROPAULINE HOUSEHOLD CODE

Titus 2:1–10 looks much like a household code. After an exhortation to "teach what is consistent with sound doctrine" (2:1), it provides advice pertaining to older men and older women (2:2–3), younger women and younger men (2:4–8), and slaves (2:9–10). But here the concern is not so much with hierarchy and power relationships (though modified by reminders about mutual obligations and religious motivations) as it is with the virtues that are proper to members of each group.

The advice to the older men (2:2) combines certain natural virtues (temperance, seriousness, prudence) and the triad of theological virtues (faith, love, and hope). The older women (2:3) are told to be "reverent in behavior" and so to avoid slanderous talk and drunkenness and to take seriously their obligation to initiate the younger women into the life of domestic virtue and Christian faith.

The instructions to the younger women and men are distinctive for their emphasis on the effects of virtuous behavior on outsiders (see 2:5, 8). The life of the younger woman (2:4–5) is assumed to revolve around the household. It is taken for granted that she will marry and have children. Recall that the opponents were forbidding marriage (see 1 Timothy 4:3), and so the insistence in 1 Timothy 2:15 that women will be saved through childbearing becomes more intelligible. In this domestic context women were expected to love their husbands and children, to be self-controlled and chaste, to manage their household well and to be kind (toward the servants?), and to be submissive to their husbands.

One theological reason for early Christian women to cultivate such exemplary and virtuous behavior was to increase respect for the Christian faith and the church among outsiders: "so that the word of God may not be discredited"

(2:5). Christians were a tiny minority in the Greco-Roman world, and the best and most effective way of furthering the Christian mission was through the good example of people who were already Christians. The kind of behavior recommended here for Christian women conformed to the highest standards of conduct in the Greco-Roman world around them.

The younger men (2:6) are urged to be "self-controlled," presumably in the area of sexual conduct. Then in 2:7–8, Titus is addressed as a representative of the younger men and is told to do good works and in his teaching activity to show himself as someone marked by integrity, gravity, and sound speech. Again, an important motive for such behavior is the positive impression that it will make on outsiders: "then any opponent will be put to shame, having nothing evil to say to us" (2:8).

Likewise, slaves (2:9–10) are to cultivate the virtues that are proper to slaves: submissiveness, respectfulness, honesty, and fidelity. It is proposed that in this way even Christian slaves can contribute effectively to the missionary program of good example: "so that in everything they may be an ornament to the doctrine of God our Savior" (2:10).

In the format of the household code, Titus 2:1–10 provides insight into what virtues were regarded as most appropriate for various categories of early Christians. It also gives a glimpse of a somewhat "domesticated" form of Christianity in which the conventional and even elite household (replete with slaves) is assumed to set the pattern for Christians living in the Greco-Roman world. And finally it suggests that early Christians had recognized and were exploiting an important sociological truth: Religions spread and grow through social networks, and new converts are attracted primarily through contact with the exemplary behavior of representatives (even if they are women or slaves!) of that religion.

GODLINESS AS A CHRISTIAN VIRTUE

The Greek word *eusebeia* can be translated in various ways: godliness, piety, devotion, worship, or religion. In pagan Greek and Latin texts *eusebeia* refers to the respect or devotion that a person has for the gods. In some circles it ranked with the classical cardinal virtues of prudence, justice, temperance, and fortitude.

In the Old Testament what was meant by *eusebeia* in Greek was conveyed in many ways, but none of them was exactly the same as the Greek concept of *eusebeia*. The writers of the Hebrew Bible expressed their concept of godliness in terms such as fear of the Lord, holiness, righteousness, fidelity, covenant loyalty, steadfastness, and so on. Perhaps because of its association with reverence for pagan gods, *eusebeia* was not a prominent word in the Greek version of the Old Testament (Septuagint) and in much of the New Testament.

Most of the New Testament occurrences of *eusebeia* appear in the Pastoral Epistles and in 2 Peter (which is generally regarded as the latest composition in the canon). The occurrence in Titus 2:13 is especially significant: "in the present age to live lives that are self-controlled, upright, and godly." The Greek adverbs in *sophronos kai dikaios kai eusebeos* clearly allude to the cardinal virtues of temperance and justice, and place *eusebeia* with them. The list appears after the household code in Titus 2:1–10 but seems directed to all Christians. Titus 2:11–14 is an interesting combination of Christian theological formulas ("the grace of God"), terms used in the cult of the Roman emperor ("bring salvation to all . . . our great God and Savior"), Jewish eschatology ("in the present age"), and the classical moral tradition (temperance, justice, piety). The passage is evidence of a new urban Christian culture that was emerging in the late first and early second century CE. Bringing together elements from various settings, this movement was creating a theological vocabulary and a conceptuality for expressing the effects of the Christ-event and for helping Christians actualize the gospel.

The frequent use of *eusebeia* in the Pastorals is a strong witness to this development. According to 1 Timothy 2:2, the ideal of Christian life is to "lead a quiet and peaceable life in all godliness and dignity." In 4:7–8, Timothy is instructed to "train yourself in godliness" because "godliness is valuable in every way, holding promise for both the present life and the life to come." While godliness can be misused as a "means of gain" (1 Timothy 6:5) or for outward show (2 Timothy 3:5), the positive Christian ideal is a form of godliness that is based on "the sound words of our Lord Jesus" (1 Timothy 6:3). In this context "there is great gain in godliness combined with contentment" (1 Timothy 6:6).

The three great Christian "virtues" are faith, hope, and love. In fact, they are more gifts from God than human accomplishments. They provide the proper theological context for all the other virtues to be pursued and acted upon (and for the vices to be avoided). While there are indications that some New Testament writers were familiar with the classical tradition of the cardinal virtues, they do not seem to have singled them out for an especially prominent place in early Christian moral teaching. Rather, without much apparent effort at systematization, early Christian teachers mentioned all kinds of virtues that seemed to be appropriate expressions of faith, love, and hope. They clearly regarded the "natural" virtues as important and commended them as part of the way of life befitting Christians. But in the final analysis "faith, hope, and love abide, these three; and the greatest of these is love" (1 Corinthians 13:13). In this context "godliness" (*eusebeia*) is a good point of connection or link between the so-called theological and the natural virtues.

SELECT BIBLIOGRAPHY

Barclay, J. M. G. *Obeying the Truth: A Study of Paul's Ethics in Galatians.* Edinburgh, Scotland: T&T Clark, 1988.

Barrett, C. K. *Freedom and Obligation: A Study of the Epistle to the Galatians.* Philadelphia: Westminster, 1985.

Kamlah, Ehrhard. *Die Form der katalogischen Paränese im Neuen Testament.* Tübingen, Germany: Mohr Siebeck, 1964.

Malherbe, Abraham. *Moral Exhortation: A Greco-Roman Sourcebook.* Philadelphia: Westminster, 1986.

Matera, Frank J. *New Testament Ethics: The Legacies of Jesus and Paul.* Louisville, KY: Westminster/John Knox, 1996.

Meeks, Wayne. *The Origins of Christian Morality: The First Two Centuries.* New Haven, CT: Yale University Press, 1993.

Vermes, Geza. *The Complete Dead Sea Scrolls in English.* London: Penguin, 1997.

Wibbing, Siegfried. *Die Tügend- und Lästerkataloge im Neuen Testament und ihre Traditionsgeschichte unter besonderer Beruchsichtigung der Qumran-Texte.* Berlin: Töpelmann, 1959.

Chapter Fourteen

Virtues and Vices: Theological Perspectives

THE SPECIFICITY OF CHRISTIAN THEOLOGICAL ETHICS

In the 1970s there was an extended debate as to whether there was something substantive about Catholic theological ethics. Prior to the Council, the famous turn to the person that Yves Congar, Marie Dominique Chenu, Karl Rahner, and others accepted and applied to their theology prompted moral theologians to begin understanding moral truth as not primarily about actions—that is, whether this action is right or wrong—but rather about persons.

Then moral theologians, notably Bernhard Häring and Josef Fuchs, began to speak about moral truth and the vision of the human being, that is, the *humanum*. Moral truth was about getting the *humanum* right.

Following Fuchs, many moral theologians began in the 1970s to ask if the *humanum* was opened to investigation by human reason. Yes, they argued: The nature of the *humanum* could be articulated by Christian or Jew, Buddhist or secular, pagan or agnostic. From the Greeks to the Renaissance, there has always been a deep interest in expressing the *humanum*.

Now we need to appreciate that though Josef Pieper did write extensively in the 1940s to 1960s on the cardinal virtues, the turn to virtue beyond Pieper did not occur until MacIntyre's *After Virtue* appeared in 1982—that is, after the debate in the 1970s on the specificity of Catholic theological ethics.

What could other traditions or Christianity itself bring to the image of the *humanum* that if it were right would not be assented to by others? This became the key question. It played itself out in a variety of contexts. For instance, could we Christians say something about the *humanum* that would not resonate with a Muslim or a Jew or a Buddhist? In the 1970s, there was a great presupposition about sharing a common *humanum*.

Prior to any era of cultural contextualization or cross-cultural context discussion, in the 1970s, in the aftermath of the warlike and rebellious 1960s, there was a new détente in shared understanding. French Marxists were speaking to French Christians; Italian communists were talking with Catholic theologians; English Anglicans were talking with English Roman Catholics. People of different traditions believed that through dialogue they would discover the hitherto unexpressed common vision of the human.

With an overwhelming sense of disdain for being so chauvinistic as to claim that we could bring something distinctive to the table of discourse over the *humanum*, Joseph Ratzinger and Hans Urs von Balthasar broke ranks and asked, "Is that all there is?" Does not faith allow us to understand the *humanum* differently?

They noted that faith helps us see what many today do not understand but that Catholics reading *Humanae vitae* could understand—that is, that there are two ends of marriage: the procreative and the unitive. The "light of faith" could so inform our reason that we could understand matters that those not in our tradition would not. Pope Benedict XVI reiterated this position recently ("Birth control teaching is beyond reason, says Pope," *The Tablet*, 11 October 2008, 33.)

The defenders of the specificity of Catholic theological ethics were not only insisting that it was distinctive, they were also naming which teachings made it so. In fact, they had a number of specific norms (like no divorce, no sex outside of marriage, no homosexual activity, no abortion, no contraception) that they held did not belong specifically to the Catholic faith and, therefore, to the Catholic understanding of the *humanum*.

As time went on, a new wave of reaction emerged. Fuchs and Häring from Rome; Louis Janssens from Louvain; Richard McCormick from the United States; Hans Küng, Alfons Auer, Dietmar Mieth, and Franz Böckle from Germany all noted that, like faith, moral theology was about the *humanum*; but these issues about homosexuality and contraception were not from revelation, but from the moral tradition.

Did revelation give us something specific regarding morals? Thomas Aquinas had written that the New Law (meaning revelation) had not added anything new to the matter of moral theology. This became the mantra of many like Fuchs who stood with Thomas on this point. What did this mean? Basically it meant that there were no new norms in the New Testament. For instance, other than the love command, the Synoptic Gospels have only one moral norm: no divorce—but Matthew and Mark have different expressions of the near-absolute teaching of Jesus, and Paul actually suspends the teaching on divorce if it were to cause one to lose the faith.

In the midst of the debate, both sides were right. Fuchs, Häring, Rahner, Küng, McCormick, and even Thomas were right to say that there were no new norms in the New Testament. There were specific norms in the moral tradition, but they were at best norms in which the tradition was building on but not deriving from the teaching of revelation. On the other hand, Ratzinger and von Balthasar were right to say that there was distinctive moral matter from Scripture, but these matters ought not be confused with matters of the tradition.

But, and here's the great "but," when Fuchs and the others raised the question about what the light of faith did bring to reason, they were faced with a question going on in moral philosophy at the time. The question was "Why be moral?" This is a question captured by many—for instance, the well-regarded American William Frankena. If the moral life was about pursuing excellence, to the point that one could give up one's life, did you need faith so as to be moral? Experience taught us that faith was not necessarily always the answer. For instance, we know that during World War II, in the name of justice and loyalty, many gave up their lives to do the moral action. Of course, for Christians, they did the moral action not only out of a moral humanism, but also because they wanted to act as Jesus would, out of charity.

Fuchs and the others said: This is what faith and charity give us, a motivation to be moral. By faith we understand God, by charity we love God. If we believe and love God, we will do what God wants. What does God want? For us to realize rightly the *humanum*. But like the humanist soldier, the Christian soldier, while having another motivation, could do the exact same thing: surrender his life for a just cause. What made us distinctive was not the substance of our morality, but rather the grounds for being moral in the first place.

Another question arose. Was the *humanum* Christ? If the *humanum* was Christ, was Christ the *humanum* even for the nonbeliever? Well, here we get the Rahnerian anonymous Christian and other like-minded claims, and Fuchs was the most Rahnerian of all moralists. The *Christus* was the *humanum*, the *humanum* was the *Christus*, but there was nothing specifically Christian that was not specifically human. By 1979, four movements conspired against this position.

First, the great détente came to an end. People began to appreciate the specificity not only of culture but of great texts. The previous belief that society could articulate the *humanum* without a cultural bias and with great unanimity seemed to be a pipe dream. Moreover, the naive presupposition that secularity being free of religion meant that it was free of any presuppositions or biases also became exposed. As we see in France today (and Paul Valadier notes this), secularity is as rooted in a tradition as Islam, Judaism, and Christianity are. There are no rose-colored glasses with which we can filter out our own culturally driven presuppositions so as to see a harmonious and universally shared image of the *humanum*.

Second, at the same time, while moving away from this naivete, we began to appreciate the local roots of moral claims. This was the work of Alasdair MacIntyre in his book *Whose Justice? Which Rationality?* which was developed by Jean Porter. Moral norms inevitably have their genesis, and their genesis is local. The *Shema* of Deuteronomy 6:4–5 might be a summons to the love of God analogous to that found in many religious traditions, but it is still the Shema.

Third, Lisa Sowle Cahill contended against Porter that the local genesis of moral norms did not mean that they were left to the silos of cultural contexts. We seek to be cross-cultural, and while mindful of hermeneutics we try to articulate the overarching points of agreement. The United Nations Universal Declaration of Human Rights is a relevant achievement of consensually articulating universal norms. Porter would concur, but she would still maintain that the source of morals begins locally and specifically. We achieve universality through globalized consensus.

Fourth, Catholic ethicists discovered the Bible. This is not a facetious comment. The great biblical scholar Fritz Tillman was forced by Rome from his work in exegesis, and so he turned for sanctuary into theological ethics. A study of the history of moral theology in the twentieth century shows us, however, that despite the mantra of reform-oriented claims to turn to the Scriptures, as a matter of fact, few did. However, in the United States, several major moralists were trained at American Protestant universities, and there they were introduced to the Bible as the source for Christian moral teaching. Lisa Sowle Cahill, Stephen Pope, and William Spohn at the University of Chicago and David Hollenbach, Margaret Farley, and Jean Porter at Yale, for instance, studied with Protestant colleagues and mentors, and were far more at home with Scripture-based ethics than Catholic students at universities like the Gregorian, Leuven/Louvain, or the Catholic University of America.

In many ways Spohn and Cahill led the way, with both recognizing that the distinctiveness of theological ethics was not in norms found in the Bible but something else: for Spohn it would be the virtues, while for Cahill it was practices. Now we could see that maybe there were no new norms in the Bible, but there *was* something new and distinctive.

While emphasizing these sources, however, we need to be mindful, as Cahill would insist, that we turn to the local sources of our moral teachings (whether of norms for action, practices, or virtues)—not simply to define ourselves, but more importantly to communicate beyond our definitions with those who also mine their texts to find moral norms, practices, and virtues.

With the renewal of virtue ethics, outlined in chapter 1, theological ethicists began to see that the New Testament had a great deal to offer about moral life. But its offerings did not come in the form of norms. In the Gospels and the Epistles, virtue and vice language and their practices appear throughout: The parables and the sayings of Jesus and Paul are formed by the virtues. Could we now say, many years after the debate in the 1970s, that there was something substantively specific to moral theology and that it was not the tradition per se, but more importantly, the Scriptures? Could we also note that inasmuch as these texts are shared with Protestants and Orthodox churches, that we might be claiming a specifically Christian theological ethics?

For instance, besides his vice lists, Paul teaches us about the triple virtues of faith, hope, and charity. These virtues are not in Plato or Aristotle; they are not constitutive of a Greek *humanum* but rather a specifically Christian one. Can we not suggest, however, that the Greeks might have had some anthropological claims that approximated these? Certainly.

Moreover, we will also see, whether in Philippians or elsewhere, that Paul endorsed humility and mercy as well as justice and forgiveness and reconciliation.

One final comment. Certainly virtues and practices need norms, and norms are articulated so as to direct our virtues and practices, but they arise out of the soil of virtue. A parent interested in a child's appreciation of friendship recommends practices and gives norms to a child precisely about friendship. Norms are not alien to virtues, but if we look to the Bible for its distinctive traits, we do not find them in norms, but rather in the virtues and practices with which early Christian communities wrestled.

Beginning with virtues, we can then develop the anthropological profile of a disciple according to Paul. For virtues convey the specifically human character traits that Paul wants us to emulate.

PAULINE VIRTUES BEYOND FAITH, HOPE, AND CHARITY

The biblical lists of virtues give us a minimalist framework. With these as with the vice lists, Paul is basically saying to the early Christians, "Please don't embarrass the community; be temperate, be faithful to your spouse and family; don't be gluttonous, lustful, or slothful." Obviously, these admonitions suggest that the community is yet extraordinarily virtuous, as the expectations in these lists are exasperatingly low.

These lists do not give us an idea of Paul's theological anthropology. But his other comments on the virtues do. We have already seen that for Paul the disciple believes, hopes, and loves. Moreover, in recognizing the possibility of a lifeless faith and a lifeless hope, we appreciate that among these virtues charity holds pride of place in Paul and in the traditions that received him.

Moreover, in the next chapters we will see that Paul calls us to be humble and hospitable, two distinctively Pauline virtues. Now I want to add five others: being merciful, faithful, reconciling, vigilant, and reliable. These ten virtues I think capture the Pauline image of the Christian disciple.

We might recognize mercy as a virtue from the Synoptic Gospels—for example, in the parable of the Last Judgment in Matthew 25:31–46 or in the Good Samaritan parable (Luke 10:25–37), defining love of neighbor as the practice of mercy. But Paul's experience of God in his conversion is precisely in terms of mercy. Paul presents himself as the worst of sinners on whom God in Jesus Christ poured out his mercy (1 Timothy 1:13, 16). Elsewhere, Paul sees mercy in God as judge (Romans 9:14–24).

I define mercy as the willingness to enter into the chaos of another. This strikes me as quite applicable to Paul. For him, just as God entered into his chaos and saved him and kept him as his own, so too Paul enters into the chaos of his communities to bring salvation and to remain faithful with them until the end. We can think of Paul's travels (and letters) as mercy journeys, entering into the chaos of the Corinthians, the Romans, the Philippians, the Galatians, and so on. Similarly, Paul expects mercy from the communities he visits (and addresses), as he brings the collection for the community in Jerusalem. In terms of the Gentiles, Paul shows a very deep mercy with regard to circumcision and the other Hebrew practices that seem too burdensome and not evidently essential for Gentiles.

Coupled with mercy is the call to be faithful. Paul's greatest and most evident demand is for the disciple to be faithful. Paul is faithful because God in Jesus Christ is faithful. Our hope is in the faithfulness of Jesus: If we stand and wait, he will come.

The call to be faithful marks the conclusions of each of his epistles. In Romans 16:1–23, he calls on the community to greet those who "risked their necks for me," those who "worked hard in the Lord," those "who were in Christ before" him. Similarly, he warns against those who sow dissension and difficulties.

In 1 Corinthians 16:1–24, Colossians 4:7–17, and 2 Timothy 4:9–21, Paul again sends greetings and admonitions focused on being faithful. Fidelity is the way the disciples of Jesus are related to one another. The entire community depends on this fidelity.

1 Corinthians 7:10–15 gives us the Pauline teaching on divorce. Faithfulness to Christ and to one another in Christ is the hermeneutic for understanding divorce: Anyone whose spouse would undue the most fundamental call to faithfulness—of being baptized in Christ—should be divorced. Not surprisingly, then, the greatest sin in the early church is apostasy. Murder and robbery were not as problematic as abandoning the one who has been and will be faithful to us.

Being faithful does not necessarily mean, however, being in unison. And for this reason, reconciliation is a virtue in need of constant practice. Paul reminds the Corinthians continually that they need to be reconciled to one another. Their fractiousness gives no evidence of being in Christ. Reconciliation, then, is the only possibility for remaining faithful: A community only exists if it has ways of being reconciled frequently.

The admonition to reconciliation comes in the same way as did the summons to mercy and faithfulness: When we were not yet deserving—in fact, when we were sinners—we received reconciliation (Romans 5:8–11). But not only are we reconciled to God in Jesus Christ and not only are we to be reconciled to one another, Paul calls us in 2 Corinthians 5:16–21 to be ambassadors of reconciliation.

The Pauline vision of virtue is an *imitatio Dei*: as God is, so we are called to be. Our experience of God is as merciful, faithful, reconciling, and so we are called to be.

And of course, the all-knowing and all-loving God is vigilant. Paul frequently calls the community to be vigilant. In Colossians 4:2, he writes that we should "continue steadfastly in prayer, being watchful in it with thanksgiving." In 1 Corinthians 16:13, he urges: "Be watchful, stand firm in your faith, be courageous, be strong."

The Christian is always vigilant. In the tradition, sometimes vigilance looks like suspicion: Christians must be on the watch for the world, the flesh, and the devil. Sometimes it becomes a benevolent vigilance, as in being ready and able to see those who are in need. But beneath these stances is the more fundamental one of being watchful for the Lord. It is like the prayerfulness of Colossians, and it is not unlike the Buddhist practice of mindfulness. By being vigilant with regard to the Lord, we will be mindful of the needs and threats around us that call us to respond.

This vigilance coupled with faithfulness finally asks us to be reliable. In the closings of many of his letters, Paul asks his readers to assume certain tasks. He counts on reliability. And often, the migratory Paul is sending not simply tasks but persons our way. When he does, as when he sends the deacon Phoebe (Romans 16:1), the response is to be hospitable. But for that form of vigilant reliability, we turn to the next chapter.

SELECT BIBLIOGRAPHY

Cahill, Lisa Sowle. "Toward Global Ethics." *Theological Studies* 63 (2002): 324–44.
Curran, Charles, and Richard McCormick, eds. *Readings in Moral Theology No. 2: The Distinctiveness of Christian Ethics.* New York: Paulist Press, 1980.

Frankena, William. *Thinking about Morality.* Ann Arbor: University of Michigan Press, 1980.

Gaziaux, Éric. *L'autonomie en morale: Au croisement de la philosophie et de la théologie.* Leuven, Belgium: Leuven University Press, 1998.

———. *Morale de la foi et morale autonome: Confrontation entre P. Delhaye et J. Fuchs.* Leuven, Belgium: Peeters, 1995.

Keenan, James F. "Virtues, Principles, and a Consistent Ethics of Life." In *The Consistent Ethic of Life: Assessing Its Reception and Relevance,* edited by Thomas Nairn, 48–60. Maryknoll, NY: Orbis, 2008.

MacIntyre, Alasdair. *Whose Justice? Which Rationality?* Notre Dame, IN: University of Notre Dame Press, 1988.

Porter, Jean. "The Search for a Global Ethic." *Theological Studies* 62 (2001): 105–21.

———. "A Tradition of Civility: The Natural Law as a Tradition of Moral Inquiry." *Scottish Journal of Theology* 56 (2003): 27–48.

Valadier, Paul. *Une Christianisme d'avenir: Pour une nouvelle alliance entre raison et foi.* Paris: Seuil, 1999.

Chapter Fifteen

Ethics in a Communal Setting: Pauline Perspectives

AN EGREGIOUS OFFENSE: 1 CORINTHIANS 5:1–5

In the first four chapters of his First Letter to the Corinthians, Paul criticizes the Christians there for their factionalism ("'I belong to Paul' or 'I belong to Apollos,'" 1:12) and for taking pride in their spiritual gifts. As Paul begins to deal with more specific issues in the rest of the letter, he treats what he regards as a particularly egregious moral failure: the case of a man who was having a sexual affair with his father's wife.

> 1. It is actually reported that there is sexual immorality among you, and of a kind that is not found even among pagans; for a man is living with his father's wife. 2. And you are arrogant! Should you not rather have mourned, so that he who has done this would have been removed from among you? 3. For though absent in body, I am present in spirit; and as if present I have already pronounced judgment 4. in the name of the Lord Jesus on the man who has done such a thing. When you are assembled, and my spirit is present with the power of our Lord Jesus, 5. you are to hand this man over to Satan for the destruction of the flesh, so that his spirit may be saved in the day of the Lord.

In 5:1 Paul first describes the man's action as *porneia,* a general term covering various kinds of sexual misconduct. He goes on to define the offense more specifically: "A man is living with his father's wife." The way in which the woman is described rules out her being the man's own mother. She was most likely his stepmother, or perhaps his father's concubine or common-law wife. While the man was clearly a Christian, it is doubtful that either his father or his stepmother was a Christian. Paul complains that having a sexual affair with one's stepmother was forbidden even by pagan law (see Gaius, *Institutes*

1.63). It was also expressly forbidden by the Old Testament Law: "You shall not uncover the nakedness of your father's wife" (Leviticus 18:8).

Such conduct, then, was morally and legally indefensible, in Paul's mind at least. What the incestuous man was thinking can only be a matter of speculation. However, in the light of the slogan used in other contexts by Corinthian Christians ("All things are lawful for me," 6:12; 10:23), it is likely that he regarded himself as having been freed (according to an overly realized eschatology) from the bonds of conventional morality. Apparently the incestuous man had received support from some like-minded Christians at Corinth. Paul expresses his anger at their spiritual pride ("And you are arrogant!" 5:2) and suggests that they should instead have been mourning and working to remove the incestuous man from their community.

As was the case with all his letters except Romans (since Paul had not founded the church there), 1 Corinthians was Paul's way of keeping up his pastoral contact with a Christian community that he had founded. In 5:3, Paul claims that even though "absent in body, I am present in spirit." And Paul had definite ideas about what the Corinthian Christians should be doing in this case. As one present in spirit, he had already pronounced a judgment of condemnation upon the man as guilty of incest, which was a crime in most cultures and certainly in the Jewish and Greco-Roman cultures in which he wrote.

As a communal response to the behavior of the incestuous man, Paul in 5:4–5 proposes a ritual of excommunication something like those practiced under Ezra in the postexilic Jewish community (see Ezra 7–10), in the Qumran community (see *Rule of the Community* 6:8–10), and elsewhere in the New Testament (see Matthew 18:15–18; 1 Timothy 1:18–20). Paul describes the ritual as handing "this man over to Satan for the destruction of the flesh" (5:5).

In this notorious case of sexual misconduct, there was no need, at least from Paul's perspective, for much communal discernment about judging the man's behavior. Rather than arguing about the merits of his behavior (which was unnecessary in Paul's view), Paul preferred to offer a strategy for dealing with the straying community member lest eventually he might infect the whole community (see the "yeast-leaven" images in 5:6–8). The Christian community had been made holy through "the power of our Lord Jesus" (5:4), and the holiness of the community must be protected by driving out "sexually immoral persons" (5:9–13).

The case of the incestuous man presents Paul at his most judgmental and authoritative. Nevertheless, he does require assent and action on the part of the Corinthian Christian community if his plan is to be followed out. What Paul intended by the ritual of excommunication is not entirely clear. On the surface it seems to be a matter of definitive exclusion from the Christian community and of handing over the incestuous man to the sphere of Satan at the last judgment. Such a procedure would imply giving up entirely on the man and his fate for the sake of the holiness of the community. However, in view of the final clause in 5:5 ("so that his spirit may be saved in the day of the Lord"), it is at least possible to regard the public condemnation of the incestuous man and the ceremony of excommunication as a kind of "shock therapy" designed to have the man face up to the enormity of his immoral behavior and eventually change his ways.

PAUL'S LETTERS AS SOCIAL
AND PASTORAL COMMUNICATIONS

The letters that Paul sent to the communities that he had founded (and to the Romans) served to some extent as substitutes for his physical presence (see 1 Corinthians 5:3). Paul is best described as a pastoral theologian. He addressed real problems of real people in the context of Christian community life. To those problems he brought the insights of Christian theology as he received them and handed them on to others (see 1 Corinthians 11:23; 15:3). In these letters he seldom gives orders or commands, preferring instead the language of exhortation ("I appeal to you," Romans 12:1). These letters, however, were read at the assemblies of the whole community, and so they naturally put great moral pressure upon those who were addressed and especially those whose behavior was judged to be inappropriate or offensive.

Among the seven Pauline letters whose origin with Paul himself is not disputed, the letter to Philemon comes closest to being a private letter. In that brief letter, Paul asks that Philemon (whom he had brought to Christian faith) to take back his runaway slave Onesimus (who had subsequently become a Christian under Paul's guidance) "no longer as a slave but more than a slave, a beloved brother" (v. 16).

What makes this more than a private letter is first of all the fact that it was addressed not only to Philemon but also to "Apphia our sister, to Archippus our fellow soldier, and to the church in your house" (v. 2). While Paul goes on to address Philemon directly in the second person singular ("you"), he praises for all to hear the faith and love that Philemon had always displayed (vv. 4–7), claims to be appealing to him "on the basis of love" rather than commanding him (vv. 8–9), reminds Philemon of the (spiritual) debt that he owes to Paul (vv. 17–21), and asks Philemon to prepare a guest room for Paul during his forthcoming visit to him (v. 23).

All these elements put great moral pressure upon Philemon. If this letter was read in the house church assembly (and how else would it have eventually become part of the canonical collection of Pauline letters?), then practically everything in the letter served to put pressure on Philemon to do "the right thing"—in this case to take Onesimus back as "more than a slave, a beloved brother" (v. 16).

The letter to Philemon, which on the surface appears to be a private letter, illustrates the extent to which every Pauline epistle was an exercise in social communication. Paul used these letters as vehicles for the ongoing pastoral care of the communities that he founded. They were intended to help members of these communities face and solve the pastoral problems that came their way. In that sense they entered into the process of communal decision making undertaken not only by the communities originally addressed by them but also by churches throughout the centuries by their inclusion in the canon of Holy Scripture. From their composition to the present, Paul's letters are social communications.

The most obvious example of the social-pastoral dimension among Paul's letters is 1 Corinthians. There he provides pastoral theological advice regarding factions within the community (1:18–25; 3:5–17), incest (5:1–5), lawsuits (6:1–11), marriage and divorce (7), food sacrificed to idols (8–10), the place of women in the community assembly (11:2–16), disruption of the Lord's Supper (11:17–34), the gifts of the Holy Spirit (12–14), the resurrection (15), and the collection (16:1–4). Paul's treatments of these topics were meant to be made public to members of the Corinthian Christian community and to enter into their process of discerning the movements of the Spirit in their community life.

In 1 Thessalonians, his earliest letter (51 CE), Paul felt compelled to defend his own ministry and to allay fears about those Christians who had died before the second coming of Christ. In three other letters (Galatians, 2 Corinthians, and Philippians), Paul defended his apostleship against the criticisms of other Jewish Christian missionaries who had been undercutting Paul's mission to the Gentiles. They were insisting that in order to be real Christians, Gentiles had to become Jews, undergo circumcision, and observe the Sabbath and the Jewish food and purity laws. In his letter to the Romans (a community that he had not founded), Paul set out to explain why Gentiles and Jews were equals in Christ and how Gentiles could be part of the people of God.

Besides these grand questions of identity and theology, Paul in his letters also tried to adjudicate local disputes internal to churches such as those between Euodia and Syntyche at Philippi and between the "weak" and the "strong" at Corinth and at Rome. As social communications, Paul's letters were intended to serve as pastoral helps for communities finding their individual and communal ways in a complex world.

A COMMUNAL CRISIS OF CONSCIENCE

Whereas in 1 Corinthians 5:1–5 Paul is at his most judgmental and authoritarian, in chapters 8–10 he shows himself to be remarkably sensitive to the complexities of Christian community life. The difference between the two texts is rooted, of course, in the moral seriousness that Paul attributed to the issues under discussion: incest versus eating food offered to idols.

The occasion for Paul's advice in 1 Corinthians 8–10 was the practice of having meat sold in the marketplace first pass through sacrificial rituals observed in local pagan temples. The details of the practice are complex, and there is no need to go into them here. The communal crisis of conscience was due to the fact that it was possible and even likely that the meat purchased by Christians at the market or served at a meal in someone else's house had been previously involved in sacrifices that had been offered to the pagan gods.

According to Paul, there were two groups of Christians at Corinth: those who saw no problem in Christians eating such food, and those who had problems of conscience about doing so. How these people should regard one another and treat one another is the topic of Paul's instruction in 1 Corinthians 8:1–11:1. Here we focus on 8:1–13 and 10:23–30.

In 8:1–13, Paul constructs a kind of dialogue between himself and the slogans that were apparently being used by those who found no problem in eating meat sacrificed to idols. While Paul sides with them on the theological level, he directs them quite forcefully not to assume that their views are shared by all Christians and are to be imposed on them.

The "dialogue" begins with Paul quoting their claim to have superior knowledge ("All of us possess knowledge"), and suggesting that true knowledge builds up the community and comes from God. Next, Paul provides the theological basis for their (and his) position with two slogans cited in 8:4: "'No idol in the world really exists' . . . 'There is no God but one.'" Since for Christians there is "one God, the Father . . . and one Lord, Jesus Christ" (8:6), the pagan gods honored by the sacrifices do not really exist. So from the perspective of Christian theology, there was no logical problem involved in eating food that had passed through pagan rituals. The logic was that because the pagan gods were figments of human imagination, there was nothing intrinsically wrong with the food that may have been used in rites honoring the pagan gods.

Most of the Christians at Corinth seem to have been converts from paganism. Not all of them saw things as clearly as did Paul and those who claimed to have superior knowledge about these matters. The temples of the various gods were part of their everyday experience, and members of their own families were very likely participating in the pagan cults and even inviting them to meals at the pagan temples. The Christians had come to faith in the one God and in Jesus as their Lord, and they had undergone baptism. But worship of the pagan gods had been part of their previous lives. While convinced intellectually by Christian doctrine, they were still linked to the pagan cults by experience and emotion. Paul diagnosed their situation in this way: "Since some have become so accustomed to idols until now, they still think of the food they eat as food offered to an idol; and their conscience, being weak, is defiled" (8:7).

Paul resumes the dialogue in 8:8 by quoting another slogan being used by the "strong" at Corinth: "'Food will not bring us closer to God.'" While Paul agreed intellectually with their position, his advice to them goes in another direction. Paul fears that their free attitude on these matters may scandalize those with weaker consciences (that is, put an obstacle in the way of another's faith, and even result in loss of faith). He fears that if a "weak" person sees a "strong" person eating in a pagan temple (at a banquet after a sacrifice), the "weak" person with still some vestigial belief in the pagan gods will conclude that it is acceptable for Christians to participate in pagan rituals and thus effectively deny belief in the one God and in the one Lord, Jesus Christ.

Here Paul is concerned less with affirming the theological correctness of the "strong" (with whom he agrees intellectually) and more with warning against the harmful potential of their "free" attitude regarding these matters for scandalizing those with weaker consciences. If their behavior might scandalize one person, then it would be better (as Paul says) to "never eat meat, so that I may not cause one of them to fall" (8:13).

Having reflected on the constraints that Paul placed on his freedom (9:1–27) and on warnings drawn from Israel's history (10:1–22), Paul quotes still another slogan being used by the strong to justify their position: "'All things are lawful'" (10:23). Being theologically correct, however, is not the essence of Christian life, since this form of life takes place in the context of a Christian community: "But not all things build up." What Paul proposes is a practical "don't ask" policy. So if one buys food in the market or if one dines at the house of another, the Christian may eat the food without inquiring about its possible connections with pagan cults. However, if one is told "this has been offered in sacrifice" (10:28), then one should abstain from eating "for the sake of conscience"—not for one's own conscience but for the conscience of the "weak" person who may have scruples on this matter.

The beginning (8:7–13) and the ending (10:23–30) of Paul's instruction about food sacrificed to idols make frequent reference to *syneidesis,* which is usually translated as "conscience." When we today use the word "conscience," we generally mean a sense of right and wrong—or more properly, the faculty, power, or principle that enables one to decide about the morality of an action. One can see how Paul has influenced the development of the term in that direction. But whether this precise meaning fits in all the occurrences in Paul's letters is less obvious.

Some translators of Paul's letters into English prefer to render *syneidesis* in its even more general and basic sense as "consciousness." The problem is more pressing for English speakers, who have two words ("conscience" and "consciousness") for the one Greek word *syneidesis*. French and Spanish, for example, use one word (*conscience* and *conciencia,* respectively) to cover both meanings and so better reflect the Greek term. In fact, the Greek word *syneidesis* can be described as conveying a meaning somewhere between "consciousness" and "conscience" in English.

Those whose *syneidesis* is "weak" (see 1 Corinthians 8:7, 10, 12) with regard to food sacrificed to idols are incorrect on the intellectual and theological levels in their evaluation of such food. They think that they must avoid what needs not be avoided, at least if one believes in only one God and one Lord, Jesus Christ. We might say that they have an "erroneous" conscience. Since Paul agrees with the "strong" that such food is in fact morally and religiously indifferent in itself, he bases his "don't ask" policy in the market or at a meal on the ground of what in his estimation is a correct and well-informed "consciousness/conscience" (10:25, 27). Nevertheless, he advises the "strong" at Corinth that they should be willing to respect their fellow Christians "for the sake of conscience . . . the other's conscience" (10:28–29) even when the "weak" are operating on objectively mistaken assumptions about food associated with pagan deities.

Paul's instruction in 1 Corinthians 8:1–11:1 was intended to help the Corinthian Christians discern a practical solution to a potentially divisive issue in their community. While on the theological level Paul sided with the "strong," he was also concerned to give equal attention to the moral hesitations felt by those with "weak" consciences. And so he urged the strong to hold on to their intellectual positions but to grow in sensitivity and pastoral accommodation to those who held other views. Being "correct" theologically does not close the process of communal discernment.

DISCERNING THE SPIRIT IN COMMUNITY

In 1 Corinthians 12–14, Paul presents a long instruction on the "spiritual" gifts (*pneumatika*), or gifts coming from the Holy Spirit. Paul's basic position is that every Christian is spiritually gifted: "To each is given the manifestation of the Spirit for the common good" (12:7). The problem at Corinth that he is addressing is the difficulty of discerning the relative value of the spiritual gifts. But the criteria that he proposes are also useful when applied to making moral decisions in the context of Christian community life.

In the context of the community assembly at Corinth, the most spectacular spiritual gift was *glossolalia*, or speaking in tongues. Despite the impression fostered by Acts 2:4 ("All of them . . . began to speak in other languages"), *glossolalia* at Corinth most likely referred to a speaker who made nonverbal sounds (grunts and groans, or perhaps more melodious noises) allegedly under the influence of the Holy Spirit. Apparently those who possessed this gift were putting themselves forward as the most spiritual persons in the Christian community. Paul's instruction provided the Corinthians with at least some criteria for discerning and judging the action of the Holy Spirit (and so the actions of Christians) in the community.

The first and most basic criterion is that the spiritual gift (and analogously, the moral decision) must be consistent with the Christian gospel, which Paul summarizes as "Jesus is Lord" (12:3). If the spiritual manifestation (or moral decision) confirms or is in accord with that gospel, then it can be regarded as coming from God through the Holy Spirit. And if it runs counter to the gospel ("Let Jesus be cursed!"), it is to be rejected. One mark of genuine inspiration by the Holy Spirit is conformity with the confession that Jesus is Lord.

A second criterion is building up the community as the body of Christ. The concept of the body as a metaphor for the community was not original with Paul. Indeed, it is a natural and even irresistible metaphor. Ask any coach or play director or chief executive. What is different in the case of the Christian community is that Christ makes it into his body. Those who are "in Christ" are related to one another through Christ, and in this way they make up the body of Christ.

The consequence of this understanding of the body of Christ is that in all their actions—whether in exercising their spiritual gifts or in making moral decisions, Christians are bound to ask, "Is this beneficial to the other members?" and "Does this build up the body of Christ?" Paul's problem with speaking in tongues was that without interpretation it remained unintelligible to anyone else and could not build up the body of Christ. And so when Paul lists the various spiritual gifts, he always places speaking in tongues at the end of his lists (see 12:10, 30).

A third criterion is love. Paul's great paean to love in 1 Corinthians 13 appears in the context of discerning the relative importance of the various spiritual gifts. His point is that love must be fundamental in the exercise of any spiritual gift (or in any moral decision): "Love is patient; love is kind; love is not envious or boastful or arrogant" (13:4).

A fourth criterion is the impression made upon outsiders (the issue of scandal). In his efforts to deflate the spiritual pretensions of those who spoke in tongues, Paul imagines a situation when the entire Christian community came together and everyone was speaking in tongues: "If, therefore, the whole church comes together and all speak in tongues, and outsiders or unbelievers enter, will they not say that you are out of your mind?" (14:23). To outsiders, such a gathering of tongue speakers might look like a madhouse.

The context of Paul's advice in 1 Corinthians 12–14 is the display of the spiritual gifts and how to discern their relative importance. However, the criteria that Paul develops here can easily be transferred to the context of communal moral decision making. The four criteria treated in this section—conformity with the gospel, potential for building up the body of Christ, love as the primary motive, and public perception—belong on any list of criteria for communal decision making in a Christian context. They surely are not the whole story, nor can they be used as a template or computer program to guarantee a correct conclusion. But failure to take account of any one of them can result in immoral behavior and so bring great shame upon the church.

THE STRONG AND THE WEAK AT ROME

Paul's letter to the Romans is often regarded as a theological treatise. One reason is that its presentation of Jesus as the good news or "gospel" of God seldom descends into the particulars of the pastoral problems facing the Christian community at Rome in the late fifties of the first century CE. However, in 14:1–15:13, Paul does take up what seems to have been a practical communal conflict at Rome between Christians who were "weak in faith" and those who considered themselves to be "strong." Two specific issues seem to have sparked off the conflict: eating (or not eating) meat, and observing (or not observing) certain days as holy. According to Paul, "some believe in eating anything, while the weak eat only vegetables" (14:2) and "some judge one day to be better than another, while others judge all days to be alike" (14:5).

Much about this controversy is unclear. It is tempting (but not at all certain) to interpret it along the lines of Jewish Christians ("the weak") versus Gentile Christians ("the strong"). However, there is not much evidence for Jewish vegetarianism (but see Daniel 1:12), and many religions besides Judaism observed holy days. Moreover, for Paul at least, these two issues were matters of indifference, and there was no question of immoral behavior as in 1 Corinthians 5. What was of greatest concern to Paul was the disruption that this conflict was causing within the Christian community at Rome and the crisis of conscience that it presented.

Rather than trying to figure out the identity of the parties in this dispute and the precise nature of their positions, the focus here will be on the reasons that Paul gives for why the strong and the weak at Rome should accept one another and try to live harmoniously in community. Most of Paul's advice is directed toward "the strong"—the group with which he agreed on the intellectual level. His advice to the strong, however, takes up the cause of the weak: "Welcome those who are weak in faith, but not for the purpose of quarreling over opinions" (14:1). His use of the term *opinions* at the outset indicates Paul's judgment that these were matters of moral indifference.

For our purposes in treating communal moral discernment, Paul's instruction in Romans 14:1–15:13 is important for the light that it sheds on how members of the Christian community should regard one another even when they disagree. Unlike 1 Corinthians 5, here there is no question in Paul's mind about sinful actions. But as in 1 Corinthians 8–10, there is a question about sensitivity to the consciences of others. Paul's basic position is stated in Romans 14:4: "I know and am persuaded in the Lord Jesus that nothing is unclean in itself; but it is unclean for anyone who thinks it unclean."

The major issue for Paul in Romans 14:1–15:13 is sensitivity to the conscience of others, even in matters that he regarded as morally indifferent. In addressing this issue, Paul points to God as the ultimate judge of all persons, to the pivotal significance of conscience in moral decisions and action, and to the example of Christ, who put the needs and the unity of others before his own pleasure.

Most of Romans 14:1–15:13 is devoted to explaining why the strong at Rome should be sensitive to the conscience of the weak. One reason is that judgment belongs to God (see 14:1–12). Therefore the strong have no right to pass judgment on the weak. All Christians have been accepted by God, belong to God, and are servants of God. Just as all (Jews and Gentiles alike) stood equally in need of the gospel, so all who have embraced the gospel (strong and weak alike) will stand as equals before the judgment seat of God (see 14:4, 8, 12). Judgment is a divine prerogative, not a human task.

A second reason is respect for the conscience of others (14:13–23). Since Christ died for the weak as well as for the strong (14:15), all Christians have the duty to "pursue what makes for peace and for mutual upbuilding" (14:19). That can mean respecting the tender conscience of another. The reason is that to force weak Christians into acting against what their conscience tells them is to lead them into sin. As Paul states: "Everything is indeed clean, but it is wrong for you to make others fall by what you eat" (14:20). And in explaining this position, Paul adds that "those who have doubts are condemned if they eat, because they do not act from faith; for whatever does not proceed from faith is sin" (14:23).

The third reason is the example of Christ (15:1–13). Paul points out that Christ "did not please himself" but instead took upon himself the insults of others so that we might stand together and glorify God "with one voice" (15:6). Therefore, in respecting the conscience of others, Christians should seek to please not themselves but their neighbors, "for the good purpose of building up the neighbor" (15:2). Moreover, Christ is the principle of unity, not of division. As Paul suggests in 15:7–13, if Christ could bring together Jews and Gentiles into the one people of God, how much more can Christ bring together Christians who take differing views about minor matters such as diet and holy days!

Paul's treatment of the conflict between the strong and the weak at Rome fits well in the context of his entire letter to the Romans and need not be regarded as a digression, afterthought, or appendix. In fact, some interpreters view it as the pastoral goal to which the whole letter was pointing from the beginning.

Having established that all people—Gentiles and Jews alike—needed the revelation of the gospel of Jesus Christ (1:18–3:20), Paul shows that faith after the example of Abraham is the way for all to share in the benefits of the gospel (3:21–4:25). Then having explained how Christ has set us free from the power of Sin, Death, and the Law (5:1–7:25) and for life in the Holy Spirit (8:1–39), Paul reflects on Jews and Gentiles constituting the people of God (9:1–11:36) and offers remarks on the ethical dimensions of new life in Christ (12:1–13:14). Paul's advice to the strong and the weak at Rome reflects his great theological insights about God as the ultimate judge of all humans, the universal scope of salvation in Christ, the nature of Christian freedom, and the unity that Christ has made possible.

SELECT BIBLIOGRAPHY

Barrett, C. K. *Paul: An Introduction to His Thought.* Louisville, KY: Westminster/ John Knox, 1994.

Collins, Adela Yarbro. "The Function of 'Excommunication' in Paul." *Harvard Theological Review* 73 (1980): 251–63.

Collins, Raymond F. *First Corinthians.* Collegeville, MN: Liturgical Press, 1999.

Doty, William G. *Letters in Primitive Christianity.* Philadelphia: Fortress, 1973.

Eckstein, H.-J. *Der Begriff Syneidesis bei Paulus.* Tübingen, Germany: Mohr Siebeck, 1983.

Forkman, Göran. *The Limits of Religious Community: Expulsion from the Religious Community within the Qumran Sect, within Rabbinic Judaism, and within Primitive Christianity.* Lund, Sweden: Gleerup, 1972.

Gooch, Paul W. "'Conscience' in the New Testament." *New Testament Studies* 33 (1987): 244–54.

Harrington, Daniel J. *Paul's Prison Letters.* Hyde Park, NY: New City Press, 1997.

Horrell, David G. *Solidarity and Difference: A Contemporary Reading of Paul's Ethics.* London: T&T Clark, 2005.

Martin, Dale B. *The Corinthian Body.* New Haven, CT: Yale University Press, 1995.

Meggitt, Justin J. "Meat Consumption and Social Conflict in Corinth." *Journal of Theological Studies* 45 (1994): 137–41.

Petersen, Norman R. *Rediscovering Paul: Philemon and the Sociology of Paul's Narrative World.* Philadelphia: Fortress, 1985.

Pierce, Claude A. *Conscience in the New Testament.* London: SCM, 1955.

Stowers, Stanley K. *Letter Writing in Greco-Roman Antiquity.* Philadelphia: Westminster, 1986.

Willis, Wendell L. *Idol Meat in Corinth: The Pauline Argument in 1 Corinthians 8 and 10.* Chico, CA: Scholars Press, 1985.

Chapter Sixteen

Ethics in a Communal Setting: Theological Perspectives

HUMILITY AS A BIBLICAL VIRTUE

For ethics in a communal setting, I believe humility is the first virtue. Wayne Meeks, however, alerts us to a concern about the distinctiveness of Christian humility. Early Christians acknowledged that their founder, leader, and savior was crucified! One could say that humility comes naturally to the Christian, but to others Christian humility may look unnatural.

We might think of a more general definition of humility as the virtue of discerning one's place in the world or the community. In this sense, it is a very postmodern virtue, inasmuch as we know since the contributions of Karl Mannheim that one's perspective is always a very particular vantage point for understanding. If perspective is everything, then locating oneself is key.

Indeed, in contemporary theology we find one meaning of the option for the poor: We locate ourselves with the poor because that is where God dwells. Knowing one's place in the community, then, is also finding one's place. If I want to be close to God, I should be close to the poor.

Mary's Magnificat (Luke 1:46–55) is precisely a hymn of humility. Mary locates her place in the world and before God. God has raised up the lowly and brought down the mighty. From this topsy-turvy order, Luke takes one of the earliest Christian hymns and by letting Mary sing it, articulates how the community knows its place before God. Luke gives us this song precisely as he begins his Gospel.

And Mary said,

My soul magnifies the Lord,
and my spirit rejoices in God my Savior,
for he has looked with favor on the lowliness of his servant.

141

Surely, from now on all generations will call me blessed;
for the Mighty One has done great things for me,
and holy is his name.
His mercy is for those who fear him
from generation to generation.
He has shown strength with his arm;
he has scattered the proud in the thoughts of their hearts.
He has brought down the powerful from their thrones,
and lifted up the lowly;
he has filled the hungry with good things,
and sent the rich away empty.
He has helped his servant Israel,
in remembrance of his mercy,
according to the promise he made to our ancestors,
to Abraham and to his descendants forever.

Mary locates for us our place in the world. But she brings us, in her humility, into a connection with mercy. Mercy, the willingness to enter into the chaos of another, is only expressed by those who are humble. By humility, we are merciful. Knowing what Christ in his humility accomplished for us, we enter in turn into that humility and can become merciful. The humble know their place in the community and are mindful of where the others in the community are.

The great challenge for Roman imperial authority was that mercy was considered a virtue practiced by the uneducated, for those who did not know better. But for Christians who emulate the humble one who in his mercy died for us, mercy is for the wise. Only by being humble can we see this new order. By entering into the world of Christ, we can become humble and merciful. This movement ought not to be missed. We saw earlier that friendship with God is not about God coming into our world, but rather, it is about our entering into God's world. Similarly, in humility we enter into the topsy-turvy world of the slain savior.

Of course, this is the world of humility that we find in the great hymn of Philippians 2:5–11. This other hymn is also about reversals, about lowliness and exaltation. But more than pertaining to Mary and the church, it pertains to Jesus Christ. This is what Paul writes:

Your attitude should be the same as that of Christ Jesus:
Who, being in very nature God,
did not consider equality with God something to be grasped,
but made himself nothing,
taking the very nature of a servant,
being made in human likeness.

And being found in appearance as a man,
he humbled himself
and became obedient to death—
even death on a cross!
Therefore God exalted him to the highest place
and gave him the name that is above every name,
that at the name of Jesus every knee should bow,
in heaven and on earth and under the earth,
and every tongue confess that Jesus Christ is Lord,
to the glory of God the Father.

The humility of Jesus is effective: it is the way that he mercifully redeems us and becomes for us the exalted Savior. A new order is born, an order filled with hope.

As mercy depends on humility, humility depends on hope. Hope is the mean between despair and presumption. When we find our place between those extremes, we are humbled, for we depend on God and we know our need for God and that inevitably we shall stand before God. We are a people who hope and trust that we are saved—sinners, but saved.

Neither the presumptuous nor the despairing know their real place in being saved. The former do not realize how they got where they are and so they are unable to locate their true histories, thinking themselves to be the mythic self-made beings. The latter do not realize that they could be among the saved.

Like Mary knowing her place in God's order, we stand in hope, inclined to mercy. This is where we should be, where God is.

AUGUSTINE AND THOMAS AQUINAS ON HUMILITY

In order to appreciate how the tradition has looked at humility, we will look at some passages by Augustine and then turn to Thomas Aquinas. We conclude looking at two works by contemporary theologians concerning the grace of self-doubt and the problem of scandal.

The foundational stance of humility as the virtue for all Christians is found in Augustine. He writes in Letter 118:

I wish you would submit with sincere piety to Him and not seek any other way to abiding truth but the one shown us by Him who, being God, knows our weakness. This way consists, first, of humility, second, of humility, and third, of humility. . . . It is not that there are no other precepts to be mentioned. But, unless humility precedes, accompanies, and follows whatever we do, unless it is a goal on which we keep our eye, a companion at our side, and a yoke upon our neck, we will find that we have done little good to rejoice in; pride will have bereft us of everything.

Though Augustine writes the following in his commentary on John, clearly we see the humble Christ of Philippians in these lines:

Wherefore did it behoove Christ to be born? Wherefore did it behoove Christ to be crucified? For if He had come to point out the way of humility, and to make Himself the way of humility; in all things had humility to be fulfilled by Him. He deigned from this to give authority to His own baptism, that His servants might know with what alacrity they ought to run to the baptism of the Lord, when He Himself did not refuse to receive the baptism of a servant. This favor was bestowed upon John that it should be called his baptism. (Tractate 5 on John 1:33)

Elsewhere, Augustine reminds us that these lessons were not learned from those who did not know better. On the contrary, they were the lessons of Christ the teacher.

We have learned, brethren, humility from the Highest; let us, as humble, do to one another what He, the Highest, did in His humility. Great is the commendation we have here of humility: and brethren do this to one another in turn, even in the visible act itself, when they treat one another with hospitality; for the practice of such humility is generally prevalent, and finds expression in the very deed that makes it discernible. (Tractate 58.4 on John 13:10–15)

In short, for Augustine, humility is the way of Christ and therefore the way of the disciple. It is not a way first and foremost to seek salvation; it is, rather, the way that the saved learn to walk precisely because they have been saved. Augustine writes:

Christ Humbled is the Way; Christ the Truth and the Life, Christ Highly Exalted and God. If thou walk in the Humbled, thou shalt attain to the Exalted. If infirm as thou art, thou despise not the Humbled, thou shalt abide exceeding strong in the Exalted. For what cause was there of Christ's Humiliation, save thine infirmity? (Sermon 92 on John 14.6)

Humility is the foundation of all the other virtues, inasmuch as it is the first virtue for those with faith, hope, and charity. By humility we stay in hope and mercy.

It leads Thomas to ask in the *Summa Theologiae* II.II.161.5 whether humility is the greatest virtue. His concerns are from Augustine. In the second objection, Thomas notes that Augustine writes in Sermon 69 from the *Word of God:* "Are you thinking of raising the great fabric of spirituality? Attend first of all to the foundation of humility." Thomas comments on Augustine, "Now this would seem to imply that humility is the foundation of all virtue. Therefore apparently it is greater than the other virtues." Then in the fourth objection, Thomas quotes Augustine's comment in *On True Religion* (16): "Christ's whole life on earth was a lesson in moral conduct through the human nature which He assumed." Thomas adds, "Now He especially proposed His humility for our example, saying (Mt. 11:29): 'Learn of Me, because I am meek and humble of heart.' Moreover, Gregory says that the 'lesson proposed to us in the mystery of our redemption is the humility of God.'"

But Thomas wants to define humility in reference to charity and, as we shall see, many other virtues. Invoking Paul in Colossians 3:14, "Above all . . . things have charity," Thomas writes, that after the theological virtues of faith, hope, and charity and after the acquired virtues of wisdom, prudence, and justice, "humility stands before all others."

In response to Augustine, Thomas basically views humility as a virtue to check pride: In a manner of speaking, this is a virtue that removes obstacles. In his reply to the second objection, Thomas says that among virtues removing obstacles, humility expels pride, but in learning to walk on the way of the Lord, the foundation for the pursuit of God is faith. In his reply to the fourth objection, Thomas similarly sees humility as little more than a weapon against pride. He writes:

> The reason why Christ chiefly proposed humility to us, was because it especially removes the obstacle to man's spiritual welfare consisting in man's aiming at heavenly and spiritual things, in which he is hindered by striving to become great in earthly things. Hence our Lord, in order to remove an obstacle to our spiritual welfare, showed by giving an example of humility, that outward exaltation is to be despised. Thus humility is, as it were, a disposition to man's untrammeled access to spiritual and divine goods. Accordingly as perfection is greater than disposition, so charity, and other virtues whereby man approaches God directly, are greater than humility.

Unlike Thomas, for Paul and Augustine, humility is more than a strategy against pride. It is a virtue of self-understanding, for knowing one's place in the community. It is a virtue that guides us to be with the poor. Humility teaches us that without seeing all as gift, seeing all as in a new topsy-turvy universe made so by God, we cannot maintain our understanding of the faith, we cannot remain in hope, and we cannot practice mercy. Of course, humility in its nature is not interested in claiming a primacy. But humility as a pious, vigilant awareness of God is a recognition that all depends on God's will; that we are only capable of doing anything by that dependence and that that dependence might call me to lower myself as Christ did.

I am actually not sure what Thomas is doing other than ordering the universe by faith and charity (and then by wisdom, prudence, and justice)—but in the postmodern world where location is everything, it seems that humility ought to claim some of the ground that Thomas took. I think Thomas is seeking humility as a movement to a lower place: Indeed, the tradition saw humility as a bending down. But I think humility is really not about an ability to move but again, about knowing where you are.

Humility, then, has special significance in the community. It has a communal feature, for if I know my place, I know it in relationship to others. I think we can find here a natural affinity to Paul's sensitivity about being saved, about knowing his place as a person indebted to Christ, convicted by his conscience, to serve Christ and the church.

CONTEMPORARY EMPHASIS ON HUMILITY

In a tribute to Charles Curran, Margaret Farley proposes the grace of self-doubt, which she calls an "epistemic humility, the basic condition for communal as well as individual moral discernment" (69). Farley is concerned with the experience of authority and its afflictions, which often make a person unquestionably self-reliant and self-assured. The grace of self-doubt is not some hyperactive stance that questions the very fundamental convictions we hold. Rather, she writes that it is a

> grace for recognizing the contingencies of moral knowledge when we stretch toward the particular and the concrete. It allows us to listen to the experience of others, take seriously reasons that are alternative to our own, rethink our own last word. It assumes a shared search for moral insight, and it promotes (though it does not guarantee) a shared conviction in the end. (69).

Allowing us to throw off the "albatross of certitude" (60), this form of humility allows us to enter into discourse rather than to tower above it. By relinquishing the power of certitude, it discovers a new authority, an authority in which the admission of ignorance might actually be a way to truth.

If truth is found, then, not by me but by us, then there must be certain virtues that aid us in our pursuit of truth.

While knowing that scandal in the church will be treated in the next chapter in the context of communal ethics and the Eucharist, I cannot leave this section on humility without considering scandal, a word that became associated with the Catholic church over the clerical sexual abuse crisis. Knowing more about scandal, particularly in the writing of Paul, might help us see just how much the virtue of humility serves ethics in a communal setting.

The *Catechism of the Catholic Church* defines scandal as "an attitude or behavior which leads another to do evil. The person who gives scandal becomes his neighbor's tempter. He damages virtue and integrity; he may even draw his brother into spiritual death" (2284). This is very different from the way the contemporary world defines scandal. For instance, Wikipedia defines scandal as "a widely publicized allegation or set of allegations that damages the reputation of an institution, individual or creed." The *Oxford English Dictionary* refers to it as "To disgrace, bring into ill repute or obloquy."

For the church, scandal is a Pauline communal vice. It is not so much about objective harm brought to an institution by another's conduct, nor is it a form of conduct that violates particular norms. It is about the need to be mindful of those community members who might misunderstand one's actions and think that one is claiming something other than one is. It is about anticipating the possibility of moral confusion that might require an understanding of the community to which we belong and an appreciation of its membership. When Paul speaks of scandal, particularly in eating idol meat (1 Corinthians 8:1–11:1), he is concerned about how the weaker members might be led into confusion as to why other members find no problem with the eating of the meat. Paul writes, "But make sure that this liberty of yours in no way becomes a stumbling block to the weak." The possibility of scandal does not arise because of an actual wrong action, but rather by a misunderstanding, a misapprehension, a confusion.

The tragedy of the church's clerical abuse scandal was not the harm that it brought to the institutional church, but that children, mothers, fathers, family members, and other parishioners could not believe that the institution's reputation was more important than they were. Often, bishops testified that they were concerned about the harm that would have been done to the church if they had acknowledged the crisis. But the Pauline concept of scandal was primarily about the harm done to other church members, particularly those who gave up their confidence in God because they were so confused and shocked by the conduct of others.

Thus the Pauline concept of scandal was not the primary object of church leaders' concern in our own time. They were more worried about the scandal arising from newspaper articles; they fretted over what people would say. And so they missed the true scandal: the impact that the cover-up had on the lives of those directly affected by the abuse and on their parents, who tried to report to the leaders all that had happened. The church scandal, rightly named, caused the faith, love, and hope of the weakest (and those who loved them) to be damaged and, in some instances, destroyed.

SELECT BIBLIOGRAPHY

Farley, Margaret. "Ethics, Ecclesiology, and the Grace of Self-Doubt." In *A Call to Fidelity: On the Moral Theology of Charles E. Curran,* edited by James J. Walter, Timothy E. O'Connell, and Thomas A. Shannon, 55–76. Washington, DC: Georgetown University Press, 2002.
Meeks, Wayne A. *The Origins of Christian Morality: The First Two Centuries.* New Haven, CT: Yale University Press, 1993.

Chapter Seventeen

Communal Ethics and the Eucharist

THE LORD'S SUPPER:
1 CORINTHIANS 11:23–26

Paul's letters were for the most part social communications intended to help Christians in the communities that he had founded deal with the pastoral problems that had arisen in his absence. They were written not so much as theological treatises as practical extensions of his ministry as an apostle who founded and developed Gentile Christian communities. This fact can leave readers today frustrated, since there is so much more that we would like to know about (for example) baptism in the early church than Paul tells us. Where was it administered? How? By whom? What formula was used? However, in Romans 6 Paul is concerned only with recalling to his readers the fundamental theological significance of baptism as participation in Jesus' death and resurrection.

Likewise, with the Lord's Supper or Eucharist, there is so much that we would like to know. But Paul alludes to the Eucharist only in 1 Corinthians 10:16–17 and 11:23–26. Nevertheless, for our purposes in dealing with Paul and virtue ethics, these texts are very enlightening precisely because their contexts (1 Corinthians 10:14–22 and 11:17–34) concern "ethical" or social issues pertaining to life in the Christian community.

The most famous Pauline reference to the Eucharist appears in 1 Corinthians 11:23–26. This passage is especially important because it contains the earliest New Testament description of the Lord's Supper:

23. For I received from the Lord what I also handed on to you, that the Lord Jesus on the night when he was betrayed took a loaf of bread, 24. and when he had given thanks, he broke it and said: "This is my body that is for you. Do this

149

in remembrance of me." 25. In the same way he took the cup also after supper, saying, "This cup is the new covenant in my blood. Do this, as often as you drink it, in remembrance of me." 26. For as often as you eat this bread and drink this cup, you proclaim the Lord's death until he comes.

The descriptions of the Last Supper in Mark 14:22–25, Matthew 26:26–29, and Luke 22:15–20, however ancient they may be, all appear in documents put in final form after AD 70. But Paul wrote 1 Corinthians in the mid-fifties of the first century, some twenty-five years after Jesus' death.

In introducing the liturgical formula of the Eucharist, Paul insists on its traditional character. What he handed on to the Corinthians about the Last Supper had been handed on to him as "from the Lord"—that is, as a tradition going back to Jesus.

Paul's description brings out many theological dimensions in the Lord's Supper. It is a meal after the pattern of Jesus' Last Supper. The element of vicarious sacrifice is suggested by the reference to "my body that is for you" (11:24). The cup is equated with "the new covenant in my blood," thus evoking Moses' action in sealing the Sinai covenant (see Exodus 24:8). Repeated sharing of the eucharistic bread and cup is interpreted as a memorial of Jesus. And there is an eschatological dimension that looks forward to the second coming of Jesus and the fullness of life in God's kingdom: "For as often as you eat this bread and drink this cup, you proclaim the Lord's death until he comes" (11:26). This very early eucharistic formula contains many basic symbols of Christian faith and of the Bible taken as a whole.

CHRISTIANS AND PAGAN WORSHIP: 1 CORINTHIANS 10

The whole dispute about Christians eating meat associated with sacrifices offered to pagan gods in 1 Corinthians 8:1–11:1 was treated in chapter 15. There we saw that on the theoretical or theological level Paul sided with the "strong," who regarded the issue as a matter of indifference since the pagan gods do not exist. However, on the community or pastoral level, Paul emphasized the need for sensitivity to the "weak," who might be scandalized to find themselves and other Christians eating such food.

In 1 Corinthians 10:14–22, near the end of his argument, Paul seems to be warning all Christians (strong and weak alike) against active, conscious, and voluntary participation in pagan worship. Here the situation seems to be an invitation to attend a meal at a pagan temple where there would be no doubt whether the food being served had passed through pagan sacrificial rituals. He tells them: "Flee from the worship of idols" (10:14). He finds Christian worship and pagan worship to be thoroughly incompatible. This is the context for his first reference to the Lord's Supper or Eucharist in 1 Corinthians 10:16–17: "The cup of blessing that we bless, is it not a sharing in the blood of Christ? The bread that we break, is it not a sharing in the body of Christ? Because there is one bread, we who are many are one body, for we all partake of the one bread."

Paul's words here recall the belief that sharing in the cup and bread is really sharing in the blood and body of Christ, and so is both sign of and a means toward full participation in the body of Christ. In this context, the Lord's Supper or Eucharist serves as a reminder of the basis of all Christian community in Christ and an encouragement toward greater unity between Christians (such as the "strong" and the "weak," who might take different positions on certain matters). Paul goes on to contrast the eucharistic cup that Christians share ("the cup of the Lord") and "the cup of demons," as well as the "table of the Lord" and the "table of demons" (10:21).

For Paul, then, the Eucharist has social implications for Christian life and community. And so as a kind of "trump card" at the end of a long argument, Paul in 1 Corinthians 10:14–22 appeals to the Eucharist as a help toward promoting mutual understanding within the Christian community and toward sharpening Christian identity vis-à-vis other forms of religious expression.

A SCANDAL PERTAINING TO THE EUCHARIST:
1 CORINTHIANS 11

What greatly disturbed Paul, according to 1 Corinthians 11:17–34, was that among the Corinthian Christians the Eucharist was becoming a source of division rather than a sign of their unity. At Corinth, it seems that the ritual celebration of the Lord's Supper was combined with a meal. This meal had become an occasion for social and economic divisions within the Corinthian community.

In 1 Corinthians 1–4, Paul had already taken up the problem of factions at Corinth. Whether he was addressing exactly the same problem of factionalism in chapter 11 is not certain. The factions here have been interpreted along several different lines: religious (allegiance to different apostles, as in 1:10–17), social (belonging to different social classes, as in 1:26–31), and economic (rich and poor members). Some combination of these factors is possible and even likely.

Paul's pastoral problem was that the meal had become the occasion for certain groups to separate themselves from the larger community. He accuses some members of gluttony and drunkenness, and he suggests that still others were going hungry. And so he quotes the Lord's Supper tradition as a reminder of and an encouragement to greater unity among all Christians at Corinth.

Following the account of Jesus' Last Supper in 11:23–26, there are warnings about celebrating the Lord's Supper "in an unworthy manner" (11:27). The issue is probably not ritual correctness or being "in the state of sin." Rather, Paul's concern was more likely with recognizing the sacred character of the Lord's Supper (and not confusing it with just another meal) and with fostering the unity that it is supposed to signify and promote. Paul goes on to suggest that certain illnesses and even some deaths within the community might have been due to "unworthy" participation in the Lord's Supper (see 11:30).

He closes by advising that if some Corinthian Christians (wealthy or upper-class ones?) want to dine with their friends, they might do so better in their own homes. But if they want to participate in the Lord's Supper, they should do so with the whole Christian community and in a worthy manner: "If you are hungry, eat at home, so that when you come together, it will not be for your condemnation" (11:34).

As in 1 Corinthians 10:14–22, so in 11:17–34 Paul invokes the Lord's Supper tradition in a social context as a help toward solving problems within the Christian community. In both cases he invokes the Eucharist to reconnect erring Christians with Jesus' death and resurrection, and to summon them to greater unity and seriousness among themselves on the basis of their shared identity of being "in Christ."

SELECT BIBLIOGRAPHY

Jeremias, Joachim. *The Eucharistic Words of Jesus.* New York: Scribner, 1966.

Kodell, Jerome. *The Eucharist in the New Testament.* Wilmington, DE: Glazier, 1988.

Lietzmann, Hans. *Mass and Lord's Supper: A Study in the History of Liturgy.* Leiden, the Netherlands: Brill, 1979.

Smith, Dennis E. *From Symposium to Eucharist: The Banquet in the Early Christian World.* Minneapolis, MN: Fortress, 2003.

Spohn, William C. "Identity and the Lord's Supper." Chap. 8 in *Go and Do Likewise: Jesus and Ethics,* 163–74. New York: Continuum, 1999.

Theissen, Gerd. *The Social Setting of Pauline Christianity: Essays on Corinth.* Philadelphia: Fortress, 1982.

Chapter Eighteen

Eucharist and Virtue

In the first chapter, I underlined the remarkable shift in theological ethics in the anthropological assertion that we are deeply relational. Previously, a fairly individualistic personal model of morality dominated Catholic theological ethics: My sins were my sins; my merit was my merit; my grace was my grace. The Christian belonged to a church, but responsibility, like identity, was not collectively understood. Though there were hints of a language that saw the church as a community of faith, for the most part those concepts were secondary. On judgment day, each of us would stand alone. We each would be accountable for our own way of living. Thus we may have had a communion of saints, but they were singularly named. We did not celebrate communities but rather heroic individuals (and we still do!).

THE SHIFT TO RELATIONAL SELF-UNDERSTANDING

We cannot underestimate the decidedly new relational point of view of the human person. From greater regard for the common good to developing a consciousness of social sin, the agenda of theological ethics has changed considerably. We might still celebrate individual lives of holiness, but we are so imbued with a discourse revolving around community that we cannot but express ourselves as belonging to a polity.

Because of this shift, I have developed a thesis regarding virtue: Instead of adopting the medieval view of virtue as perfecting particular powers (e.g., will, reason, passions, etc.), I proposed the virtues as perfecting ways that we are related. I proposed that we are related in three fundamental ways: to all people without partiality, to particular persons by special relationships (family, friendship, citizenship, etc.), and to ourselves uniquely. I proposed too that each of these relationships has corresponding virtues (justice, fidelity, and self-care) and saw prudence as the virtue that mediates the development of these at times contradicting forms of relationship. Do family relationships always negate personal needs? Should we always abandon family members in the pursuit of justice? And so on. I will return to my thesis and its claims in the last chapter on relationships and sexual ethics. But here I want to underline the historical development of this shift to a relational anthropology. I suggest that there are several sources for the shift.

First, throughout the twentieth century, progressively, Catholic and Protestant theologians highlighted the primacy of charity and/or love. We saw earlier, in chapter 10, that Gerard Gilleman's work in the 1950s on the primacy of charity was a catalyst for many subsequent works on charity. The two most important subsequent works were Edward Vacek's work on love (already mentioned in the same chapter) and Gene Outka's work on *agape.* After them, Timothy Jackson highlighted the relevance that the primacy of love has on social justice teachings. While before we may have thought of law (which enjoined individuals) as the point of departure for theological ethics, today we think of love as the foundation of moral theology.

Second, feminists developed an anthropological foundation for their claims that was specifically relational. Long suspicious of their contemporary ethicists' heavy dependence on autonomy, feminists insisted on an alternative point of view. This was especially clear in the works of Lisa Sowle Cahill, Cristina Traina, and Margaret Farley. Not surprisingly, they began to write not only about conscience and love, but also about how that love would be realized in family, in parenting, and in community. While today we can think of many moral theologians writing on family, we have to appreciate that before the feminist movement, family was rarely engaged as a topic for moral theological reflection.

Third, the Western European advocates of autonomous ethics, who emphasized the call to heed and develop the personal Christian conscience, began to critique their earlier writings as insufficiently relational. While not abandoning an autonomous ethics, they insisted on the autonomous agent as constitutively relational. As fine as this development has been, the autonomous conscience still dwarfs any relational self-understanding of conscience.

Fourth, writers from other continents pointedly distanced themselves from their American and European counterparts and argued that their native anthropologies were not as alienating and autonomous; they contended that their traditional understandings of humanity were in fact much more communal than elsewhere. This was especially the position of African ethicists like Bénézet Bujo, who specifically contrasted African tribal practices of collectivity against the more autonomous tendencies of the West. Nonetheless, Bujo, like others, uncritically upheld African traditional practices as egalitarian when in fact they too were part of deeply patriarchal values. There may have been circles of relationships, but these circles were still hierarchically defined.

Fifth, at the same time, within Catholic theological ethics, the once-firm boundary distinguishing fundamental morals from social ethics began to become much more porous. This was especially the case, again, for feminists. Cahill, for instance, brought the entire common good tradition into sexual ethics and began writing not only about chastity or responsible sexual conduct, but also about matters of justice in human sexual relationships. In time, she would do the same in bioethics. By bringing in the social justice tradition, she could put issues of access and fair treatment at the top of the bioethical agenda. In similar ways, Margaret Farley and Cristina Traina thought and wrote. Other feminists too broke down the divisions between fundamental moral theology and social ethics. Black Catholic feminists known as *womanists* as well as Latina theologians holding a *muerista* approach to ethics insisted on matters of equity and justice as paramount to contemporary ethics. Moreover, they began to retrieve women's practices of creating more relational worlds of life as integral to the work of moral theology.

WORSHIP AS THE EMBODIED PRACTICE OF FUNDAMENTAL MORAL THEOLOGY

In light of these developments, William Spohn wrote his landmark work on Scripture and ethics. In it, he claimed that virtue ethics, precisely in its anthropological interests in a deeper level of embodied relationality, most recommended itself as a worthy hermeneutics for understanding the Scriptures.

Notably, at the conclusion of his book, Spohn turned to worship as the practice that shapes Christian community and identity. Specially, in the practice of the Eucharist, we find the spiritual practice where this relational identification with Christ is regularly fostered. In the practice of the Eucharist we become what we do (or eat and drink): We become the body of Christ.

This transformation is effected by the grace-filled presence of Jesus himself in the Eucharist. And for this reason, the Eucharist is therefore the paradigm of the community of faith. Through the Eucharist, we become like Christ.

But is the Eucharist in fact transformative? Do people leave the Eucharist with more a sense of being constitutively in Christ than they believed beforehand? Do they similarly understand their fellow-communicant as belonging to the very same body?

In the previous chapter Daniel Harrington described the scandal of the Corinthian community in which the Eucharist was becoming a source of division

rather than a source of unity. Is that the same reality today? Is the Eucharist still
an occasion for strife? Or is it the sanctuary that the Hunchback of Notre Dame
recognized, where protection and not division is the overarching concern?

Certainly the tension between what we actually do become in the Eucharist and what we could become in the Eucharist captures the tension that all
Christians recognize in our understanding of God's kingdom as now but not
yet. The divinely appointed and divinely assisted initiative encounters human
shortcomings.

To bridge the gap, we might ask ourselves, "What is the theological ethical way of worshiping?" Other churches do ask that question. For instance,
the Greek Orthodox theologian Joseph Woodill writes that liturgy is where
we become illuminated about how we are to be conformed to God. Liturgy
is where we understand ourselves as the people we are called to become. In
liturgy, we Christians stand in community before God as a people saved and
called to be sanctified.

Interestingly, sacramental theologians are even more mindful of this question. Donald Saliers brokered in many ways the discourse on the relationship
between liturgical theology and ethics. More recently, Bruce Morrill has
furthered this interest by addressing how the theologies of Saliers, Johannes
Metz, and Louis-Marie Chauvet see the church and the liturgy as the place
where our sinfulness and our hopes become expressed in an expectation of
faith pursuing justice.

THE MORAL PRACTICES OF THE LITURGY OF THE WORD

What then are the practices that help shape such virtuous conformity as a
response to the gift of God in the Eucharist? How do our prayerfulness, our
hospitality, our community, our participation, our gestures, and our use of
music and language in the liturgy allow us to be shaped by the one we seek?
Do we not eat the one bread and drink from the one cup?

So as to understand the Eucharist as the locus for becoming a community
of disciples in the way that Paul exhorted us to become, let us simply consider
the liturgy as a series of embodied practices that are transformative by God's
grace and by our participation in them.

We begin by signing ourselves with the cross. Klaus Demmer calls that
an effective sign: It effects the change we seek. For Demmer, the cross must
make a real difference in our lives. Specifically, as Paul informs us, the cross
frees us from Sin and Death. Like Paul, Demmer does not mean this in some
sort of conceptual way. He means that we need to see that guilt and shame
should have no lasting claim on our lives. Guilt and shame have no lasting

claim on us not because we are good, but because Christ by the cross has taken away our sins. When we sign ourselves by the cross, we are getting ourselves into the practice of seeing that we have been set free from guilt so as to be free to live for ourselves and for others. Similarly, by the cross we are free of the lasting claim of death. When we sign ourselves by the cross, do we see our fears as taken away? Do we sense our being freed from guilt and shame, sin and death? We need to become more aware of the effect that the practice of signing ourselves can have. It is a sign not only of being claimed by Christ but also a sign of identifying ourselves with his freedom from sin and death so as to serve one another. It is the sign of our liberation.

One of the horrendous twists in history has been when Christians have used the cross to shame, imprison, exile, torture, or otherwise harm other persons. As a sign of the gift of our liberation, it is above all an expression of God's mercy. That Christians have used the cross as some sort of weapon of their own to promote their purported righteousness over others' purported wickedness is the great Christian obscenity. Whenever we separate our understanding of the cross from God's mercy, we inevitably risk again morally deplorable conduct, for we forget how our righteousness was won. For this reason the practice of cross burning in the United States was so obscene: In whitened, hooded sheets, members of the Ku Klux Klan burned the cross as a symbol of racial threat and racial violence.

The sign of the cross ought to make us truly humble, and so after the practice of the signing of the cross, we turn in the Eucharist immediately to the Kyrie, through which we call upon God's mercy. Through the cross we are signed by our redemption, but on the road to sanctification we call for mercy. This communal practice highlights the ongoing reconciliation of ourselves with God; we never celebrate the Eucharist without it. It is a remarkably habitual liturgical practice.

Following the pursuit of mercy, we sing to give God glory, an act of gratitude for the cross of Christ and for God's mercy. Together, these three practices prepare us to receive the narrative of revelation, the story of Jesus Christ.

Stanley Hauerwas makes the telling claim that the Christian task is to get the narrative of Jesus right. He uses the accounts of Peter, who understands that Jesus is the Christ but refuses to acknowledge suffering and death as constitutive of the task of the Messiah. Peter gets the name of Jesus right, but not the narrative. He resists it all the way through the Garden of Gethsemane and into the courtyard, right up until the crucifixion itself. Peter assumed that suffering and death ought not to be the way to salvation. Not until Christ has suffered, died, and is raised, does Peter finally get the story of Jesus right.

Similarly, we too are called to get the story of Jesus right. How then in the Eucharist do we do that? How do we receive the text? How do we get the

reception right? Here I often think of the community gathered: Is it expect-
ant? Is it awaiting the revealed word of God? Is it complacent or fearful about
what is to unfold?

And what about the preacher? How does the preacher help us be shaped by
the narrative so that we understand it as it is? Does the preacher understand the
task of bringing the Word and its meaning into the life of the community?

The reception of the narrative of Jesus takes us then to the confession of
faith, wherein we become incorporated into the fundamental claims of the
church itself. That confession of faith leads us in turn to the prayer of the
faithful, to the beseeching of the church for the church, the body of Christ.
For what do we pray? Are our prayers formative? Do they bring us to a deeper
appreciation of how we are constituted in Christ? This, after all, is the first
(and only) chance to add something to the liturgy: Here we can by our prayers
get our own narrative right.

THE MORAL PRACTICES OF THE EUCHARIST

In light of the way we have been formed in prayer by Christ the Word, we
are called to enter the liturgy of the Eucharist. Here we enter into an extended prayer that calls for us to remember. In doing so, we turn to the act
of memory, our most affective, historical, rational practice. Here the Italians
call the practice of remembering *ricordare*: to bring back our hearts to our
recollections. But before we remember the narrative, we preface it, we define
ourselves, with the priest, with the community, and with God, and so we sing
"Holy, holy, holy" and "Hosanna."

Then in the Eucharistic Prayer we enter into the narrative that shapes us,
a narrative told again and again, that calls us into the reception of the same
bread and the same cup. By entering the narrative of deliverance, of humility,
and of mercy, we become, like Christ himself, characters in the narrative of
salvation. The story of our salvation leads inevitably to the self-understanding
that just as Jesus' death was for us, so too is the meal for us. But the narrative
of our salvation does not end with us; rather it empowers us as a community
of disciples to follow Christ and serve and feed others with the word and
sacrament.

As we move to the point that we, as a people, participate in the meal, we
recognize the need to be reconciled with one another yet again. We exchange
the greeting of peace and we acknowledge our need for mercy as we call on
the Lamb of God.

As reconciled and humbled recipients of peace and mercy, we receive now
the body and blood of Christ. We are called to take and eat, not sit and watch.

We eat what we are called to become, the one body of Christ. We are now, like the Twelve, full participants in salvation history.

As the liturgy concludes we are blessed for the road of sanctification. Having been fed, fortified, and sustained on the journey of the community of discipleship, we turn to serve God and one another.

SELECT BIBLIOGRAPHY

Bordeyne, Philippe, and Bruce Morrill, eds. *Sacraments: Revelation of the Humanity of God: Engaging the Fundamental Theology of Louis-Marie Chauvet.* Collegeville, MN: Liturgical Press, 2008.

Bujo, Bénézet. *The Ethical Dimension of Community: The African Model and the Dialogue between North and South.* Nairobi, Kenya: St. Paul, 1997.

Curran, Charles, Margaret Farley, and Richard McCormick, eds. *Feminist Ethics and the Catholic Moral Tradition.* New York: Paulist Press, 1996.

Hauerwas, Stanley. *A Community of Character.* Notre Dame, IN: University of Notre Dame Press, 1981.

Jackson, Timothy. *The Priority of Love: Christian Charity and Social Justice.* Princeton, NJ: Princeton University Press, 2003.

Keenan, James. *Ethics of the Word: Voices in the Catholic Church Today.* Lanham, MD: Rowman & Littlefield, 2010.

———. *A History of Catholic Moral Theology in the Twentieth Century: From Confessing Sins to Liberating Consciences.* New York: Continuum, 2010.

Keenan, James, and Thomas Kopfensteiner. "Moral Theology out of Western Europe." *Theological Studies* 59 (1998): 107–35.

Morrill, Bruce. *Anamnesis as Dangerous Memory.* Collegeville, MN: Liturgical Press, 2000.

———. *Divine Worship and Human Healing: Liturgical Theology at the Margins of Life and Death.* Collegeville, MN: Liturgical Press, 2009.

Outka, Gene. *Agape: An Ethical Analysis.* New Haven, CT: Yale University Press, 1977.

Saliers, Donald, E. Byron Anderson, and Bruce Morrill, eds. *Liturgy and the Moral Self: Humanity at Full Stretch before God.* Collegeville, MN: Liturgical Press, 1998.

Spohn, William. *Go and Do Likewise: Jesus and Ethics.* New York: Continuum, 1999.

Traina, Cristina. *Feminist Ethics and Natural Law: The End of the Anathemas.* Washington, DC: Georgetown University Press, 1999.

Uzukwu, Elochukwu E. *A Listening Church: Autonomy and Communion in African Churches.* Maryknoll, NY: Orbis, 1996.

Woodill, Joseph. *The Fellowship of Life: Virtue Ethics and Orthodox Christianity.* Washington, DC: Georgetown University Press, 1998.

Part Four

THE VIRTUES AND
SOCIAL AND SEXUAL ISSUES

Chapter Nineteen

Social Ethics: Pauline Perspectives

STAY AS YOU ARE: 1 CORINTHIANS 7:21–24

For most Bible readers in the twenty-first century, Paul's advice to Christian slaves that they should remain in the social condition in which they were called by God to Christian faith (that is, as slaves) is among the most outdated and even outrageous parts of Scripture. But precisely because it is so outdated and outrageous, 1 Corinthians 7:21–24 can provide a useful entry into both the possibilities and the problems of Paul's teachings on social matters.

> 21. Were you a slave when called? Do not be concerned about it. Even if you can gain your freedom, make use of your present condition now more than ever. 22. For whoever was called in the Lord as a slave is a freed person belonging to the Lord, just as whoever was freed when called is a slave of Christ. 23. You were bought with a price; do not become slaves of human masters. 24. In whatever condition you were called, brothers and sisters, there remain with God.

Slavery was a social and economic fact in the Roman Empire (and in most other ancient societies). People became slaves by being conquered in battle, through loss of property and other financial failures, by the death of parents and other guardians, and even by selling themselves into slavery (to cover debts or raise their standard of living). It had little to do with racial identity.

The essence of slavery is belonging to another person, being the property of another. Not only did people in the Greco-Roman world find slavery not unusual or shocking, but great thinkers like Aristotle regarded slavery as perfectly natural: "It is clear then that some men are by nature free, and others slaves, and that for these latter slavery is both expedient and right" (*Politics* 1255a). It has been estimated that at Corinth in Paul's time, one-third of the population were slaves and another third had been slaves at some time in their lives (Collins, 279). Thus slavery was a very much a reality in Paul's world.

In the Greco-Roman world, slaves had a certain measure of mobility and freedom, much more than African slaves in eighteenth- and nineteenth-century America had. They could own property, take on additional jobs, and even become teachers, philosophers, political officials, and doctors. It was also possible to be emancipated by buying one's way out of slavery, by an act of kindness on the owner's part, or by being "sold" to one of the gods (sacral manumission). Even when freed, however, the former slave still had some obligations toward the master. While some slaves sought freedom by running away, this act was regarded as illegal; runaways were often hunted down and punished on the grounds that they were the owner's legal property.

In the New Testament world, the institution of slavery was a social fact. And even the uprisings led by slaves such as Spartacus were not primarily concerned with overthrowing the institution of slavery. What was especially important for slaves was the identity of one's master. As Collins observes, "In Paul's social world, where most people were slaves, the fact that one was a slave was not so important. What was important was whose slave one was" (286).

The literary context for Paul's advice to Christian slaves in 1 Corinthians 7 is a part of his instructions to Christians who are married (7:1–16) and unmarried (7:25–40). The instructions about ethnic identity (7:18–19) and social status (7:21–23) are bounded and punctuated by three calls to remain in the condition in which one received the call from God to become a Christian (7:17, 20, 24). The following concentric (ABA) outline emerges from 1 Corinthians 7: A—advice to the married (7:1–16); B—advice to Jews/Gentiles and to slaves/free persons (7:17–24); and A—advice to the unmarried (7:25–40). Paul's teachings about the married and unmarried are treated at length in chapter 21.

For the central section in 1 Corinthians 7, it is possible to discern an ABABA outline, in which the basic principle of staying in the ethnic and social condition in which one was called (7:17, 20, 24) is illustrated with reference to one's ethnic identity (7:18–19) and social status (7:21–23).

Where Paul is coming from in 1 Corinthians 7:21–24 is clear from his reiteration of the principle of social stability: "In whatever condition you were called, brothers and sisters, there remain with God" (7:24; see also 7:17 and 20). The operative words are "with God." This is not a utopian blueprint for the perfect society. Rather, Paul's advice arose, first of all, out of the theological conviction that in Christ all gender, ethnic, and social distinctions had been made relative: "There is no longer Jew or Greek, there is no longer slave or free, there is no longer male and female; for all of you are one in Christ

Jesus" (Galatians 3:28). In other words, in light of the Christ-event the great sociological distinctions are not very important any longer. And so rather than spending one's physical and spiritual energies on these matters, in Paul's view one should channel them into the service of God and his Messiah.

A second theological conviction underlying Paul's advice is the recognition that God (and his Messiah) is the only master who is worth serving as Lord. Recall the importance of who one's master was in the Greco-Roman world. Those who answered God's call to become Christians accepted God (and his Messiah) as their true master. And so those who were legally slaves at the most profound level were really the servants of God. And those who were legally free had become at the most profound level "slaves" in that they acknowledged God (and his Messiah) as their true "Lord" (*Kyrios*).

A third theological conviction underlying Paul's advice here is the belief that with the full coming of God's kingdom there would soon be a dramatic transformation of the world. The point is made most clearly in Paul's later advice to unmarried persons: "For the present form of this world is passing away" (7:31b). This sentence provides the background for much of the advice in 1 Corinthians 7. In Paul's eschatological perspective there need not be much concern about reforming society or developing a utopian social vision, precisely because the irruption of God's kingdom in its fullness would render all such plans unnecessary. Moreover, the sociopolitical influence of a tiny religious movement (probably no more than two thousand persons in the world were Christians at the time of 1 Corinthians) would have amounted to practically nothing at all. There is no equivalent to Plato's *Republic* or Aristotle's *Politics* in the New Testament.

Two ancillary issues that arise in 1 Corinthians 7:21–24 deserve comment here. In 7:21b, Paul takes up the case of slaves who had the opportunity to gain their freedom. His advice, expressed in the imperative *mallon chresai* in Greek, is ambiguous. It can be taken positively to mean "avail yourself of the opportunity" or negatively as "make use of your present condition now more than ever." The positive reading better fits with the Greek vocabulary and grammar, while the negative reading is more consistent with the thrust of Paul's advice in the 7:21–24 and in the chapter as a whole.

Another issue is the "redemption" Christology alluded to in 7:23: "You were bought with a price; do not become slaves of human masters." There may be an allusion here to the practice of sacral manumission whereby a slave could be sold (at least symbolically) to a god. The "price" in the case of Christians was provided by God in Jesus' passion and death. The result was that now slaves and free persons alike have God (and his Messiah) as their Lord and Master. All have been redeemed ("bought") or ransomed through Christ. This is another example of Paul's (or a predecessor's) developing a christological point on the basis of a social institution that would have been familiar to all his readers.

In summary, Paul's social teaching is hard to label as either utopian or realistic, or as either progressive or conservative. It was shaped primarily by his theological convictions about the Christ-event, God as the only master worth serving, and the coming kingdom of God, as well as the minority status of the Christian movement within the Roman Empire. Thus the relevant Pauline texts provide more of a challenge than a social blueprint.

PROBLEMS FOR PHILEMON AND PAUL

The shortest among the Pauline epistles is the letter to Philemon. In it Paul writes from prison to intercede with Philemon on behalf of Philemon's runaway slave, Onesimus. Here with an eye toward better understanding Paul's "social ethics," we explore the problems that this request posed for Philemon and the fact that Paul wrote to him from prison.

Paul had brought Philemon to Christian faith. This was something that both Philemon and Paul seem to have regarded as very important and positive (see v. 19). Philemon seems to have been a wealthy man, at least wealthy enough to own slaves and to let the local Christian community use his house as the place for their gatherings. Paul addressed his letter not only to Philemon but also to "Apphia our sister" (probably Philemon's wife) and "Archippus our fellow soldier" (most likely in the "campaign" for the gospel) as well as "the church in your house." The implication is that Paul's letter would be read in the assembly of Christians at Philemon's house, and that there would be great social pressure on Philemon to accede to Paul's request.

The slave belonging to Philemon who was named Onesimus (which means "useful" or "profitable") had run away from the household of Philemon. He eventually found his way to Paul, who was in prison somewhere (more likely at Ephesus than in Caesarea Maritima or Jerusalem). There under Paul's instruction, Onesimus became a Christian and developed a personal relationship with Paul. The time had come for Onesimus to return to the house of Philemon. But as a runaway slave he faced severe punishment from his master. Paul's letter to Philemon is a plea that Onesimus be taken back without recrimination and now as a beloved brother.

Some of the reasons that Paul offers are personal and pragmatic. Playing on the meaning of Onesimus' name, Paul notes that the slave who had been "useless" can now be "useful" both to Philemon and to Paul (v. 11). And near the end of the short letter, Paul uses financial terminology to remind Philemon about his own spiritual debt to Paul and to suggest that now Philemon "owes" a favor to Paul (vv. 18–19). In the middle of his plea, Paul claims that he played with the idea of having Onesimus remain with him as some kind of assistant as a way of getting recompense from Philemon (v. 13). But in the end Paul decided to send Onesimus back to Philemon.

The thrust of Paul's request is expressed in v. 16. Paul wants Philemon to accept Onesimus "no longer as a slave but more than a slave, a beloved brother—especially to me but how much more to you, both in the flesh and in the Lord." The least that Paul is asking is that Philemon accept Onesimus back into his household as an equal at least on the spiritual level; that is, as a fellow Christian (see Galatians 3:28).

This kind of request from Paul the prisoner to Philemon the wealthy householder about the slave Onesimus would have had important social and economic ramifications. In a culture that was very conscious of status, class, and hierarchy, it would have been regarded as shameful (an important matter in this society) for a rich person like Philemon to act as if a runaway slave like Onesimus were his equal in any way. And yet Paul was asking Philemon to take Onesimus back as "a beloved brother."

Was Paul also asking that Philemon set Onesimus free? The answer is not clear, and most exegetes are very cautious about supposing that he was doing so (see 1 Corinthians 7:17, 20, 24). However, the phrase "no longer as a slave" in v. 16 could suggest that Paul had in mind the manumission of Onesimus. Likewise, Paul's closing comment to Philemon ("knowing that you will do even more than I say," v. 21) could also be taken as a subtle hint that Paul expected that Philemon might free Onesimus.

If Paul really was suggesting freedom for Onesimus, then Philemon's problems would increase dramatically. After all, according to law and custom, Onesimus was Philemon's "property," and so Philemon would incur some financial loss. Moreover, he might set a dangerous precedent whereby slaves with Christian masters might become Christians only to increase their prospects of being freed. Finally, Philemon's social peers—householders and slave owners—would very likely be angry at his lack of solidarity with them regarding the institution of slavery. He would be in effect tampering with one of their deeply held cultural assumptions (that some people are by nature meant to be slaves) and contributing to the ruin of the entire economy and social fabric (which was built to a large extent on slave labor). So in requesting that Philemon accept Onesimus back as "a beloved brother," Paul was presenting Philemon with some big social and ethical problems.

Paul's own problem was that he was in prison when he wrote to Philemon. In the salutation Paul identifies himself (with some pride) as "a prisoner of Christ Jesus" (v. 1; see also v. 19) and speaks about his "imprisonment for the gospel" (v. 13; see also vv. 10 and 23). His letter to the Philippians (see especially 1:12–26) was also written from prison. And the Deuteropauline letters (Colossians, Ephesians, and the Pastorals) take Paul's imprisonment as their setting in life.

In Philippians 1:12–26, Paul presents a remarkably positive meditation on his imprisonment as an opportunity to spread the gospel. All that Paul really cared about was that Christ would be proclaimed (see 1:18). So he shows how his imprisonment had good effects not only on the "imperial guard" (presumably his jailers) and his timid Christian allies in preaching but also on his Christian opponents (1:13–17). As Paul faced the possibility of his own death (and one must ask, What was the charge against him that carried the death penalty?), he reasoned in 1:19–26 that if he died, then he would be more fully with Christ, and that if he lived, he would have further opportunities to carry on his ministry of preaching the gospel. Either way, Paul could not lose. He summarized the situation in this way: "For to me, living is Christ and dying is gain" (1:21).

In his many references to his imprisonment, Paul never makes clear precisely what imprisonment meant concretely. Was he in a prison building, or was he under some kind of house arrest? He clearly could receive visitors like Onesimus and could carry on correspondence with his coworkers and with the communities he had founded. According to Acts 28:16, when Paul came to Rome, he "was allowed to live by himself, with the soldier who was guarding him." But it is difficult to determine under what actual conditions his "prison" letters to Philemon and to the Philippians were composed.

It is even more difficult to figure out why Paul was in prison at all. When Paul refers to "my imprisonment for the gospel" (Philemon 13), he suggests some connection between his imprisonment and his evangelistic activity. But what was the precise activity that got Paul into trouble with the Roman legal system?

In Acts it is suggested that the local Jewish communities resented Paul's interpretations of the Jewish Law and so reported or delated him to the Roman officials (even though they were themselves skeptical about any criminal wrongdoing on Paul's part). The statement attributed to Claudius Lysias in his letter to the governor Felix in Acts 23:29 is typical of Luke's approach: "I found that he [Paul] was accused concerning their law, but was charged with nothing deserving death or imprisonment." Whereas Paul's own statements are too vague, Luke's explanations are probably too colored by his theological concerns with Jewish rejection of the gospel, his effort to draw parallels between Jesus and Paul, and his concern to placate the fears of Roman officials in his own time.

We may never know what precise legal charges were made against Paul by the Roman officials. We can at least speculate that they may well have found in Paul's gospel some teachings that they perceived as having dangerous religious and political implications. These officials had a hard time in classifying the new Christian movement. Its members did not build temples, offer sacrifices, or have priests. In Paul's time most of them were Jews, and yet they did not insist that new non-Jewish members should become Jews and accept circumcision, observe the food and purity laws, or keep the Sabbath rules.

It is possible and indeed likely, however, that Paul's theological views and their social implications did get Paul into serious trouble with the Roman officials to the point of their imprisoning him. In 1 Corinthians 8:6, Paul cited as a general Christian belief the conviction that "for us there is one God, the Father from whom are all things and for whom we exist, and one Lord, Jesus Christ, through whom are all things and through whom we exist." Such a confession of faith would naturally call into question the existence of the many gods in the Greek and Roman pantheons, and might (and did, as the book of Revelation shows) even preclude Christian participation in the Roman civil religious rites and in worship of the Roman emperor as divine in particular.

The gospel that Paul preached also had potentially subversive social implications. The self-consciousness of the Christian community as the people of God, the body of Christ, and the charismatic community rendered all other social arrangements (family, city, empire, etc.) of secondary importance. Moreover, the ideal of celibacy undertaken as a sign of total dedication to the coming kingdom of God threatened to disrupt the social system, which was built to a large extent upon marriages arranged between powerful families. Likewise, where there was talk about Christians being "no longer slave or free" (Galatians 3:28), the economic and social consequences for what was a slave-based economy were very serious indeed. There must have been more to Paul's imprisonments than simply his public preaching of Jesus' death and resurrection and jealous opposition on the part of other Jews.

CHURCH AND STATE

While Paul's gospel may have contained within itself the seeds of tension between the church and the Roman Empire, the existence of that empire also facilitated the spread of early Christianity in several ways. Through the development of a system of good roads and a sustained campaign to rid the Mediterranean Sea of pirates, the Roman Empire made travel by land and by sea much safer than it had been before. Also, it offered a relatively stable and comprehensive political structure in which Christian communities and their apostles could live and work. The use of Greek as the common language (with Latin as a second option) meant that Christians from all parts of the Roman Empire could communicate. And the Roman Empire provided at least the rudiments of a common culture (often promoted as part of the civil religion) to unify some very different peoples.

The classic New Testament "church and state" text appears in Romans 13:1–7. That passage assumes a remarkably positive view of the Roman Empire and urges the Christians at Rome to cooperate with Roman government officials and to pay their taxes. While Paul's cooperative approach is echoed in some other texts (1 Timothy 2:1–2; Titus 3:1; 1 Peter 2:13–17), other New Testament views of the Roman Empire include the very negative approach in Revelation and the cautious approach of Jesus in Mark 12:13–17 and parallels. For a full discussion of these texts, see our *Jesus and Virtue Ethics* 111–119. The point is that there is no one, uniform perspective on "church and state" or on the Roman Empire in the New Testament.

Paul's own perspective on the Roman Empire is presented in Romans 12–13, chapters devoted to spelling out the ethical implications of the gospel. In this literary setting, Paul provides ethical advice (*paraenesis*) on various topics pertaining to Christian life. While Romans 13:1–7 stands out in this immediate context because of its relatively sustained and focused argumentation, it does not seem to be an interpolation by a later editor (as some scholars have suggested). Rather, the passage appears to represent Paul's own advice on what should be the Roman Christians' attitude toward the Roman Empire.

The thesis or basic principle is respect for the established political hierarchy: "Let every person be subject to the governing authorities" (13:1a). The first argument in support of this stance (13:1b–2) is that the existence of political authorities is in accord with God's will, and therefore cooperation with them is expected by God. The second argument (13:3–4) is that those who do what is good and right will have nothing to fear from the political authorities. The two arguments are summarized in 13:5: "Therefore, one must be subject not only because of wrath but also because of conscience." The practical consequence of this position is that Roman Christians should pay their taxes to the government and give the government officials the honor and respect that are due them (13:6–7).

On the surface, at least, Paul in Romans 13:1–7 promotes a cooperative and respectful attitude toward the Roman Empire. Once one goes beneath the surface, however, the interpretation of this text becomes more complicated. First of all, the text presumes an ideal system of government that reflects and promotes God's will and is founded upon the principles of justice and fairness. But that was surely not always (if ever) the case with the Roman Empire. The most obvious counterproof would be the execution of Jesus of Nazareth under Pontius Pilate, the Roman governor of Judea. So one can object that Paul here proposes a utopian vision of the state that in fact was found nowhere at all (recall that the root meaning of "utopia" is "nowhere").

Throughout church history, Romans 13:1–7 has been repeatedly presented as expressing the Christian doctrine of "church and state." Repressive governments have often tried to use this text to discourage political dissent and resistance on the part of committed Christians. For example, part of the political strategy of the South African apartheid regime was to appeal to this passage to keep black Christians in line. However, neither the repeated use nor the abuse of this text can make Paul's advice here into a universal philosophical-theological principle. Attempts to do so have been undercut by the variety of perspectives on the Roman Empire in the New Testament and by church history itself.

The interpretation of Romans 13:1–7 is best approached in terms of the concrete historical situation in which Paul wrote to the Roman Christians. Paul was addressing a small community of Christians in the very capital of the Roman Empire. In 49 CE, the emperor Claudius had expelled all Jews (including Christian Jews) from Rome because of some kind of political unrest among them, perhaps involving disputes about "Christ." Only in 54 CE were the Roman Jews (including Christian Jews) allowed to return. The tensions between Gentile Christians and the returning Christian Jews were at least in part the occasion for the composition of Paul's letter to the Romans.

In such a highly charged political situation, Paul presented in Romans 13:1–7 advice that would certainly cause no trouble for the Christians at Rome. Any imperial official who gained access to Paul's letter could find nothing subversive or revolutionary here. And any rational person with religious beliefs would agree that a government that operates in accord with God's will and the principles of justice deserves cooperation and respect from its subjects. In this particular context, however, Paul's wish may have been father of his thought.

Interpreters of Romans 13:1–7 must also take account of a passage that appears in close proximity: "For salvation is nearer to us than when we became believers; the night is far gone, the day is near" (13:11b–12a). If we assume that "the day" is the eschatological Day of the Lord, then it would seem that Paul did not expect the Roman Empire to last much longer. With other Christians, he expected that the kingdom of God would soon be fully manifest and that the Roman Empire (and every other human empire) would disappear. (For apocalyptic scenarios in Paul's letters, see 1 Thessalonians 4:13–5:11 and 1 Corinthians 15.) At the heart of much of Paul's "social" teaching seems to have been the conviction that "the present form of this world is passing away" (1 Corinthians 7:31). On the topic of "church and state," then, Paul's advice in Romans 13:1–7 is better viewed as pragmatic and temporary rather than as utopian and metaphysical.

SOCIAL INSTITUTIONS WITHIN THE CHURCH

Paul wrote his letters at a time (51 to 58 CE) when there were probably around two thousand Christians in the world, and the churches that he had founded had been in existence at most for a few years. There was simply not the mass of people or the time span for elaborate Christian social institutions to have taken shape. However, it is possible to glimpse the beginning of two such institutions pertaining to lawsuits among Christians and to the collection for the poor.

The problems of lawsuits between Christians is treated in 1 Corinthians 6:1–11. There Paul expresses his horror and frustration that Christians were engaging in legal actions against one another before non-Christian judges. The cases were most likely what in modern judicial systems would be handled in small claims courts. In 6:1, Paul characterizes the judges as *adikoi,* a term that suggests that the judges were not only pagans but also unjust or crooked (in a system where bribery and other forms of chicanery were common). Paul's solution was that such legal matters should be kept within the Christian community.

Paul argues his case first by appealing to the identity of Christians as "the saints" and to their eschatological role as judges of the world. These people were "saints" insofar as they had been called and chosen by God, the Holy One. They are also to judge the world along with the Twelve at the last judgment (see Luke 22:30 and Matthew 19:28). Paul's reasoning in 1 Corinthians 6:1–2 was that if Christians can be trusted by God to participate in the last judgment, surely they can be trusted by fellow Christians to adjudicate minor legal matters among themselves.

Therefore Paul was astonished that Corinthian Christians were having recourse to unjust pagan judges (6:3–4) and not finding one of their own to decide their legal cases (6:5–6). Moreover, he wonders why these Christians were so litigious at all ("Why not rather be wronged?" 6:7) and why they were committing deeds that resulted in such legal actions.

When Paul wrote this letter (56–57 CE), the church at Corinth was small and fragile. Although it had attracted some elite members, according to Paul himself "not many of you were wise by human standards, not many were powerful, not many were of noble birth" (1 Corinthians 1:26). Paul was concerned with the public image of a small community whose members were now suing one another in open court. His solution was that they should keep their legal problems "within the family" in order to protect the public reputation of the church.

What started as an understandable answer to an embarrassing situation within a tiny church eventually developed into an elaborate legal system (canon law, ecclesiastical courts, and even ecclesiastical prisons) administered by and within the church. As events in recent years have shown, this internal legal system has also provided cover for pedophiles and other predators whose public exposure has become the source of great embarrassment for the church. In Paul's historical situation there may have been good reasons for Christians to keep their legal disputes "within the family." But such a policy when pushed too far has had disastrous consequences for the reputation of the church in recent times.

Another social institution internal to the early church that Paul promoted was the collection for the Christian community at Jerusalem. The project seems to have been part of the agreement that Paul reached with the "pillar apostles" (Peter, James, and John) in Jerusalem to gain approval for his ministry of preaching the gospel to non-Jews: "They asked only one thing, that we remember the poor" (Galatians 2:10). In writing to the Corinthians, Paul urges them to put aside some money for this collection "on the first day of the week" (1 Corinthians 16:2). And in Romans 15:25–26, Paul describes his plans to bring the proceeds of the collection to Jerusalem as a sign of gratitude and unity on the part of Gentile Christians to members of the "mother church" in their time of need.

However, Paul's most extensive treatment of the collection appears in 2 Corinthians 8–9, which is aptly described as the first Christian fundraising letter. Here Paul combines rhetorical skill and Christian theology to urge the Corinthian Christians to be generous. On the human level he proposes the generosity displayed by the Macedonian churches as a model to imitate and surpass in a kind of "holy rivalry" (8:1–6). He insists that such giving is voluntary but pleads that they not put Paul to shame by failing to give (9:1–5). On the theological level, Paul describes God as the origin of all good things and as one who "loves a cheerful giver" (9:7). He also appeals to the example of Christ, who "though he was rich, yet for your sakes he became poor, so that by his poverty you might become rich" (8:9). He includes considerations of social justice: "It is a question of a fair balance between your present abundance and their need" (8:13–14). And he clinches his appeal at two points with biblical quotations: Exodus 16:18 in 8:15, and Psalm 111:9 in 9:9.

The collection was an important project for Paul. It was a concrete sign of unity among the churches. It was a way for Gentile Christians to express their indebtedness to the Jewish Christians of Jerusalem. And it was an early effort at combining Christian charity and social justice. In 2 Corinthians 8–9 Paul offers a model for all Christian fundraisers and sets an example for such appeals to generosity in giving throughout church history.

DEUTEROPAULINE HOUSEHOLD CODES

The classic statement about the social structure of the household in the Greco-Roman world appears in Aristotle's *Politics*. He notes that the household is the most basic form of a social institution in the *polis* ("city"), and in its most basic form the family that constitutes a household consists of "master and slave, husband and wife, father and children" (*Politics* 1253b).

The slave is described by Aristotle as "a living possession" and a "minister of action" (1253b–1254a). As noted above, Aristotle maintained that slavery is entirely natural: "It is clear, then, that some men are by nature free, and others slaves, and that for these latter slavery is both expedient and right" (1255a). As property and as destined for servitude by nature, slaves live under the rule of the master of the household.

The dominion of the patriarch over the household is absolute, according to Aristotle: "The rule of a household is a monarchy, for every house is under one head" (1255b). And the husband has absolute power over the wife by "nature," since according to Aristotle "the male is by nature superior, and the female inferior; and the one rules, and the other is ruled; this principle, of necessity, extends to all humankind" (1254b). If wives are subject to the master as to a king, even more so are the children.

There is much about hierarchy and "nature" in Aristotle's description of the household. But there is little or nothing about human relationships, mutual responsibilities, and love. It is against this intellectual background that we must read the New Testament household codes and try to see where they agree with and where they differ from Aristotle and those who thought as he did about the household.

The Deuteropauline letter to the Colossians 3:18–4:1 contains the oldest Christian example of a household code. Composed most likely by a disciple of Paul around 80 CE at Ephesus rather than by Paul directly, this letter emphasizes the perfect sufficiency of Jesus' life, death, and resurrection to bring about right relationship with God and even cosmic reconciliation. The heart of this letter is an early Christian hymn preserved in 1:15–20 that celebrates Christ as the Wisdom of God and as such the first in the order of creation and the first in the order of redemption. After the salutation and thanksgiving (1:1–11), the letter to the Colossians provides a theological instruction on the universal lordship of Christ (1:12–2:23), an exhortation on the rule of Christ in the life of believers (3:1–4:6), and the final greetings and blessing (4:7–18). The household code appears in 3:18–4:1 as part of the exhortation.

18. Wives, be subject to your husbands, as is fitting in the Lord. 19. Husbands, love your wives and never treat them harshly. 20. Children, obey your parents in everything, for this is your acceptable duty in the Lord. 21. Fathers, do not provoke your children, or they may lose heart. 22. Slaves, obey your earthly masters in everything, not only while being watched and in order to please them, but wholeheartedly, fearing the Lord. 23. Whatever your task, put yourselves into it, as done for the Lord and not for your masters, 24. since you know that

from the Lord you will receive the inheritance as your reward; you serve the Lord Christ. 25. For the wrongdoer will be paid back for whatever wrong has been done, and there is no partiality. 4:1. Masters, treat your slaves justly and fairly, for you know that you also have a Master in heaven.

In form and content the Christian household code in Colossians 3:18–4:1 stands in large part in the tradition of Aristotle's *Politics*. It considers the same three relationships: wives and husbands (3:18–19), children and parents (3:20–21), and slaves and masters (3:22–4:1). It assumes that there is a natural hierarchy that controls each relationship. The major concern is order. Wives are subordinated to husbands, children to parents, and slaves to masters. The expectation that there will be slaves in the household and the disproportionate attention given to obedience by slaves to masters imply that this code is written from the perspective of the social elite.

What distinguishes the Christian household code in Colossians from the one in Aristotle's *Politics* is the emphasis on mutuality and the religious dimension. The subordination of wives to husbands is said to be "fitting in the Lord," and husbands are told to love their wives and "never treat them harshly." Children are urged to obey their parents as their "acceptable duty in the Lord," while fathers are exhorted not to provoke their children lest they become discouraged. And slaves are commanded to obey their earthly masters, while their masters are counseled to treat their slaves "justly and fairly." Both are told to recognize that their real master is the Lord. The slaves are to serve their masters in the belief that they "serve the Lord Christ" (3:24), and masters are to be kind to their slaves on the assumption that they "also have a Master in heaven" (4:1).

While much of Aristotle's framework and hierarchy remains in place, the Christian household code in Colossians insists on mutual responsibilities from each party and effectively relativizes all these personal relationships by holding up God as the only true Master and Lord.

The Deuteropauline letter to the Ephesians as a whole is a revised and expanded version of the letter to the Colossians. It is actually less a letter than an essay or synthesis of key aspects of Pauline theology that was written by a student or admirer of Paul in the late first century. Even the place name in the address to the saints "in Ephesus" is suspect on text-critical grounds, and the epistle tends to treat general issues rather than concrete local problems. Using the letter to the Colossians as his major source, the author of Ephesians gave particular attention to the church understood not simply as a local entity (the church at Corinth or at Rome) but as a worldwide and even a cosmic reality (the body of Christ).

The household code in Ephesians 5:21–6:9 is a longer version of the one in Colossians 3:18–4:1 discussed above. It is prefaced by a sentence that highlights the theme of mutual obligation and the religious dimension that run through the household code in Colossians: "Be subject to one another out of reverence for Christ" (Ephesians 5:21).

The most extensive additions appear in the section devoted to wives and husbands (5:22–33). In fact, the author of Ephesians seems interested much more in Christ and the church than in marriage partners. He views the marriage relationship as an opportunity to reflect on the relationship between Christ and the church. He notes that just as the husband is the "head" of the wife, so Christ is the "head" of the church, which is his body (5:23). He goes on to show that the church is the object of Christ's love (5:25), that Christ's sacrificial death was undertaken on behalf of the church (5:25), that Christ initiated the process that has created the community of baptized persons (5:26–27), that we are "members of his body" (5:30), and that the marriage union reflects the even greater unity that binds together Christ and his church (5:32).

The section devoted to children (6:1–3) is strengthened by an appeal to the biblical commandment to "honor your father and mother" along with the promise of happiness and a long life for doing so (see Exodus 20:12; Deuteronomy 5:16). And in 6:4 fathers are instructed to bring up their children "in the discipline and instruction of the Lord."

The section about slaves and masters (6:5–9) is somewhat abbreviated in comparison with Colossians 3:22–4:1. Its relative conciseness serves to highlight the reminders that slaves have Christ as their real master and are ultimately responsible to Christ at the last judgment, and that masters have the same Master to whom they too will be responsible at the last judgment. Thus the slave-master relationship is relativized by the image of Christ as Lord and the prospect of the last judgment.

SELECT BIBLIOGRAPHY

Bartchy, S. Scott. *Mallon chresai: First-Century Slavery and the Interpretation of 1 Corinthians 7:21*. Missoula, MT: Society of Biblical Literature, 1973.

Collins, Raymond F. *First Corinthians*. Collegeville, MN: Liturgical Press, 1999.

Cullmann, Oscar. *The State in the New Testament*. New York: Scribner, 1966.

Disbrey, Claire. *Wrestling with Life's Tough Issues: What Should a Christian Do?* Peabody, MA: Hendrickson, 2008.

Grassi, Joseph A. *Informing the Future: Social Justice in the New Testament*. New York: Paulist Press, 2003.

Harrill, James A. *The Manumission of Slaves in Early Christianity*. Tübingen, Germany: Mohr Siebeck, 1995.

Harrington, Daniel J. *The Church according to the New Testament*. Franklin, WI: Sheed & Ward, 2001.

Horsley, Richard A., ed. *Paul and Empire: Religion and Power in Roman Imperial Society.* Harrisburg, PA: Trinity Press International, 1997.

Longenecker, Richard N. *New Testament Social Ethics for Today.* Grand Rapids, MI: Eerdmans, 1984.

MacDonald, Margaret Y. *Colossians and Ephesians.* Collegeville, MN: Liturgical Press, 2000.

Martin, Dale B. *Slavery as Salvation: The Metaphor of Slavery in Pauline Christianity.* New Haven, CT: Yale University Press, 1990.

Mitchell, Alan C. "Rich and Poor in the Courts of Corinth: Litigiousness and Status in 1 Corinthians 6.1–11." *New Testament Studies* 39 (1993): 562–86.

Pilgrim, Walter E. *Uneasy Neighbors: Church and State in the New Testament.* Minneapolis, MN: Fortress, 1999.

Rosner, Brian. *Paul, Scripture, and Ethics: A Study of 1 Corinthians 5—7.* Leiden, the Netherlands: Brill, 1994.

Schiavone, Aldo. *The End of the Past: Ancient Rome and the Modern West.* Cambridge, MA: Harvard University Press, 2002.

Chapter Twenty

Social Ethics:
Theological Perspectives

Daniel Harrington points to the very complex way that Paul, in expectation of the imminent coming of the kingdom, shapes a community that remains at once in its traditional relationships with one another and with the state and yet begins to anticipate an entirely new order of equality and discipleship.

I want to offer further reflections on the ethics for being social in the church and the world. Here I am not taking the long tradition of social ethics, per se, with its encyclicals and notions of the common good, social justice, and subsidiarity. Rather, I want to develop today, just as Paul did two millennia ago, the way for being ethical in the church. I propose seven points of consideration. I conclude, developing at length, the overarching virtue of hospitality, which I believe helps define Christianity.

SEVEN POINTS FOR CONSIDERATION

First, Paul gives us a social ethics without giving us kingdom stories. As we tried to emphasize in our first book on the Synoptic Gospels, Harrington and I saw in the parables of the kingdom a set of images that shaped the horizon of expectations for the early church. Without the kingdom parables, we have no frequent evocation about the nature of the kingdom prepared for us. There is no just judge of Matthew 25; there is no vineyard owner who pays the last first; there is no king who invites the homeless into his banquet, while weeding out the ungrateful. Likewise there is no literary motif that highlights the difference between the kingdom of this world and the kingdom of the next where a good thief is welcomed, where Lazarus lives, which like a mustard seed or like a grain of yeast is present though emerging. Nor does Paul give us the beatitudes or antitheses that adequately and somewhat comprehensively offer us an anthropological profile of the qualities for being a citizen of the kingdom. In short, the Synoptic Gospels offer a great deal of material about the kingdom that we simply cannot find in the earlier writings of Paul the pastoral theologian.

A social ethics, without the kingdom images and attributes, forces us to look at the dispositions and practices that actually do exist and in turn ought to exist. For this reason the Pauline letters have an immediacy in them that we do not find in the Synoptic Gospels. While the Synoptic Gospels point to the future, we see Paul concerned about specific practices of the early church members. We see concretely what he expects, not for the future, but now. He admonishes and commends his followers according to the practices they engage. He dislikes disunity and outward strife, and urges reconciliation; he takes up collections and extends concern not just within a local church but among the churches.

Second, Paul's concerns are still ours today. Read the newspapers. Have times changed? The news that San Bernardino's diocese was going to sue the archdiocese of Boston, well, this sounds worse than Corinth! Think of the sexual abuse scandal. How is the notion of scandal understood? Is it in a Pauline way? How have the weakest been affected? Or is it in a contemporary way? What will the powers that be say? Ought we not to have an understanding of scandal that is more Pauline and interpersonal and less about image? We need to recognize that in the self-understanding of now but not-yet, often we are with the not-yet. And for that reason, we can see that Pauline concerns from two millennia ago are still here.

Third, Paul's interest in the unity of the body of Christ is sustaining. Here he offers us an organic understanding of the community of faith into which each member is called. The one who is baptized and who calls on the name of the Lord enters into the body of Christ—which captures this visceral, organic, integrated unity in which the parts, like the members, are each recognized for their distinctive role in the community.

In this body, each person has his or her attributes, talents, and competencies, and each has his or her respective yet corresponding roles. These differing skills and dispositions are integrated into the fullness of the community. Therefore there is a society, a people, and a way that we are identified first by our "incorporation" into the body of Christ.

That notion of incorporation seems appropriate. By belonging to the body of Christ, we change our self-understanding, for there is a certain way that we surrender our individual prerogatives in order to be and remain incorporated. Even the skills that we develop may be more for the community than for ourselves.

Fourth, is this an alternative community? Does this community live as a political alternative to the contemporary "secular" community? I do not see that. Certainly like the writers of the other New Testament texts, Paul wants the standards of the Christian community to be greater than those of contemporary communities. In fact, Paul finds often that Christians do not even live up to those minimal standards of other communities. But Paul is hardly seeing the community existing as an alternative to contemporary life. Such sectarianism is not evident in Paul's letter to the Romans.

Nonetheless, theologians like Stanley Hauerwas and John Howard Yoder urge us to understand the Scriptures as forming an alternative community. For Hauerwas, the church does not have a social ethics; it is one. The social task of the community is not to serve the needs of the world but to be true to the narrative of what the church is called to be. The more truly church we are, the more we embody, rather than practice, a social ethics.

I think that today we understand ourselves as belonging to so many different communities that decisively to belong to one community that disassociates itself definitively from others seems to me unfathomable. I am a Christian, specifically a Roman Catholic who belongs to a religious order with a distinctive charism. By being a Jesuit, I define myself by vows through which I bind myself to this order for life. Moreover, I submit my will, my sexuality, and my income to that same order. It is hard to think of any church having such a claim on its members as does a religious order. Still, I do not live in a hermetically sealed universe.

I am an American of Irish descent, born and raised as a native New Yorker (Brooklynite, even), and for many years now a resident of the Commonwealth of Massachusetts. I am like these people because I am these people. Still, I have to choose between the Yankees and the Red Sox, and that is definitively a cultural choice.

Still, I have lived in Italy for six years and some of my ways of looking for the good life are less inspired by the United States and more by Europe. I have taught many times in the Philippines and feel as much at home in the Ateneo de Manila as I do in all the other Jesuit communities to which I have belonged. One of my closest friends is from Hong Kong and his Confucian cultural formation has become a part of me. Sure, I'm a New Yorker, but there are a lot of accretions here.

I am a theologian. A friend of mine once said to me, "Jim, you are such a theologian. You think and talk and express yourself as a theologian." Yet I am not always a theologian, even when I am in my office. Thus, I belong to a Catholic university that takes most of my concerns, energies, and work. As Catholic as Boston College is, it is also a university with attendant expectations that at times take me in a direction not at odds with Catholicism, but certainly less specifically and identifiably Catholic.

Moreover, many of the colleagues I most admire are feminists, some who remain decisively Catholic while others do not. In either case, I believe in good parts of their agenda and find myself critical of the world and of religion when it ignores their critique.

I belong to a pretty Catholic family, though my sister-in-law is Jewish and now my nephews, hers and my brother's children, are Jewish as well. I have never been so attentive to Passover, Yom Kippur, and Rosh Hashanah.

I just am not able to define myself uniquely with a single entity or identity. My faith so identifies me, yet not such that it excludes me from the world.

Nonetheless, I am a Christian who belongs to identifiable but not exclusive communities. I am shaped by my faith and I have more of a vested interest in my church than almost anything else in my life. I do not define that church as an alternative, but I do define myself within it. I love Paul—not because he separates me, but because he incorporates me.

Fifth, for this reason I believe that whatever community we belong to (Catholics, scholars, Jesuits, priests, New Yorkers, Yankees fans, friends of Manila, etc.), humility is pivotal. But I believe that for the Christian formed in faith and love by Christ, that humility is a particularly relevant virtue for building up a strong social fabric. As I said earlier, humility is knowing your place in God's world: sinner but saved, the one called into freedom by the blood of Christ, the one who understands his or her place within the body of Christ.

Humility requires me to be willing to be mentored by my leaders; to imitate those who imitate Christ; and to heed the authority of the Lord, my conscience, and my (divinely appointed) leaders. Here in understanding humility as knowing one's place, we can see humility not as inhibiting but as expressing the many gifts of the community members. Humility, then, is not a personal or private disposition but an important social one, for me and for all of us.

Sixth, reconciliation is an essential practice of the church. A friend of mine, John O'Malley, says that where two or three are gathered, there is bound to be an argument; and for that reason, there is always a need for reconciliation. Thus we recognize that reconciliation is essential for human relationships.

But as sinners we recognize the need for reconciliation with God and with one another. We saw earlier that in the liturgy, we practice reconciliation regularly, whether in the Kyrie, the sign of peace, or the Agnus Dei. If we believe that we can grow in faith, hope, and love, then we believe that reconciliation is an essential virtue and practice for growth in the Lord. Without it, we would not have hope.

Paul even wants us to be ambassadors of reconciliation. This is as much a call to serve the church as it is to serve the world. As a people who know that we sin against God and against ourselves, in light of the history of our own sinfulness, we recognize the intrinsic necessity of reconciliation. Indeed, in light of the humbling effects of the sexual abuse crisis, we have seen the overarching need, not only for reconciliation, but also for public liturgies of repentance by priests and bishops so as to heal the harm and bind the community together.

Our world needs reconciliation. We see the enormous sufferings of war and genocide where people hate ethnic groupings of people. The anonymity of hate today is astonishing. People may not know an Israeli or a Palestinian, an Iraqi or an American, a Korean or a Japanese, but they hate them. If hate is so pervasive, then reconciliation must be in idle.

We see it in our own boorish cultural wars, where we are identified frequently not by our communities but by our opposition. Of course, reconciliation depends deeply on respect, and so little respect for the person exists in so many societies.

Seventh, I think the great witness of the church is to hospitality. I teach at Boston College in Chestnut Hill, and in the middle of this campus, David Hollenbach helps run a center for human rights and refugees. His work dovetails with the work of Jesuit Refugee Services and Catholic Relief Services; both are fully focused on the needs of those who have no home or homeland, and welcome those who seek to find rest and welcome elsewhere. In a grossly problematic world where wealth is so extraordinarily distributed unjustly, the church is called to be hospitable.

A CLOSER LOOK AT HOSPITALITY

In the field of ethics, hospitality emerges particularly out of scriptural and early church studies. The Hebrew Bible opens with God creating the first man and woman, placing them in the Garden, and giving them all that they need. Whether God walks in the Garden with them, protects them in their exile, or later leads the descendants of Abraham into the promised land, the God of the Hebrew Bible tends to our needs as a host ministers to a guest. The divine practice of hospitality becomes normative for God's chosen people and is rewarded when, for instance, Abraham welcomes the three mysterious visitors at Mamre (Genesis 18:1–15), Lot provides sanctuary to the angelic guests at Sodom (Genesis 19:1–23), Joseph hosts his brothers in Egypt (Genesis 45:4–15), Rahab hides the messengers of Joshua (Joshua 2:1–21; 6:17), and the wealthy woman of Shumen greets Elisha (2 Kings 4:8–17). Since hospitality is normative, any act of inhospitality is an offense to God; nowhere is the offense more clearly described than in the destruction of Sodom (Genesis 19:24–29).

The hospitality of God in the Garden contrasts evidently with the inhospitality of humanity toward Jesus. From start to finish Jesus is rejected and reviled; yet, he is the paradigm of hospitality, whether at Cana (John 2:1–11), the Last Supper, or on the beach (John 21:4–12). His dying words are themselves an act

of hospitality, as he assures the good thief of a place of welcome in the world
to come (Luke 23:43).

Just as Abraham and his descendants practiced an *imitatio Dei* in their exercise
of hospitality, so Christians in the new dispensation practiced an *imitatio Christi*.
Wayne Meeks remarks that the specifically Christian beliefs about Jesus' actions
and God's actions through him affected their code of conduct. One of those sets
of action concerned hospitality. As in the case of Sodom, the most severe judgment in the New Testament (damnation) is for the inhospitable, whether the rich
man who ignored Lazarus (Luke 16:19–31) or those at the last judgment who
failed to minister to "the least" (Matthew 25:31–46). Jesus does not simply warn
us with parables; rather, he constantly admonishes those closest to him when
they are inhospitable—as when they try either to keep the children away (Mark
10:13–16; Matthew 19:13–15; Luke 18:15–17) or to send his listeners away
hungry (Mark 6:32–44; Mark 8:4–10; Matthew 14:13–21; Luke 9:11–17; John
6:1–14). In fact, the clearest admonition against inhospitality is directed against
Martha for her complaining (Luke 10:38–42). Ironically, this passage was long
considered (wrongly) an endorsement of the superiority of the contemplative
life; but contemporary writers see in Martha's failure to be really hospitable an
occasion to reinforce the message of the previous parable of Jesus—the Good
Samaritan, the quintessential story of welcoming (Luke 10:29–37).

Major theologians from Augustine to Venerable Bede have commented
on this parable's evident christological structure, in which the Samaritan is
Christ who encounters the stranger, the exiled Adam, wounded by sin, lying on the road outside the city (which is Paradise), where the priest and the
Levite (the Law and the Prophets) are unable to do anything for him. But the
Samaritan (Christ) washes his wounds and brings him to the inn (which is the
church), where he pays (that is, redeems him) and promises to return so as to
take him to the place where he lives. The Good Samaritan parable is a story
of Christ as the hospitable one who brings us into the church as a temporary
shelter where we await his return.

Hospitality is not found only in the Gospels. For the itinerant Paul and his
co-evangelizers, hospitality had a special significance. Throughout his letters
we find concrete accounts of the hospitality that he, Timothy, Titus, and others receive (Philemon 22; Romans 16:1–2, 23; 1 Corinthians 4:17; 16:10–11;
2 Corinthians 8:16–24; Philippians 2:19–23). That hospitality extends into a
Philippian financial support group for Paul and his coworkers as they preach
in other provinces (2 Corinthians 11:8–9; Philippians 1:5; 4:10–20). In particular, the Corinthians are especially praised for their hospitality (1 Clement
1:2; 10:37; 11:1; 12:1, 3).

The accounts of hospitable practices are paralleled by summons to hospitality that are fairly pervasive in early Christian texts. The letter to the

Hebrews (13:2) admonishes the readers, "Do not neglect hospitality, for by this means some have unwittingly hosted angels." In the *Shepherd of Hermas* (38.10), hospitality is promoted as prominent among the Christian virtues. In endorsing hospitality, the early church identified itself both with the guest preachers and the hosting local community and in both cases considered them "resident aliens" as First Peter notes so eloquently. Likewise, the letter to the Hebrews reminds us that "we have no enduring city, but we await one that is coming" (13:14). In turn, this identity led to a sensitivity to all "aliens," as Justin wrote in his *First Apology* (67.6).

Hospitality then is deeply tied to Christian identity: the patron who welcomes the guest who brings news of the real homeland. This insight played out significantly in the earliest development of the church, as both a sending and a receiving church, for the church that sent out its missionaries knew that the other local church would receive them. That local church was little more than an assembly (*ekklesia*) gathered in some patron's home, on whose hospitality the *ekklesia*, in turn, depended. As the *ekklesia* grew, it did so in its ability to receive guests/members. In time, the church itself took over the role of patron and served as host; that turn from individual to communal patron finally led to the appointment of a bishop for the local church who then served as the community's leader, exercising the hospitality that an individual patron once performed (1 Timothy 3:2; Titus 1:8; Hermas 104.2).

We cannot underestimate the role that hospitality had in the rise of Christianity. Rodney Stark argues that "Christianity was an urban movement, and the New Testament was sent down by urbanites" (147). But those urban areas were dreadful; he describes the conditions as "social chaos and chronic urban misery." This was in part due to the population density. At the end of the first century, Antioch's population was 150,000 within the city walls, or 117 persons per acre. New York City has a density of 37 persons per acre overall, and Manhattan with its high-rise apartments has 100 persons per acre. Moreover, contrary to early assumptions, Greco-Roman cities were not settled places whose inhabitants descended from previous generations. With high infant mortality and short life expectancy, these cities required "a constant and substantial stream of newcomers" in order to maintain their population levels. As a result, the cities were comprised of strangers. These strangers were well treated by Christians who, again contrary to assumptions, were not all poor. Through a variety of ways of caring for newcomers, financially secure Christians welcomed the newly arrived immigrants. This welcoming then was, as we saw above, a new form of incorporation. Stark notes:

> Christianity revitalized life in Greco-Roman cities by providing new norms and new kinds of social relationships able to cope with many urgent urban problems.

> To cities filled with the homeless and impoverished, Christianity offered char-
> ity as well as hope. To cities filled with newcomers and strangers, Christianity
> offered an immediate basis for attachments. To cities filled with orphans and
> widows, Christianity provided a new and expanded sense of family. (161)

This new incorporation was distinctive. Certainly, ethical demands were imposed by the gods of the pagan religions. But these demands were substantively ritual; they were not neighbor-directed. And while pagan Romans knew generosity, that generosity did not stem from any divine command. Thus a nurse who cared for a victim of an epidemic knew that her life might be lost; if she were a pagan, there was no expectation of divine reward for her generosity; if she were a Christian, this life was but a prelude to the next where the generous were united with God. Stark concludes:

> This was the moral climate in which Christianity taught that mercy is one
> of the primary virtues—that a merciful God requires humans to be merciful.
> Moreover, the corollary that *because* God loves humanity, Christians may not
> please God unless they *love one another* was entirely new. Perhaps even more
> revolutionary was the principle that Christian love and charity must extend
> beyond the boundaries of family and tribe, that it must extend to "all those who
> in every place call on the name of our Lord Jesus Christ" (1 Cor. 1:2). . . . This
> was revolutionary stuff. Indeed, it was the cultural basis for the revitalization of
> a Roman world groaning under a host of miseries. (212)

Meeks and Stark, along with many other recent scholars, direct us to hospitality as one of the key identifiable traits of early Christians. These studies are congruent with the work of contemporary ethicists who, likewise, turn their interests to hospitality, though often unaware of the data from early church studies. Thomas Ogletree, for instance, has invoked a variety of philosophical thinkers to awaken the Christian ethicist to the importance of hospitality. We saw earlier that Stanley Hauerwas has claimed that the primary ethical task for the church is to live the Gospel narrative as authentically as possible. The church, says Hauerwas, is not to preach to the world, but rather is to embody in itself the life of Christ. Thus, rather than being both the sending and receiving church, Hauerwas's *ekklesia* is singularly receiving and thus hospitality becomes an acutely important virtue. More recently, Christine Pohl takes a critical look at hospitality and analyzes the power inequities that occur in any guest-host relationship. But Pohl turns to the Scriptures and discovers in both the Hebrew and Christian Bibles that often the host was once an alien and thus understands the normative significance of being marginal. She captures what so many who write about hospitality miss: that the host must understand the perspective of the alien, and that this was precisely the richness of hospitality throughout the Scriptures.

SELECT BIBLIOGRAPHY

Jones, L. Gregory. "The Virtues of Hospitality (2 Kgs 4:8–17; Lk 10:38–42)." *Christian Century* 109 (1992): 17–24.

Koenig, John. *New Testament Hospitality: Partnership with Strangers as Promise and Mission.* Philadelphia: Fortress, 1985.

Malherbe, Abraham. *Social Aspects of Early Christianity.* Baton Rouge: Louisiana State University, 1977.

Meeks, Wayne. *The First Urban Christians.* New Haven, CT: Yale University Press, 1983.

Ogletree, Thomas. *Hospitality to the Stranger: Dimensions of Moral Understanding.* Philadelphia: Fortress, 1985.

Pohl, Christine. *Making Room: Recovering Hospitality as a Christian Tradition.* Grand Rapids, MI: Eerdmans, 1999.

Scroggs, Robin. "The Social Interpretation of the New Testament." *New Testament Studies* 26 (1980): 164–79.

Sordi, Marta. *The Christians and the Roman Empire.* Norman: University of Oklahoma Press, 1986.

Stark, Rodney. *The Rise of Christianity: A Sociologist Reconsiders History.* Princeton, NJ: Princeton University Press, 1996.

Yoder, John Howard. *The Priestly Kingdom: Social Ethics as Gospel.* Notre Dame, IN: University of Notre Dame Press, 1984.

Chapter Twenty-One

Relationships and Sexual Ethics: Pauline Perspectives

MARRIAGE AS THE USUAL PATTERN: 1 CORINTHIANS 7:1–7

First Corinthians 7 is the most comprehensive treatment of sexual morality that appears in the Pauline corpus and indeed in the whole New Testament. Here and in most of the rest of 1 Corinthians, Paul is responding to a series of queries raised by the Corinthian Christians on a variety of issues. It appears that one such question (see 7:1b) provided the occasion for Paul to give a fairly full treatment of what can be called sexual morality.

> 1. Now concerning the matters about which you wrote, "It is well for a man not to touch a woman." 2. But because of cases of sexual immorality, each man should have his own wife and each woman her own husband. 3. The husband should give to his wife her conjugal rights, and likewise the wife to her husband. 4. For the wife does not have authority over her own body, but the husband does; likewise the husband does not have authority over his own body, but the wife does. 5. Do not deprive one another except perhaps by agreement for a set time, to devote yourselves to prayer, and then come together again so that Satan may not tempt you because of your lack of self-control. 6. This I say by way of concession, not of command. 7. I wish that all were as I myself am. But each has a particular gift from God, one having one kind and another a different kind.

In the first part of the opening verse ("Now concerning the matters about which you wrote," 7:1a), Paul notes that now he is responding directly to questions raised by the Corinthians, whereas up to this point in the letter he had been commenting on reports that he had received about factions and other problems in the community. The second part of the verse ("It is well for a man not to touch a woman") was most likely a maxim or slogan current in some circles among the Corinthian Christians, and not Paul's own teaching.

While in the early Greek manuscripts there was no punctuation (there was no such convention), the New Revised Standard Version and other modern translations are correct in supplying quotations marks here. As the rest of the chapter shows, the maxim does not fully reflect Paul's own position. Rather, 1 Corinthians 7:1b is a statement that Paul takes up in order to correct and modify it.

It appears, then, that some Corinthian Christians were promoting complete sexual abstinence. Why they did so is not clear. Their program may have been grounded in an overly realized eschatology, whereby enthusiastic Christians imagined that they could and should live an "angelic" life (see Mark 12:25) already. Or they may have been influenced by the practice of certain pagan cults that demanded temporary sexual abstinence in connection with their rituals. Or perhaps they were impressed by the personal example of celibacy given by Jesus and Paul, and wanted all to emulate them. Whatever the precise rationale may have been, it seems that some Corinthian Christians were proclaiming that "it is well for a man not to touch a woman." In response Paul felt the need to correct and modify their position.

As stated in 1 Corinthians 7:2–4, Paul's own position is that for most Christians marriage and sexual relations within marriage constitute the general norm. What is striking and unusual (given the patriarchal culture of the Mediterranean world in the first century) is Paul's insistence on parity and mutuality between husband and wife.

Paul's basic teaching is presented in three parallel statements. In 7:2 he explains that as a way of avoiding sexual misconduct (*porneia*) it is advisable that each Christian man have a wife and each Christian woman have a husband. And then in 7:3, Paul assumes that there will and should be sexual relations within marriage. In the Greek text he uses the term *opheilon* (literally, "something owed, a debt") to describe what the NRSV translates as "conjugal rights." The point is that spouses owe one another access to sexual relations within marriage. In 7:4, Paul takes his theme of mutual obligations even further. Here he insists that in marriage the spouses give to one another authority over their own bodies. Now the husband has "authority" over the wife's body, and the wife has "authority" over the husband's body.

So according to Paul, marriage is the general norm for Christians. He regards marriage as a protection against sexual misconduct (*porneia*), and takes very seriously the mutual obligations that married persons take upon themselves. In some ways Paul's view here is the extension of the biblical ideal of married persons constituting "one flesh" (see Genesis 2:24; Mark 10:8; Matthew 19:6). What is most important is Paul's insistence on parity and mutuality between husband and wife. They have the same rights and the same obligations within the marriage relationship.

Having delivered his basic teaching about Christian sexual morality (sex within marriage is the general norm) in a frank and even earthy manner, Paul introduces in 7:5–6 temporary sexual abstinence within a marriage as a possible exception. While allowing this practice, he presents it as an exception and lays down three guidelines: Both marriage partners must agree to it; it should be for spiritual purposes ("prayer"); and it should be only temporary ("for a set time"). Paul's fear seems to be that if these guidelines are not followed, the profession of sexual abstinence may result in greater sin and scandal "because of your lack of self-control" (7:5). Paul's comment in 7:6 ("This I say by way of concession, not of command") implies that he is not ordering married persons to undertake sexual abstinence. Rather, his point seems to be that it is allowed if the three conditions are met. And the assumption is that sexual relations within marriage remain the general norm.

Paul rounds off his treatment of marriage and celibacy within marriage by pointing to his own example: "I wish that all were as I myself am" (7:7a). What does that mean? At least it implies that when he wrote to the Corinthians Paul was not married (see 7:8) and that he was practicing celibacy. Some scholars contend that Paul was once married but his wife had died (see the discussion below on 7:8–9). They assume that since rabbinic Jewish teachers generally were married in fulfillment of the biblical command in Genesis 1:28 ("be fruitful and multiply"), Paul must have been married. However, while it is possible that Paul was indeed a widower, there is no mention of his wife or children in the New Testament. And there is no positive evidence that John the Baptist or Jesus was ever married, and some Jewish groups (Therapeutae, Essenes) practiced celibacy. Moreover, the scholars' assumption is largely based on rabbinic evidence that is much later than the time of the New Testament.

Whether Paul was a widower or never married, he does put forward celibacy as a high ideal, even higher than the normal married state. Perhaps those Corinthian Christians who were promoting celibacy as the norm took their inspiration and encouragement from Paul's example. Paul, however, dampens their enthusiasm by insisting that celibacy is a gift from God that is given only to certain persons (see Matthew 19:12). Marriage and sex within marriage, not celibacy, is the usual way for most Christians. It is the duty of each Christian to discern whether his or her gift is marriage or celibacy: "But each has a particular gift from God, one having one kind and another a different kind" (7:7b).

OTHER TEACHINGS IN 1 CORINTHIANS 7

Paul's instruction about marriage in 1 Corinthians 7 falls into three major sections: advice to married persons (7:1–16), the principle of remaining in the condition in which you are called (7:17–24), and advice to unmarried persons (7:25–40).

Advice to Three Groups of Married Persons (7:8–16)

Having established marriage as the norm and celibacy as a praiseworthy exception for Christians, Paul goes on in 1 Corinthians 7 to give advice to married persons whose marital status lay somewhat outside these general norms: widowers and widows (7:8–9), those contemplating divorce (7:10–11), and those in mixed marriages (7:12–16).

The first group (7:8–9) consists of widowers (literally "the unmarried") and widows. Since the Greek term *agamoi* appears as a masculine plural noun and in parallelism with the feminine plural term for "widows" (*cherai*), the interpretation as "widowers" seems sound. Moreover, Paul provides advice to those who had never been married later in the chapter (see 7:25–40).

Here Paul counsels widowers and widows to "remain unmarried as I am" (7:8). That is, they are urged to remain celibate after the death of their spouses. It should be noted that Paul's comment here is the best textual evidence that he himself had been married and lived as a celibate widower. However, Paul also recognized that if sexual self-control (a Stoic ideal) became too much of a personal burden, it would be better for those widowers and widows to marry again than to "burn" with sexual passion.

The second piece of advice (7:10–11) very likely addressed a real case in the Corinthian Christian community in which a woman was going to divorce her husband. While in the Jewish law only the man could initiate divorce proceedings, in Roman law (and Corinth was a Roman colony) a woman could divorce her husband. The fact that the woman is mentioned first in 7:10–11 strengthens the impression that Paul may be dealing here with a specific case at Corinth.

The basic principle is "no divorce." The background of this strict teaching seems to be the teaching of Jesus himself (see Mark 10:1–12; Matthew 5:31–32; 19:1–12; Luke 16:18). And Paul makes this explicit when he claims that his teaching here is not his own creation but rather came from Jesus: "not I but the Lord" (7:10). In his paraphrase of Jesus' teaching Paul insists "that the wife should not separate from her husband . . . and that the husband should not divorce his wife." Thus he adapts Jesus' teaching that was first formulated in a Jewish context (where women could not divorce) to a Greco-Roman context (where they could), and in fact overrides or trumps both legal systems by forbidding divorce entirely. This teaching supports the ideals of parity and mutuality in marriage that were enunciated above in 7:2–4.

In a parenthetical comment in 7:11, Paul gives a divorced woman the option to remain unmarried (and presumably celibate) or to be reconciled to her husband. Since mixed marriages are treated in the next section (7:12–16), it seems that the advice in 7:10–11 is directed to situations in which both spouses are Christians. Its strict teaching is based on the biblical ideal of spouses constituting "one flesh," the teaching of Jesus, and the concept of Christian marriage as involving exclusive and lifelong commitment to one's spouse.

To those in mixed marriages (7:12–16), Paul's advice is striking for its surprisingly tolerant attitude and its apparent willingness to allow an exception to the "no divorce" position just enunciated. The situation envisioned here seems to be a case in which one partner in a marriage had become a Christian and the other had not. Bear in mind that the Christian community at Corinth had been in existence for only a few years, and that everyone in it had only recently become a Christian. Unless both spouses had adopted Christianity as their religion, the fact of a mixed marriage (that is, between a Christian and a non-Christian) was bound to create problems.

In introducing his counsel on this matter, Paul asserts that he has no direct teaching from Jesus on this issue but is speaking on his own: "I say—I and not the Lord" (7:12a). His pastoral solution is to ultimately leave the decision up to the non-Christian spouse. In 7:12b–13, he takes up the cases first of the Christian husband with a non-Christian wife and then of the Christian wife with a non-Christian husband. In neither case is the Christian spouse encouraged or even permitted to initiate divorce proceedings on his or her own.

Paul gives two reasons why a Christian should stay in a mixed marriage if the non-Christian partner consents to do so. The first reason (7:14) is what can be called the idea of holiness by association; that is, the concept that the unbelieving spouse (and the children) can somehow be made holy by contact with the Christian spouse. See Exodus 29:37 and Leviticus 6:18 for the Old Testament roots of this concept. The second reason ("It is to peace that God has called you," 7:15c) is to preserve peace within the marriage and also between families, since arranged marriages between "good" families were common at the time.

But what if the non-Christian spouse declines to continue the marriage with the Christian spouse? This case is treated in 7:15ab. As noted above, Paul left the decision up to the non-Christian spouse and urged the Christian to respect the spouse's decision: "But if the unbelieving partner separates, let it be so" (7:15a). In such a case the marriage ends.

May the Christian spouse remarry in such a case? According to 7:15b, "the brother or sister is not bound." The Greek term *ou dedoulotai* is even stronger and means "not enslaved." In other words, when the non-Christian spouse ends the marriage, the bonds of marriage no longer exist between the Christian and the non-Christian spouses. While it is not stated explicitly, the possibility of remarriage by the Christian spouse seems likely. This exception to Jesus' teaching about "no divorce" has traditionally been called the Pauline privilege. Matthew (see 5:32 and 19:9) also seems to allow divorce and re-marriage for the case of *porneia* (which seems to refer to sexual misconduct on the wife's part; see *Jesus and Virtue Ethics*, 149–154).

The final verse in Paul's pastoral advice about mixed marriages (7:16) can be read as an expression of either optimism or pessimism. The NRSV provides an optimistic rendering: "Wife, for all you know, you might save your husband. Husband, for all you know, you might save your wife." This version holds out the hope to the Christian spouse that he or she can commu-nicate holiness to the spouse (see 7:14) and perhaps even bring the spouse to Christian faith. The translation in the Revised Standard Version suggests that a more cautious and even pessimistic attitude may be warranted: "Wife, how do you know whether you will save your husband? Husband, how do you know whether you will save your wife?" Of course, there was no punctuation in the ancient Greek manuscripts to guide our reading. However, given the surprisingly tolerant and positive tone of 7:12–15, it seems more likely that the NRSV's optimistic translation is warranted.

The Principle of Remaining in the Condition in Which You Are Called (7:17–24)

Between his advice to married persons (7:1–16) and to unmarried persons (7:25–40), Paul enunciates the principle upon which much of his teaching about sexual morality is based: "Let each of you remain in the condition in which you were called" (7:20). In fact, this same principle is also stated in slightly different forms at both the beginning (7:17) and the end (7:24) of the passage (see the discussion in chapter 19).

The principle of stability is illustrated with reference to ethnicity (7:18–19) and to social status (7:21–23). In the first case Paul urges those who had been circumcised (Jews) to remain as they are and not to undergo "epispasm," the medical procedure meant to cover over the effects of circumcision (see 1 Maccabees 1:15). Likewise, those who had never been circumcised (Gentiles) should not seek to be circumcised. The reason is that in Paul's view both conditions have become matters of indifference. What really counts now is "obeying the commandments of God" (7:19).

So also in matters of social status (slave or free), Paul's basic position is that these are not very important. This is so because whoever is in Christ, whether that person is slave or free, has been bought with a price (Jesus' pas-sion and death) and is truly freed for life in the Spirit.

What do these illustrations about ethnicity and social status have to do with sexual morality? And what does the principle about remaining in the condition in which you were called have to do with sexual morality? The clue comes below in 7:26, when Paul gives advice to unmarried persons: "I think that, in view of the impending crisis, it is well for you to remain as you are." The "impending crisis" here seems to refer to the events surrounding what Paul and other early Christians expected would take place with the second coming of Christ, the resurrection of the dead, the last judgment, and the fullness of God's kingdom (see 1 Corinthians 15).

Paul apparently believed that only a short time remained before these events ("the birth pangs of the Messiah") would come to pass. And since one's ethnic, social, and marital status would remain in force during "the last days" (the interim period between Jesus' resurrection and the definitive display of God's reign), whatever advice that Paul gives on these matters was necessarily provisional and temporary. As always, Paul writes as a pastoral theologian. He envisions society not as so stable as to be fixed forever (like Aristotle) but rather as so fleeting and passing as not to merit the concern and energy of those who had already been "bought with a price" (7:23). This fact, of course, raises the question about the abiding significance of Paul's teaching about marital relationships (and other matters) in 1 Corinthians 7. Can these interim teachings still matter for Christians some two thousand years later?

Advice to Unmarried Persons (7:25–40)

Whereas in 7:1–16 Paul gave counsel to various married persons, in the rest of his instruction (7:25–40) he directs his attention to unmarried persons and applies his principle of stability ("remain as you are," see 7:17, 20, 24) to their situations while leaving open the possibility of its modification in some cases.

The way in which Paul opens his advice ("Now concerning virgins") suggests that here as elsewhere in 1 Corinthians he is responding to a query raised by the Corinthian Christians. The word *parthenos* is usually translated as "virgin," but it can and does also refer simply to an unmarried person. Concerning them it is Paul's considered opinion (*gnome*) that "it is well for you to remain as you are" (7:26). It is important to recall that this opinion and all the other views expressed in 1 Corinthians 7 are presented in view of "the impending crisis." In this apocalyptic context, Paul in 7:27 urges engaged persons (those "bound to a wife") to stay engaged and others not to enter into engagement, while conceding in 7:28 that those who marry do not sin.

Paul's advice to the unmarried in 7:25–28 is strengthened by an exhortation in 7:29–31 that reinforces the eschatological context. Since "the appointed time has grown short" (7:29), Christians should live as if they were already living in the age to come: "For the present form (*schema*) of this world is passing away." In this context Paul wants the Corinthian Christians to be able to concentrate on pleasing the Lord. And so he explains in 7:32–35 that married persons must naturally focus on pleasing their spouses, whereas unmarried persons are free to give their entire attention to pleasing the Lord. Paul notes that the goal of his advice to unmarried persons is only "to promote good order and unhindered devotion to the Lord" (7:35).

In 7:36–40 Paul takes up two other cases concerning unmarried persons: a man in an engagement to a woman (7:36–38), and a woman whose husband is now deceased (7:39–40). While the precise nature of the first case has been interpreted in various ways throughout the centuries, the most likely reading takes it to concern a man whose sexual impulses toward his fiancée are becoming too strong to control. Here Paul says that he does well to marry, though refraining from marriage might be even better. In the second case (7:39–40), a widow is free to marry whomever she wishes, but "only in the Lord." The latter phrase may mean that she should marry a Christian man or at least a man who will not prohibit her from practicing her Christian faith. But again Paul regards the widow as "more blessed if she remains as she is" (7:40).

In 1 Corinthians 7, Paul is responding to questions posed by new and (sometimes overly) enthusiastic Christians. The occasion for his advice here seems to have been the invitation to comment on a slogan that had become current among the Corinthian Christians: "It is well for a man not to touch a woman" (7:1b). This slogan may even have originated among the women at Corinth. Or perhaps it came (also) from male Christians who regarded themselves as already living a kind of angelic existence. In this passage as elsewhere in 1 Corinthians, Paul is writing as a pastoral theologian. He had founded the church at Corinth, and this letter to the Corinthians served as the vehicle for him to continue his guidance of these new Christians. In his responses to pastoral problems, Paul brings to bear his convictions about Christian faith.

One of those convictions was that "the present form of this world is passing away" (7:31) in favor of "the world to come." In this apocalyptic context Paul offers advice on an interim basis for the period between Jesus' resurrection and his second coming. It is in this framework that he teaches that it is best to "remain as you are" and that celibacy is in principle preferable to marriage. The reason for celibacy is to allow greater freedom to attend "to the affairs of the Lord, how to please the Lord" (7:32). At the same time celibacy undertaken on these terms is a witness to the conviction that "the present form of this world is passing away" (7:31).

Nevertheless, Paul always remains the pastoral realist. While celibacy undertaken on behalf of the kingdom of God (see Matthew 19:10–12) may be better, he recognizes that the normal pattern for Christians is marriage between man and woman lived out in a spirit of parity and mutuality (7:2–4). And at every step of his instruction he readily concedes that if sexual desire is becoming too strong an issue in a person's life, then it is better for that person to marry. The hermeneutical question that 1 Corinthians 7 (and the rest of Paul's teaching on sexual morality) poses is this: Can Paul's pastoral-theological advice worked out in an intense apocalyptic context serve as the basis for a Christian sexual ethics that is valid and applicable for the ages?

"NO LONGER MALE AND FEMALE"?

While 1 Corinthians 7 contains the longest and most comprehensive treatment of sexual morality by Paul, other important teachings on or related to this topic are scattered throughout the Pauline corpus. In Galatians 3:28, in what has become one of the most famous verses in the Bible, Paul proclaims:

> There is no longer Jew or Greek, there is no longer slave or free, there is no longer male and female; for all of you are one in Christ Jesus.

In fact, this sentence seems to have originated as an early Christian baptismal statement or slogan, which Paul quotes as common ground between him and the Galatian Christians. In the context of Paul's argument in Galatians 3, the most relevant member is "there is no longer Jew or Greek," since Paul is trying to show that it is by faith after the example of Abraham (and not by "the works of the Law") that Jews and Gentiles alike are members of God's people in Christ. The phrase "no longer male and female" echoes Genesis 1:27 ("male and female he created them").

According to Galatians 3:28, the most important identity marker for Christians is their being "in Christ": "for all of you are one in Christ Jesus." This identity came about in faith and baptism. It transcends all differences in ethnic background ("Jew or Greek"), social status ("slave or free"), and gender ("male and female"). Being in Christ is the most important thing, so important that all other distinctions are secondary.

SEXUAL IMMORALITY/FORNICATION

In 1 Thessalonians 4:3–8 (Paul's earliest letter, written around 51 CE), Paul describes abstaining from *porneia* ("sexual misconduct") as the "will of God, our sanctification" (4:3). Here *porneia* may cover many kinds of sexual misconduct. Or it may be taken more restrictively to refer to fornication. As a way to avoid such misconduct, Paul urges those who are tempted along these lines to enter into marriage and to live with their spouses "in holiness and honor" (4:4). He especially warns against drawing fellow Christians into such sins (4:6). In 4:7–8 he insists that such activities will be judged severely by God ("the Lord is an avenger in all these things"), are contrary to the vocation of the Christian ("God did not call us to impurity but to holiness"), and are offenses not only against other humans but also and especially against God and the Holy Spirit.

GENDER ROLES

Despite Galatians 3:28, social and gender distinctions have not been rendered entirely nonexistent. For example, in writing to Philemon, Paul acknowledges that Onesimus remains Philemon's slave even while pleading that Philemon take him back now as a "beloved brother." Likewise, in 1 Corinthians 11:2–16, Paul appears astonished that in the assemblies of the Corinthian Christians gender differences were being blurred. Whether the precise issue was head coverings (veils) or hairstyles has been a matter of vigorous debate among scholars. But in either case the underlying issue seems to have been that in these assemblies it was becoming hard to distinguish between the males and the females. Some scholars even refer to the problem as a kind of "spiritual transvestitism," perhaps inspired by too literal a reading of the part of Galatians 3:28 that said "there is no longer male and female."

Notice that Paul assumes that women do pray and prophesy in the assembly: "Any woman who prays or prophesies with her head unveiled disgraces her head" (11:5). Here Paul does not insist on women's silence, notwithstanding 14:33–36, which seems to include another Corinthian slogan (14:33–35) and Paul's negative response to it (14:36). He does insist that in the Christian assembly men should look like men and women should look like women.

To ground his position, Paul brings out arguments from several sources: (1) the order of "headship" in salvation history—God, Christ, husband, wife; (2) Scripture (Genesis 1:27; 2:18, 22–24); (3) nature, in giving woman longer hair than men; and (4) the lack of any custom or tradition allowing the blurring of gender differences in the churches. However unpersuasive these arguments may sound today, they do reflect a tension at least for Paul between a transcendent theological principle (in Christ "there is no longer male and female") and what he perceived to be a dangerous abuse in the Corinthian assembly, where some people seemed to be taking it too literally.

INCEST

Among the abuses at Corinth that most scandalized Paul was the case of a man who was having a sexual affair with his father's wife (or concubine): "A man is living with his father's wife" (1 Corinthians 5:1). See the full discussion in chapter 15. The woman was most likely not the man's own mother (that would be too horrifying!) but rather his stepmother or at least his father's mistress or concubine. This activity was technically incest, and so was forbidden by the Old Testament (see Leviticus 18:8; 20:11) and by Roman law. Paul's anger was directed not only at the offender but also at the Corinthian Christian community for its failure to condemn such shocking behavior.

In his physical absence, Paul instructs the Corinthian community to conduct a rite of excommunication for the offender. His instruction is full of judicial language ("I have already pronounced judgment"), and his advice is that the community "hand this man over to Satan." This extreme procedure may have been intended to shock the offender into the recognition of his sinful behavior "so that his spirit may be saved in the day of the Lord" (5:5). His sin of incest is condemned by Paul as contrary to the holiness of the church and as antithetical to the meaning of Christ's sacrificial death (5:6–8). At the close of 1 Corinthians 5, Paul warns against even associating with sexually immoral persons who may be within the Christian community (5:9–13).

PROSTITUTION

The ancient port city of Corinth had a reputation as a center for sexual immorality in general and for prostitution in particular. It appears that some Corinthian Christians continued to visit prostitutes with the justification that "all things are lawful for me" (1 Corinthians 6:12). Paul rejects their declaration of unlimited freedom and condemns their consorting with prostitutes as contradictory to belief in the resurrection: "The body is meant not for fornication but for the Lord. . . . God raised up the Lord and will also raise us by his power" (6:13–14).

To consort with prostitutes makes a mockery of the concept of the body of Christ (6:15–17). Recall that in Paul's anthropology the body (*soma*) is the person in relationship. One who is in relationship to Christ in the body of Christ should have nothing to do with the body of a prostitute. For one who is a member of the body of Christ and thus "one flesh" with Christ to have sexual relations with a prostitute is inappropriate behavior: "Should I therefore take the members of Christ and make them members of a prostitute?

Never!" (6:15). Likewise, to engage in fornication and other forms of sexual immorality (6:18–20) is an offense against the body of Christ and so against one's own body.

HOMOSEXUALITY

While there seem to be references to homosexuality in the Pauline lists of vices in 1 Corinthians 6:9–10 ("male prostitutes, sodomites") and 1 Timothy 1:9–10 ("sodomites"), the only extended coverage of the issue appears in Romans 1:26–27 (see *Jesus and Virtue Ethics,* pp. 166–67, where all the relevant biblical texts on homosexuality, including Romans 1:26–27, are treated). Following Jewish tradition (see Wisdom 13–14), Paul views the pagans' failure to recognize and honor God in creation as their primary sin. According to Paul, from this primary sin they fell into idolatry, then into homosexuality, and finally into all kinds of evil conduct listed in 1:29–31. Jews like Paul regarded homosexuality as a pagan vice. See Leviticus 18:22 and 20:13 for the Old Testament condemnations of homosexual activity.

Paul condemns homosexual activity as contrary to "nature." But what did Paul understand by "nature?" According to many scholars today, what was regarded as "natural" in sexual relations for Paul and his contemporaries was the dominance of the male over the female. In a Jewish context this pattern was viewed as having been intended by God the Creator. With these assumptions there could be no "natural" sexual relations between two women or between two men. In writing about homosexuality, Paul uses some very emotional and negative terms: "degrading passions . . . unnatural . . . consumed with passion for one another . . . shameless acts." Thus Paul condemns any sexual activity that deviates from the heterosexual "norm" supplied by "nature."

PAUL'S SEXUAL ETHIC

In summary, Paul's sexual ethic is restrictive, eschatological, and relatively favorable for women. It is restrictive in the sense that its ideal of monogamous marriage between husband and wife rules out polygamy, as well as fornication, adultery, consorting with prostitutes, and homosexual activity. It puts forward the lifelong union of male and female as the norm, and counsels that this union be lived out in mutual concern and love. And it praises celibacy undertaken to please the Lord and to prepare for the imminent coming of the kingdom of God as an even more perfect form of life for those to whom God has given the gift.

Paul's sexual ethic is eschatological. This dimension comes out most clearly in 1 Corinthians 7. But it underlies most of Paul's teachings on sexual morality in his other letters. Paul was convinced that "the present form of this world is passing away" (1 Corinthians 7:31) and that it would soon yield to the new age of the fullness of God's kingdom (see 1 Corinthians 15). Like other apocalyptically minded Jews, Paul expected a time of testing that he described as the "impending crisis" (7:26). In this context, Paul's basic advice was that everyone should remain in the condition (married or unmarried) in which God had called them to Christian faith. And the real justification for celibacy in this context is that it is a gift from God that allows the person to focus one's whole self on "the affairs of the Lord, how to please the Lord" (7:32).

Paul's sexual ethic is—perhaps surprisingly so to twenty-first-century readers—favorable to women, at least relatively so in the context of Jewish and pagan *mores* in the Roman Empire. By forbidding polygamy, by encouraging parity and mutuality in marriage, by imposing a strict sexual ethic on men (no adultery or consorting with prostitutes), by condemning child abandonment and infanticide (generally performed on girls), by radically restricting the man's right to divorce, and by making celibacy an option for women, Paul and other early Christian teachers gave to Christian women a stability and even a degree of freedom that were otherwise not available to them. On the whole, early Christianity was liberating for women, and women in turn were good for Christianity in their active participation in the life of the Pauline churches (see Romans 16:1–16), in drawing their husbands and other relatives to the church (see 1 Corinthians 7:14, 16), and in bearing children who would become Christians (see 1 Timothy 2:15).

SELECT BIBLIOGRAPHY

Balch, David, ed. *Homosexuality, Science, and the "Plain Sense" of Scripture.* Grand Rapids, MI: Eerdmans, 2000.

Baumert, Norbert. *Woman and Man in Paul: Overcoming a Misunderstanding.* Collegeville, MN: Liturgical Press, 1996.

Brawley, Robert L., ed. *Biblical Ethics and Homosexuality.* Louisville, KY: Westminster, 1996.

Brooten, Bernadette. *Love between Women.* Chicago: University of Chicago Press, 1997.

Brown, Peter. *The Body and Society: Men, Women, and Sexual Renunciation in Early Christianity.* New York: Columbia University Press, 2008.

Collins, Raymond F. *Divorce in the New Testament.* Collegeville, MN: Liturgical Press, 1992.

————. *Sexual Ethics and the New Testament: Behavior and Belief.* New York: Cross-road, 2000.

Deming, Will. *Paul on Marriage and Celibacy: The Hellenistic Background of 1 Corinthians 7.* Cambridge, England: Cambridge University Press, 1995.

Ellis, J. E. *Paul and Ancient Views of Sexual Desire.* London: T&T Clark, 2007.

Gagnon, Robert A. J. *The Bible and Homosexual Practice: Texts and Hermeneutics.* Nashville, TN: Abingdon, 2001.

Instone-Brewer, David. *Divorce and Remarriage in the Bible: The Social and Liter-ary Context.* Grand Rapids, MI: Eerdmans, 2002.

MacDonald, Margaret Y. "Early Christian Women Married to Unbelievers." *Studies in Religion/Sciences Religieuses* 19 (1990): 221–34.

————. "Women Holy in Body and Spirit in the Social Setting of 1 Corinthians 7." *New Testament Studies* 36 (1990): 161–81.

Osiek, Carolyn, and David Balch. *Families in the New Testament World.* Louisville, KY: Westminster, 1997.

Scroggs, Robin. *The New Testament and Homosexuality: Contextual Background for Contemporary Debate.* Philadelphia: Fortress, 1983.

Siker, Jeffrey S., ed. *Homosexuality in the Church.* Louisville, KY: Westminster/John Knox, 1994.

Soards, Marion L. *Scripture and Homosexuality: Biblical Authority and the Church Today.* Louisville, KY: Westminster/John Knox, 1995.

Stark, Rodney. *The Rise of Christianity: A Sociologist Reconsiders History.* Princ-eton, NJ: Princeton University Press, 1996.

Watson, Francis. *Agape, Eros, Gender: Towards a Pauline Sexual Ethic.* Cambridge, England: Cambridge University Press, 2000.

Yarbrough, O. Larry. *"Not Like the Gentiles": Marriage Rules in the Letters of Paul.* Atlanta, GA: Scholars Press, 1985.

Chapter Twenty-Two

Relationships and Sexual Ethics: Theological Perspectives

In light of the recent controversies arising from the sexual abuse scandals that have broken out throughout the world, laity and clergy have been calling for a more urgent and credible articulation of Catholic sexual ethics. Presently intransigent debates occur throughout the church about the moral legitimacy of particular sexual actions. Those of us in virtue ethics are more interested, however, in positing a theological agenda that primarily refers to the type of persons we ought to become. We do not avoid discussion about particular actions, but we believe that if we want to have a credible theological ethics in general and an equally credible sexual ethics in particular, then we need to begin where as the people of God we resonate with one another regarding commonly held truths and insights. We believe that there is much more that unites us than divides us.

Toward this end, I propose a virtue ethics for relationships and sexual ethics. First, I explore the virtue of chastity. Then I consider again my proposal on contemporary cardinal virtues. I conclude by developing a sexual ethics on the foundation of these four virtues.

CHASTITY

When we think of Catholic sexual ethics, we think naturally of chastity. The *Catechism of the Catholic Church* places its discourse on chastity within the context of the sixth commandment (2331–2400), which specifically acknowledges chastity's reference to sexuality. In the *Catechism*, chastity helps us integrate the gift of sexuality. On the practical level, chastity functions in two ways: It invites us to understand ourselves as enhancing our lives whenever we seek to integrate our sexuality within ourselves as relational persons; and it offers strong, regulatory norms of abstinence.

The first function is a positive appreciation of sexuality, embodiment, relationality, and maturing sexual intimacy. Appreciating sexuality as gift, chastity invites the Catholic to see the need for understanding the special ways that sexuality brings us together within the love of God. Chastity calls the Catholic to develop this positive appreciation incrementally throughout her or his life.

The latter function promotes an abstinence, whether very narrowly in terms of a marital chastity that teaches that Catholic spouses should abstain from sexual relations outside of marriage, or for that matter any sexual activity that would in itself be anti-procreative; and more broadly in denying any sexual expressions that are genitally intimate outside of marriage.

Chastity promotes a considerable Christian realism about the challenges of sexuality in the modern world. Christian chastity is particularly important in engaging those who are growing to realize that the gift of sexuality requires a great deal of appreciation and prudential reflection, and that the innate inclination to realize sexual desires needs to be checked by a realistic appraisal of one's own maturity and willingness to commit to another. In short, Christian chastity has always brought a sense of reality to much discussion on sexuality—though contrarily, Christians have sometimes not spent enough time considering how much of a gift sexuality actually is.

But is this enough to teach a sexual ethics? Do we need something more than chastity for a contemporary sexual ethics? I believe we do, and I take my cue from the *Catechism* itself, which suggests we look to the virtues for further moral instruction.

MORE VIRTUES FOR HUMAN RELATIONSHIPS

As we begin to construct an ethics for relationships, we need to remember three points made throughout this book. First, the virtues help us move from the question of self-understanding ("Who are we?") to the question of goals ("Who ought we to become?"), through the question of means ("How do we get there?"). Second, these questions are framed in a relational self-understanding of humanity. For us, virtues do not perfect individual powers within individual persons; rather, they perfect ways that we are related. Third, there are three ways that we are related: generally, by which we treat all persons impartially and equally; specifically, wherein we treat partially those with whom we have particular relationships; and uniquely, where we are accountable to our very selves. Corresponding to these ways of being related are virtues that develop those relationships: justice, fidelity, and self-care. These virtues are but names for the ways we try to realize rightly the relationships that we have. In other cultures they have other names, but in essence, I think every culture proffers these three sets of relationships as constitutive of moral living. Moreover, every culture uses virtue language for talking about treating people, even strangers, fairly; for maintaining faithfully and loyally the relationships we have through friendship, family, work, and citizenship; and for being responsible for and accountable to one's very self.

I propose these three virtues as cardinal. The fourth cardinal virtue is prudence, which determines what constitutes in the concrete the just, faithful, and self-caring ways of being related. Finally, the two older virtues from the patristic and medieval eras, fortitude and temperance, exist to support the realization of the other four.

Here then we see that virtue ethics intersects with natural law. Natural law is the universally accessible study through human reason of a normative anthropology and of the attendant practices that realize that anthropology. Articulating that normative vision is problematic, however, since we each perceive the natural law from our own context. Despite the problem, Christian ethicists try to perceive the *humanum* with the eyes of faith. Thus, we believe that our perception will be prompted by our faith, and that what we see will have a particular urgency because of the narrative of salvation history. Thus, virtue ethics is the attempt to articulate the normative anthropology of the natural law.

I believe that these *thin* and skeletal virtues become *thickened* and enfleshed in different cultures in different ways. For instance, some understanding of justice (the willingness to be impartial and to give to each his or her due) is presumably present in every culture. Justice in the United States, however, is affected considerably by the American esteem of personal autonomy and its respect of personal rights. Autonomy thickens justice, inasmuch as we would not give "the due" to any persons without their consent. Our healthcare system, for instance, so powerfully protects the rights of the individual that we could not imagine justice in a healthcare system that did not privilege informed consent. This American understanding of justice differentiates itself from justice in the Philippines, where an emphasis on "smooth interpersonal relationships" governs most social relationships. Similarly, through autonomy, American understandings of fidelity also depend on the importance of mutual consent. In the Philippines, the strong emphasis on cohesion, unity, and peace clearly provides the yeast for translating fidelity into ordinary life.

Cultures give flesh to the skeletal cardinal virtues. This thickening differentiates, then, one virtue in one culture from a similar one in another. Justice, fidelity, and self-care in a Buddhist culture have somewhat similar and somewhat different meanings than they do in a liberal or Confucian context.

When it comes to thickening in Catholic culture, we need to turn to the virtue of mercy, which I have argued over the years is the trademark of Catholicism. In Catholic cultures, mercy thickens our understanding of the virtues. Inasmuch as mercy is, as I define it, the willingness to enter into the chaos of another so as to respond to their need, mercy thickens justice by taking into account the chaos of the most marginalized. Mercy does not temper justice, as so many believe; rather, mercy prompts us to see that justice applies to all, especially those most frequently without justice, those abandoned to the chaos of the margins. In Catholic cultures, mercy prompts justice both to find the neglected, the persecuted, and the oppressed, and to bring them into the solidarity of humanity by assisting them in the pursuit of their rights.

Similarly, fidelity in the many relationships we enjoy is enfleshed by mercy. Mercy helps Catholics see from the start that no relationship is without its chaos and that every relationship requires the merciful practice of reconciliation. In Catholic marriages, for instance, the balm of mercy prompts spouses to enter one another's chaos and to forgive each other not once or twice but seventy times seven times (see Matthew 18:22).

Finally, the Catholic practice of self-care urges each person, through mercy, to enter into the deep chaos of one's own distinctively complicated life. By the examination of conscience, we believe that the loving, merciful light of Christ illuminates every dimension of the soul and helps us see what we need to do in the care of ourselves.

DEVELOPING A RELATIONAL SEXUAL ETHICS OUT OF THESE CARDINAL VIRTUES

When these virtues are applied to us as relational sexual beings, we see how each has a very particular agenda relevant for sexual ethics. Together they offer a comprehensive sexual ethics. I saw this developed at length by one of my former doctoral students, Ronaldo Zaccharias, SDB, from Brazil, who employed these virtues precisely for a Brazilian educational program of Christian sexual ethics. He took the four virtues that I have proposed, and after seeing them as Catholic—that is, as thickened by mercy—he applied them to particular cases so as to elaborate a Catholic sexual ethics.

In light of the conversations I had with him, I want to expand on some of the insights we shared. First, justice as it applies to sexual ethics is really about each of us learning to appreciate the other person with a dignity that belongs to being human and in the image of God. In sexual relations, justice always prompts us to see the other as subject and not as an object; justice leads us to recognize the importance of never taking advantage of another for the sake of fulfilling our own desires or needs. Justice requires therefore that we see the person to whom we are attracted (or "in love with," "romantically involved with," or "dating") as a person with a dignity that cannot be compromised.

Justice in sexual ethics does not simply apply to the person we are dating or marrying. Justice informed by mercy makes us more sensitive to any sense of inequality or indignity that afflicts our neighbor. A justice informed by mercy is vigorously alert to those who are particularly vulnerable. The abuse of children by clergy is a violent violation of Catholic justice. It reminds us again and again why justice is so important in a sexual ethics. Thus, the sexual abuse of the vulnerable adult, long overlooked in the recent crisis, calls us to a sexual ethics that privileges justice. Rape of anyone is seen as a flagrant act of injustice.

In sexual ethics, this Catholic sense of justice calls us to recognize when others are denigrated, therefore, by the commercialization of sex, from prostitution to the kidnapping and transport of minors—what today we call human trafficking.

Justice in a sexual ethics moves us to enter into the chaos of those whose dignity is compromised by sexual inequities as well. Here we especially think of the ongoing work of establishing the God-given equality of women. Justice in sexual ethics requires us to recognize, support, and promote the equality of the genders, with the understanding that such work still has much to accomplish.

Still, justice is particularly relevant in promoting more egalitarian understandings in heterosexual relationships where, as elsewhere, women still do not enjoy the status of equality in so many forms of life. But justice is not simply attentive to abuse and compromise in marriage. Clear-eyed justice ought to see the chaos of the lives of poor women and their lack of adequate power—this especially in a world where millions of people have HIV/AIDS and the rates of infection among women and particularly teenage girls continues to escalate unabated.

Moreover, because justice is a forward-looking virtue, it prudently anticipates a way of seeing society more respectful of persons, their bodies, and their expressions of sexuality. A justice informed by mercy looks to those who because of sexuality (histories of abuse, sexual dysfunction, orientation questions, etc.) cry out for protection, sanctuary, support, and hospitality. On the question of orientation, the beginning of justice would seem to be that church leaders could learn more about the experiences and self-understanding of gay and lesbian persons, especially those who are devoted members of the church and also those in ministry.

A Catholic justice informed by mercy in the context of sexual ethics can be taught in our classrooms, in our religious education programs, or from the pulpit. It helps us see that our sexuality, where we are most capable of expressing, receiving, and mutually sharing love, is the embodiment of our most vulnerable dimensions. It is where through intimacy we leave ourselves open to the other. For this reason the church's long history of privileging justice easily extends its interest into the realm of sexual ethics.

Justice is not alone among the virtues. All societies call us to be faithful to the long-standing, particular relationships we have. Fidelity differs from justice in that the latter calls us to treat with impartiality all people, while fidelity recognizes that we each are constituted by a variety of specific interpersonal relationships. A fidelity informed by mercy then leads us toward approaching prudently and fearlessly those whom we love. It demands that we privilege the particular relationships that we enjoy.

Fidelity requires us not only not to end or walk out of loving relationships but more importantly to defend and sustain them. Fidelity requires that the entirety of each of our relationships must be embraced and that, informed by mercy, we are always called to stand with those whom we love, especially in their chaos.

Fidelity teaches us that in our sexual relationships we must consider the other in all his or her specificity. Therefore, fidelity demands an honesty to the sexual expression of the relationship. Fidelity calls us never to abandon our lover, to recognize rather that our sexual love must deepen, embrace, and extend through intimacy.

But by being informed by mercy, Catholic fidelity anticipates the chaos of our sexuality and sexual relationships. Fidelity teaches us to be no fool in entering sexual relationships. It reminds us that entering into a sexual relationship with another means entering into an intimate complexity, where we need to recognize the inevitable yet unpredictable moments of upheaval and confusion attendant to such intimacy.

Catholic fidelity therefore privileges dialogue. It seeks to make a couple capable of communicating as best they can their needs, hopes, fears, and desires. This fidelity helps the Christian grow further in love and in humanity. It sees sex itself as a language that expresses in a variety of ways the human person in openness and in pursuit of the other.

This fidelity becomes particularly relevant when children are born into the sexual relationship. Catholic fidelity does not simply mean no divorce or separation. It is not primarily defined by negatives. Rather it seeks to convey the bond into which a child is born. For this reason, Catholics are intensely interested in the nature of marriage as the place where faithful love and pro-creativity concretely flourish.

Self-care is another virtue in which the person recognizes the call to be accountable for oneself. This brings with it a particular competency to not let oneself be taken advantage in any relationship, sexual or otherwise. Instead it calls for a recognition of knowing one's own capabilities, whether and when one can sustain a sexual relationship. It recognizes that while fidelity seeks to look to the other and to the relationship, self-care reminds us that we need to be responsible to ourselves in sexual relationships as well.

Often people enter sexual relationships before they are actually capable of being able to sustain one. They do harm to the other and to themselves. For this reason, persons around the country and elsewhere constantly encourage younger people to delay sexual experiences and relationships—not because sex is bad but because sexual relationships are demanding and require a maturity that engages not just justice and fidelity, but self-care as well. Self-care also prompts people not to succumb to cultural disvalues that encourage casual sexual experiences.

Conversely, self-care might also lead us to acknowledge that we have long been inhibited and fearful of intimacy, touch, or sexual expression. Prudential self-care informed by mercy leads some people to delay sexual intimacy as precipitous, but for others it gently prods them to seek sexual love that has long been an object of fear and dread.

A self-care informed by mercy prompts us to attend to our own personal histories where areas of need or particular vulnerability need to be recognized rather than repressed. Interestingly, many of us are more willing to entertain and stand with another's chaos than with our own. Our pride basically keeps us from seeing the more messy side of ourselves, where our hopes, needs, and vulnerabilities exist. Self-care invites us to be as patient with ourselves as we are with others and invites us to not look to sexual experiences as a way, for instance, of resolving problems of self-esteem. Self-care invites us to see sexuality and sexual relationships as goods to be pursued but precisely within a virtuous context.

Not only are sexuality and sexual relationships goods, but by self-care we are called to understand ourselves as embodied and alive with passions, which are goods as well. Virtue prompts us not to be indulgent but rather to take these goods seriously and to see whether we really appreciate these goods as such and whether we can develop the *askesis*, or discipline, to grow passionately, bodily, sexually to maturity.

The turn to virtue ethics gives us space as a community of faith to talk about basic character traits, dispositions, and stances that members of the community ought to develop to be faithful, loving Catholics. That space, when taken seriously, will inevitably lead to discussion on the particular practices attendant to the virtues that we believe need to be cultivated, and those practices will eventually be prescribed accordingly. But now we need at least to elaborate on who we ought to become as a community of faith, and from there develop an anthropology for a sexual ethics. I suggest that we start with being a people shaped by mercy in the pursuit of justice, fidelity, self-care, and prudence.

SELECTED READINGS

Burggraeve, Roger. "From Responsible to Meaningful Sexuality: An Ethics of Growth as an Ethics of Mercy for Young People in This Era of AIDS." In *Catholic Ethicists on HIV/AIDS Prevention*, edited by James Keenan, 303–16. New York: Continuum, 2000.

Cahill, Lisa Sowle. *Between the Sexes: Foundations for a Christian Ethics of Sexuality.* New York: Paulist Press, 1985.

———. *Sex, Gender, and Christian Ethics.* New York: Cambridge University Press, 1996.

Cahill, Lisa Sowle, T. Frank Kennedy, S.J., and John Garvey, eds. *Sexuality and the U.S. Catholic Church: Crisis and Renewal.* New York: Crossroad, 2006.

Curran, Charles, and Richard McCormick, eds. *Dialogue about Catholic Sexual Teaching.* Mahwah, NJ: Paulist Press, 1993.

Farley, Margaret. *Just Love: A Framework for Christian Sexual Ethics.* New York: Continuum, 2006.

Grabowski, John. *Sex and Virtue: An Introduction to Sexual Ethics.* Washington, DC: Catholic University of America, 2004.

Guindon, André. *The Sexual Language: An Essay in Moral Theology.* Ottawa, ON: University of Ottawa Press, 1976.

Gudorf, Christine. *The Body, Sex, and Pleasure: Reconstructing Christian Sexual Ethics.* Cleveland, OH: Pilgrim Press, 1994.

Keenan, James. "Ethics and the Crisis in the Church." *Theological Studies* 66 (2005): 117–36.

———. *The Works of Mercy: The Heart of Catholicism.* Lanham, MD: Rowman & Littlefield, 2008.

Kelly, Kevin. *New Directions in Sexual Ethics: Moral Theology and the Challenge of AIDS.* London: Geoffrey Chapman, 1998.

Pope John Paul II. *The Theology of the Body.* Boston: Daughters of St. Paul, 1997.

Selling, Joseph, ed. *Embracing Sexuality: Authority and Experience in the Catholic Church.* Aldershot, England: Ashgate, 2001.

Zaccharias, Ronaldo. "Virtue Ethics as a Framework for Catholic Sexual Education: Towards the Integration between Being and Acting in Sexual Education." STD diss., Weston Jesuit School of Theology, 2003.

Epilogue:
Paul, Dietrich, Martin, and Bernhard

Years ago, before I started teaching with Dan Harrington, he taught the course alone. After his first time teaching on Scripture and ethics, he asked me if I had an essay I wanted to recommend to him to amplify his course and broaden its scope. I gave him an essay on how the early church lived out the gospel of Jesus and the Gospels about him. Dan was surprised. He was expecting an essay by a contemporary moralist speculating on a moral problem in one of the Gospels. Instead I gave him an account of how the gospel/Gospels were received and lived. It was then that we decided to work together.

I want to finish this project on the same note. How has Paul been received and lived out? To answer that question, I want to reflect on how three twentieth-century figures lived: Dietrich Bonhoeffer, Martin Luther King Jr., and Bernhard Häring.

DIETRICH BONHOEFFER (1906–1945)

Some time ago, I was watching a PBS broadcast on my favorite theologian of the twentieth century, the German Lutheran Dietrich Bonhoeffer. The show was not that great, but it did me good to be watching Bonhoeffer. When I was a student I read two volumes of his writings, and I was struck by his notion of "religionless" Christianity, to say nothing of the depth of his commitment to Jesus Christ and to all people. I was also struck by the awful irony that Bonhoeffer was executed just days before Hitler took his own life. His death captures the violent waste of life in that war.

At one point in the show, as Bonhoeffer was being questioned by the Gestapo, they read to him Romans 13. They wanted to know, "Why are you not cooperating with the state to which God ordains allegiance?" Bonhoeffer insisted that he

211

was cooperating. But later when he was back in his cell, the prison guard who had grown somewhat sympathetic with Bonhoeffer asked him outright, "Are you lying directly to the Gestapo? And if so, how do you disobey the word of God?" Bonhoeffer answered with a case. "If, in order to demonstrate his own power, a teacher demands from a student in front of the entire class to know whether the student's father returned home again last night drunk, is the student obliged to tell the truth?" The guard responded, "No." Bonhoeffer remarked, "Right you are, for the teacher has abused his power and has no right to the truth."

It was an interesting bit of ethics, not virtue ethics mind you, but casuistry or case reasoning—a topic we did not cover in this book. It reminds me, at the end of this book, of all that we did not do. We did not do casuistry, and there is so much of it in Paul. In fact, two major works in the twentieth century were both on Paul's casuistry, one by Edward Long and the other by Kenneth Kirk. So if you want to do more on Paul and ethics, read about his casuistry. I do this to make you feel a little unsatisfied, to help you think that maybe you did not get as much as you thought you did. That is a little bit of a Pauline move, you know, to stir you up.

But back to Bonhoeffer. Bonhoeffer was a vocal spokesman against the state. He may not have said what the state should be—that is, he might not have been able to offer a normative description of the state—but his experience of God through the Scriptures and particularly through Paul helped him see what was wrong with his state. He could trust the spirit/Spirit in him.

I think that Bonhoeffer is the greatest Christian martyr to stand against the injustices of the Nazis, one who not only preached against these injustices but also actively plotted to destroy, in faith, Hitler. Where did his justice come from?

Like Bonhoeffer, Paul does not give us an idea of the just state; there is certainly not the slightest seed of a Platonic Republic here. But from Paul, Bonhoeffer found his voice and his conviction: He knew this state needed to be denounced.

Bonhoeffer is better understood when we understand Paul's conversion as a normative experience, and when we understand their common faith in the forgiving power of God that could not reject another human being as worthless but saw others as always redeemable. In the experience of the Nazi persecution, Bonhoeffer found his neighbor, much as the Samaritan did. But not because Luke prompted him; rather, Paul did.

I have always thought of Bonhoeffer's conscience as Pauline. He has to preach, he has to speak, he can't relent. He is alight with the Spirit.

MARTIN LUTHER KING JR. (1929–1968)

We turn here to another figure for justice in the twentieth century and see how Martin Luther King Jr. called upon fellow ministers and asked them if they were true Christian ministers. King's notion of justice might have derived from the Synoptic portraits of Jesus as well as from others, from Niebuhr to Gandhi. But above all, Paul was in his pocket when he traveled about.

King trusted his experience, he trusted the Spirit, and he trusted Paul. And so he appealed to the apostle Paul when he spoke to his fellow ministers. In his "Letter from a Birmingham Jail," he wrote to the white ministers: "Just as the apostle Paul left his little village of Tarsus and carried the gospel of Jesus Christ to practically every hamlet and city of the Greco-Roman world, I too am compelled to carry the gospel of freedom beyond my particular hometown. Like Paul, I must constantly respond to the Macedonian call for aid."

Bonhoeffer and King are enormous figures on the landscape of the twentieth century. They remind us that when we look at virtue ethics and Paul, we need to look not only at Paul's words but at his person as well. For he repeats on occasion that great insight from virtue ethics, to look for the right by acting as the virtuous or prudent person would. In 1 Corinthians 11:1 Paul urges, "Be imitators of me, as I am of Christ." In 1 Thessalonians 1:6 he acknowledges, "And you became imitators of us and the Lord." By looking to them we see Paul expressed. We see in them a sense that the prayer of Romans 8:27 has entered into them. The Spirit speaks for and through them. The person of Paul indeed affected them and also affects our understanding of them.

We might think of Paul in the twenty-first century as quoting his own texts from Romans on homosexuality or on obeying authority, or, from elsewhere, imposing on us the household codes. In short, we might think of Paul as quoting his own particular teachings, and that being like Paul means repeating his writings.

We must remember, however, that Paul's primary identity was more as pastor than as teacher, more as convicted of Christ than of an idea, and more able to read in whatever place the signs of the times. Like him, Bonhoeffer and King preeminently understood and responded to the signs of the times. Like him, they were pastors, whom we remember for their exhortations, for their witness, and for their personal convictions. They were the pastors of the twentieth century who witnessed to the truth. By imitating Paul, they got to right teachings and right actions.

BERNHARD HÄRING (1912–1998)

Not everyone animated by Paul is a pastor. But if they are theologians, they certainly are pastoral. In my view, Bernhard Häring was the preeminent pastoral moral theologian of the twentieth century.

Häring's experience of World War II shaped the breadth and depth of his later work in moral theology: The war empowered him to stand and witness to truth in the face of a criminal regime. In *My Witness for the Church* he writes, "During the Second World War I stood before a military court four times. Twice it was a case of life and death. At that time I felt honored because I was accused by the enemies of God. The accusations then were to a large extent true, because I was not submissive to that regime" (132).

His wartime experiences convinced him that in crises people realize their true selves and reason from the depths of their commitments. He witnessed how many uneducated Christians recognized the truth, were convicted by it, and stood firm with it. Häring found truth primarily not in what persons said but in how they acted and lived. The war experiences irretrievably disposed him to the agenda of developing a moral theology that aimed for the bravery, solidarity, and truthfulness of those committed Christians he met in the war.

In his *Embattled Witness*, he comments not only on the heroism but also on the loss. He saw during the war "the most absurd obedience by Christians toward a criminal regime. And that too radically affected my thinking and acting as a moral theologian. After the war, I returned to moral theology with the firm decision to teach it so that the core concept would not be obedience but responsibility, the courage to be responsible" (23–24). He realized therein the need to develop not a conforming, obediential moral theology, but rather one that summoned Christians to a responsive and responsible life of discipleship.

Häring would write on freedom, a freedom for conscience to be responsible. Noticeably different from his predecessors, Häring privileged human freedom as foundational to moral goodness. For Häring, freedom is the possibility of responding to God's call to do God's will. But that freedom is itself a gift. As God calls, God provides. Sin is the refusal to accept the gift and the call of freedom; it is therefore the defeat of freedom and the entrance into slavery.

There are many reasons for Häring's turn to freedom: the Fascist and Nazi movements that imprisoned millions across the European continent, the subsequent developments in the philosophy of existentialism, the incredibly obsessive control of the manualist moral theologians and the ever-encroaching Vatican dictates, the Soviet expansionism into Eastern Europe, and the growing appreciation in ordinary European culture of human freedom. Moreover, several theologians, particularly his doctoral director, Theodor Steinbuchel, had been writing on freedom.

Raphael Gallagher offers another reason for his turn to freedom: revelation in general, and Paul in particular. Häring has 2,031 scriptural citations in *The Law of Christ*, and 659 come from Paul, "the apostle of Christian freedom." These glad tidings are precisely that which makes us free. We have law as a pedagogue, teaching us how to proceed and revealing to us, forensically, our sins. But the gospel, the law of Christ, makes us free to follow him. Paul's message in Galatians rings true in the life experiences of Häring, particularly those during the war. By his own testimony, Häring was free to stand and witness. Personal freedom is the foundation for doing good and for doing moral theology. It is the life lived as a disciple of Christ.

SELECT BIBLIOGRAPHY

Bonhoeffer, Dietrich. *The Cost of Discipleship.* New York: Macmillan, 1966.

———. *Letters and Papers from Prison.* New York: Macmillan, 1972.

Gallagher, Raphael. "Bernhard Häring's *The Law of Christ:* Reassessing Its Contribution to the Renewal of Moral Theology in Its Era." *Studia Moralia* 44 (2006): 317–51.

Häring, Bernhard. *Embattled Witness: Memories of a Time of War.* New York: Seabury Press, 1976.

———. *The Law of Christ.* Paramus, NJ: Newman Press, 1961.

———. *My Witness for the Church.* Mahwah, NJ: Paulist Press, 1992.

Kirk, Kenneth. *Conscience and Its Problems: An Introduction to Casuistry.* New York: Longmans Green, 1927.

Long, Edward. *Conscience and Compromise: An Approach to Protestant Casuistry.* Philadelphia: Westminster Press, 1954.

Washington, James, ed. *A Testament of Hope: The Essential Writings of Martin Luther King, Jr..* San Francisco: Harper & Row, 1986.

Index

217

About the Authors

Daniel J. Harrington, SJ, is professor of New Testament studies at the Boston College School of Theology and Ministry. He is the author of numerous books, including *How Do Catholics Read the Bible?* and *The Church according to the New Testament*.

James F. Keenan, SJ, holds the Founders Professorship in Theology at Boston College. He is the author of a number of books, including *Moral Wisdom* and *The Works of Mercy*.

Together, Harrington and Keenan are the authors of *Jesus and Virtue Ethics*.

LaVergne, TN USA
16 September 2010
197309LV00004B/2/P